MEMOIRS OF A NAVY MAJOR

by

Richard J. Nowatzki

LCDR USN (Ret)

To BARBARA
with BEST wishes
Richard J Nowatzki
8/14/2014

Second Edition - 2013

Manufactured by Paul Baker Printing
220 Riverside Ave. Roseville, CA. 95678

Printed in the United States of America

For Aida

PROLOGUE

I can remember a time, when my number two son, Billy, who was very young, said to me, "Tell me about the 'olden days' Dad."

As I recall, I was busy, doing something at the moment and never did get around to responding to his request. I have often thought about that incident and, recalling my own childhood, I realized that I had received little information from my mother about her younger days and absolutely none from my father. I would have enjoyed hearing about their early lives and times and I am sure, if I had, I would have known and understood them much better than I actually did.

My parents were both born in 1889. My father lived to be 70 and my mother lived to be 86. They are both gone now and their unique stories have gone with them.

I decided that this would not happen to my children and grandchildren. For better or worse, I was going to record the story of my life while I still had the ability to do so. This then, was the genesis and inspiration for this book. These then, are my remembrances of how it was, during my "olden days".

Richard J. Nowatzki
LCDR USN (Retired)

CONTENTS

1   The Early Years   1
2   Saint Thomas the Apostle   8
3   The Teen Years   19
4   Boot Camp   30
5   The Hornet   37
6   World War Two   48
7   Doolittle's Tokyo Raid   56
8   Hawaiian Operations   64
9   The Battle of Midway   72
10 South Pacific Operations   77
11 Condition Two   89
12 The End of the Hornet   97
13 New Caledonia   114
14 Guadalcanal   120
15 PT Boats   130
16 Back Home   159
17 Civilian Life   173
18 The Korean War   179
19 Civilian Life Again   198
20 The Electronics Tech   203
21 The Warrant Officer   220
22 The Shipyard Years   235
23 Hawaii   242
24 Vietnam   255
25 The end of the Navy Years   265
26 The Traffic Business   276
    Epilogue   285

ILLUSTRATIONS

Following page 287

Photos of my youth
Boot Camp
PT Base Melville, Rhode Island in 1943
Family photo, 1945
USS Hornet (CV-8)
USS Walke (DD-723)
USS Onslow (AVP-48)
USS Pollux (AKS-4)
Yokosuka, Japan, 1951
Sasebo, Japan, 1951
1959, Warrant Officer
1961, Hunter's Point, Naval Shipyard
1964, Nagoya, Japan
1964, Yokosuka Japan
1964, Naval Air Station Alameda
1973, Navy Retirement
2004, California
1964, Subic Bay, Philippines
Back Cover(credit Robert Fish – Hornet Museum)

1
THE EARLY YEARS

I was born on June 28,1923,in Freeport, Illinois a small town, northwest of Chicago, near the Wisconsin border. Freeport is famous for being one of the sites of the seven "Lincoln, Douglas debates" when Abraham Lincoln debated the question of free or slave States with Illinois Senator, Steven A. Douglas.

I was the fifth, and last, child of William and Izora Nowatzki. I had two older brothers and two older sisters. William, the eldest, was ten years old when I was born. Then came Dorothy, then Marian and then Paul who was about eighteen months old when I arrived. I believe that my father worked on the railroad as a Fireman then. The Engineer operates the train and the Fireman shovels the coal into the boiler. In any case, I do not think he stayed with the railroad too long, I always remember him as a house painter.

Shortly after my birth, we moved to another small Illinois town, on the western outskirts of Chicago, called Elmhurst. This is the first house that I can actually recall. It was a two story, single family house with a basement. The outside of the house was covered with Kelly-stone, a type of stucco with small green stones imbedded in it. I remember we had a big vegetable garden in the back and a large front lawn. I used to watch my mother as she planted pansies around the border of the front lawn. I believe that these must have been her favorite flowers for she had so many of them.

Human memory is a strange thing. Certain events can impress themselves on your mind and remain with you during your entire life. I may have been two, or at the most three, when I ran into the kitchen, of our Elmhurst house, to escape a

1

honey bee that had been attracted to me.

My mother asked me why I had come running in. When I explained about the bee, she said, "Be nice to the bees and they will be nice to you." I went back outside with my new found wisdom, no longer worried about my friend, the bee. I can still recall the hot summer day as I played in the vegetable garden. Suddenly, the honey bee was back, circling my head. I held out my hand, palm up, to show I was being friendly. The bee landed on my outstretched palm and immediately stung me. I ran screaming back into the house and I do not think that I ever really completely trusted, or blindly followed, my mother's advice again. Whenever she told me anything after that occasion, I took it with a grain of salt.

Since I was the baby of the family, I followed my brother Paul's lead. Whatever he wanted to do, we did. I didn't believe that I had any choice in the matter. On this particular day, my mother was at the sewing machine and I was watching her operate it.

I was about three and Paul was therefore about four and a half. Paul stuck his head in the door way and silently motioned for me to follow him. I trailed him down into the cellar and he walked over to where there were huge stacks of news-papers piled up against one of the basement walls. Paul still had not spoken but I can remember him smiling at me as he pulled a large wooden kitchen match from his pocket. He struck the match against the cement floor and lit it.

Then he set fire to the newspapers. Thank goodness my mother smelled the smoke in time to come down and extinguish the fire before it got out of control. She then proceeded to whale the tar out of us and put us both to bed to await the home coming of my father.

When he arrived and heard the story, he came in and really tore into us, whipping us both

2

severely with his belt until he felt he had made his point.

This particular event taught me that I could not safely follow my brother Paul without being held accountable for his actions as well as my own. I had to use my own judgment and I no longer trusted him. I tried to steer clear of him after that and learned to play by myself. As I look back over my life, I realize that this particular occasion, and its aftermath, caused us to each go our own way as we grew up and resulted in a rift between us that never really closed. We were brothers, but we were never close friends. I liked him and admired his craftsmanship, he was very gifted whenever he built anything, but we were as acquaintances, not brothers.

We moved to an apartment in Chicago when I was about four. Only then, they did not call them apartments, they called them flats. Certain happenings went into my long term memory that still come to mind, from time to time.

I can recall walking down the street with my mother as a tall, strange, man walked toward us. I looked up and smiled at him and was completely taken by surprise when he passed by without saying hello to me or even acknowledging that I existed. Until that very moment, I had evidently assumed that everyone, everywhere, knew me. I must have had a tremendous ego.

I remember the huge snow storms and blizzards during the Chicago winters with the dark stormy skies and the long icicles hanging from the roofs and gutters. I still love to look up at night and see the snowflakes falling past a lighted window or street lamp. At times like that, during a heavy snowfall, all the normal sounds are muffled and the everyday surroundings take on an exotic aura where everything seems different and exciting. After the snow has been there for a few days, becoming grimy and slushy, the delight is gone. However, while the snow is falling, it is a magical time.

In the spring and summer we had severe thunder and lightning storms that were always accompanied by dark, forbidding, skies. A routine summer day would turn into a day of excitement when the skies darkened, the wind whipped up and heavy rain storms swept through the city, making the streets and gutters run with torrents of water. Sleeping at night in a snug bed, while the thunder rolled ominously through the heavens, was an exhilarating experience for me. To this day, I enjoy a really, rousing storm. It peps me up and puts a zing into the air.

Of all the seasons, my favorite is the Autumn of the year, sweater weather. I really enjoy the bright colors as the tree foliage gets ready for winter. I can remember as a child, in the Fall of the year, lying on my back atop a large pile of leaves that someone had raked up and watching the white clouds scud by as I lay there. Enchanted by the occasion and catching a pleasant whiff of smoke, almost as of incense, from another pile of leaves, some distance away, that was being burned.

I discovered that you can get a completely different perspective on who and where you are by looking up and studying the rest of the universe. You can almost lose yourself in your imagination as you study the sky and the cloud formations. It was always a jolt when I would eventually look away and realize where I was, lying in a pile of leaves in Chicago.

One day, while playing outside, one of our neighbors, a boy of about my age, asked me if I was a Protestant or a Catholic. I told him I did not know, I did not know what the words meant. I went into the house and asked my mother. She informed me that we were Catholic. I asked her

what the words meant and she told me that I would
find out later. I went back out to tell the boy
that I was a Catholic, but, he had already gone.
  There I was, primed with the latest information
and no one to tell it to.
  One of my most vivid, early, memories occurred
when my brother Bill came racing into our Chicago
flat, waving a newspaper and hollering, "He made
it. he made it." It was 1927, I was four years
old and Charles Lindbergh had just completed his
historic flight across the Atlantic to Paris,
France. You could hear the newsboys shouting,
"Extra, extra, read all about it."
  In those days of no television and the earliest
beginnings of radio, whenever anything exciting
happened, the daily newspapers, who normally put
out a morning or evening paper, put out a special
edition, called an "extra" and newsboys ran
through the neighborhoods hawking their extras.
The general public could not resist the newsboys
and their papers sold like hot cakes.
  Speaking of the beginnings of radio, we took a
train one day to visit our relatives in the
country, outside of Chicago, Aunt Lola, Uncle Ray
Williams and their five children. They were my
cousins, John, Ella, Margaret, Hazel and Chuck.
Aunt Lola was my mother's sister. I was about
five at the time and the thing that fascinated
me, making this particular visit memorable, was
Uncle Ray's radio. It was called a "Crystal Set."
It was not very large, about the size of a cigar
box and had a pair of earphones attached to it.
You put on the earphones, then touched a short,
thin wire, called a cat's whisker, to a small,
lumpy, glassy looking rock, about the size of a
dime, which was called a "crystal." You would
tune the radio in by probing the crystal with the
cat's whisker until you heard a broadcast station
in your ear phones. You would hear either voices

or music. It was an amazing experience, for all of us. Not long after that episode, my father got a radio for himself and became an avid listener of short-wave broadcasts. He used to send postcards to broadcasters all over the United States to let them know that he heard them. He would describe the time that he heard them and the strength and clarity of the signal. He received answers from all of them thanking him for the information.

An event occurred about this time that convinced me that I had to steer completely clear of my brother Paul. It was a Saturday morning and our parents went shopping. In our dining room, we had an RCA Victrola record player. This machine was about the size of a four drawer file cabinet. You would raise the top to play the records. It was made of expensive, polished, hardwood, either oak or mahogany. It was spring driven and had a handle protruding from the side. When you wanted to play a record, you had to wind it up first. Paul decided to play a record. I reminded him that we were not allowed to touch it. Paul said, "They will never know, unless you tell them." Then he proceeded to wind it up. He evidently over did it and we both heard the spring snap as it broke.

I still remembered what happened after the fire episode and we both waited in terror for our mother and King Kong to come home.

My mother was a small, petite, five foot tall woman. My dad was over six feet tall and weighed about 240 pounds, and had a hair-trigger temper.

They finally returned and I can still visualize the events till this day. It was almost like it had been rehearsed. My father came into the house carrying a bag of groceries. Without saying a word, he set the bag of groceries on the dining

room table, stepped directly over to the
Victrola, turned the handle once, spun around
towards Paul and me as he simultaneously
unbuckled and pulled off his belt. He grabbed me
first and whipped me unmercifully for several,
long, minutes. Then he reached for Paul, but Paul
had seen enough and ran for his life. My father
began chasing him around the large dining room
table but he could not catch him. Paul knew that
if he allowed himself to be caught, he would
suffer the beating of his young life.

After about five laps around the table, my
father was out of breath and he stopped next to
me. He glared at me and said, "Why don't you show
some spunk like your brother Paul?" Then he
grabbed me again and gave me Paul's whipping.
Paul was delighted about the outcome of this
event and I was outraged.

After this episode, my father admired Paul's
guts and considered me a wimp. I was just younger
and law-abiding. I don't consider that as being a
wimp. I became convinced that my dad actually did
not like me or have any use for me. I did not
think that I could ever expect fair play from
him. I always obeyed him, but I no longer tried
to please him. I actually came to dislike him. I
kept my feelings totally hidden, but I am sure he
sensed the way I felt about him. I tried to never
give him any trouble. I kept out of his way as
much as I could, biding my time until I would
finally, one day, be free of his control.

I avoided Paul after this fiasco. I always liked
and admired him for having the nerve to run from
our father, but I never would trust him. He
recognized this and it caused no end of problems
between us. Unfortunately, we became two brothers
that never got along with each other. I kept
completely clear of him as we grew up to ensure
that I would never again be embroiled in one of
his escapades

2
SAINT THOMAS THE APOSTLE

We were living near the University of Chicago, on the southeast side, when I started school in 1928. I went to Kindergarten and First Grade at Ray School, a public school. I remember my First Grade teacher, Miss Blodgett. She was a large, tough, woman who had been a nurse in France, during the latter part of World War One, She did not take any sass from anyone and instilled her strong sense of patriotism in all of us. When she told us stories about George Washington, she made us feel as if she had personally known him.

I can recall her asking me to bring a piece of rope from home. The next day, I proudly handed her the length of rope I had remembered to bring and she promptly tied me into my seat. Evidently, I had been roaming around the classroom whenever I felt like it and she took direct action.

My mother saved a Chicago newspaper article, from 1929, that listed my name and address, along with twelve other Ray School students. We were found to be, "Without physical flaw," we were in perfect condition. It was part of a health project, sponsored by the National Congress of Parents and Teachers. Seventy-two were involved in the study. It would be interesting to look up the other twelve people now, to learn what happened to them during the last sixty-plus years. Their names were listed and I still have the article.

Unfortunately, 1929 was also the year that the "Great Depression" started when Wall Street crashed, crippling the Stock Market. America wound up with an average 25% unemployment rate. I

was not aware of it at first, but I soon found
out that there was a vast difference between
those with money, or good jobs, and those who
were just scraping by.

My sisters, Dorothy and Marian, and my brother
Paul, were all attending a private, Catholic
school, Saint Thomas the Apostle. The Nuns asked
my mother why I did not also attend their school.
She informed them that she could not afford to
send us all there. The High School tuition for my
sisters was $5 each, per month, and my brother's
tuition in Grammar School was $2 per month. In
addition, all students had to purchase their own
books.

The Nuns told my mother that they would allow
Paul and me to attend for $1 each per month and
we could buy used books. However, we would be
required to donate the books, back to the school
at the end of each term.

I did not want to transfer from Ray School as I
got along very good there, but when you are six
years old, you have no vote. I knew nothing about
the special tuition arrangements, until I, and my
classmates, heard it from the Nun who was our
Second Grade teacher. Evidently, I did something
to upset her. I recall her standing me up, in
front of the class and saying that the rest of
the students were paying "full tuition" while I
was paying "half price." I was not showing the
proper gratitude for the school's charity.

When I went home for lunch, I told my mother
what had happened and she told me about the
special tuition arrangements she had with the
school. She also told me that, "Times were
tough." My father worked as a painter and
decorator, jobs were uncertain and money was
tight.

I noticed that my classmates, both boys and
girls, tended to avoid me after that event. Many
of the students came from well to do families
and, since my teacher had successfully down

9

graded me in front of them, I never became real
friends with any of them. What I did not realize,
until much later, was that I would be a part of
this same group of students for seven years as we
were promoted together to each succeeding grade.

This may have been a blessing in disguise. Since
I was left alone by my classmates, I concentrated
on my lessons. I probably learned more than I
might have, if I had been a popular student.
However, I have never, in my heart, forgiven that
particular Nun for her thoughtless, ignorant
action in picturing me as a charity case in front
of my peers. The best I can say in her defense is
that she was probably just plain socially stupid.

I remember one incident that happened in Third
Grade. Our routine was to stand next to our desk
and recite our prayers, aloud, before classes
started and ended. We had been studying about
Abraham Lincoln during the morning and we were
getting ready to leave for lunch.

As we stood, saying our prayers, Justin,
standing in front of me, whispered over his
shoulder, "Abra, was a ham." It made me laugh and
the Nun heard me. She stopped the prayers, made
me empty out my desk and pack up all of my books.
She informed me that she was expelling me from
the class for laughing during prayers.

I had to lug my books all the way home, about
six blocks. When I arrived, my mother asked why I
had brought every thing home, I explained what
had happened. She told me to eat lunch and return
to school. She said the Nun did not have the
authority to expel me.

When I got back, I told the Nun that my mother
had told me to return to school. Not knowing what
would happen next, I just stood there while she
stared at me. Then she said, "We will ask the
class."

She made me stand in front of the room, facing
them, holding all my books. I was very
uncomfortable. She said "Students, shall we let

Richard rejoin the class?" I knew I was not
popular, but I was not prepared for the loud,
unanimous "No" that rang out from the class. It
surprised and depressed me. I looked over at
Justin and, to his credit, he did not join in the
response from the class. I turned around and
walked out of the room and the Nun came running
after me. She asked me where I thought I was
going and I told her, "Back home." I guess the
game had gone on long enough for her and she told
me to return to my desk and put my books away. I
hated to go back into that room, but I gritted my
teeth and returned. Oddly enough, Justin and I
liked each other after that episode.

On one occasion, during Catechism class, I made
a huge mistake, I asked a question.

Learning your Catechism is a requirement in
Catholic schools. It is a process in which a
series of standard questions are asked and you
are required to respond instantly with the
correct response, like a parrot, or robot, word
for word, no deviations are allowed. My big
mistake was in thinking about the response to the
question, "Who is God?"

Things may have changed, but as I recall, in
those days, the correct response was, "God always
was and always will be."

I was curious about this answer and held up my
hand. The Nun said, "Yes Richard?" I asked her,
"Didn't he have to start, somewhere?" She stared
at me with a look almost of revulsion, as if I
had crawled out from under a rock. She did not
answer, she turned the class over to one of her
favorite students and took me immediately to the
Mother Superior's Office, the Head Nun.

The Catechism question was related to her and I
was asked to repeat my question, which I
innocently did. The Mother Superior stared at me
with that same strange look. She did not answer
me, but picked up the phone and called the
Priest's Rectory, a nearby building where they

11

lived. A priest appeared in a few moments, the Catechism question was relayed to him and they told me to again ask my question. Now, no one has yet, ever tried to answer me. All I ever received in response was a strange stare. By now, I am apprehensive and remained silent in front of the Priest. They assured me I had nothing to fear. I asked him, "Didn't he have to start somewhere?"

This time the Priest stared at me and I could almost see him shudder. He took me firmly by the wrist and pulled me next door to the church. He started sprinkling holy water on me and I could see he was very upset.

Now, I will admit that I was afraid of my own father, but that did not extend to anyone else. I certainly was not frightened by the priest. I jerked my wrist away from his grasp and asked him, "What did I say that was so bad?" He glared down at me, pointed his finger at my nose and, in a loud voice, said, "You are what we call, a Doubting Thomas."

That was a strange answer when you realize that the church we were in was named for Thomas the Apostle, the original Doubting Thomas. However, I now knew better than to ask any more questions.

We spent the rest of the morning in the church while I did penance and the priest prayed for my soul. I have never forgotten that they were unable to answer me. I received a very good elementary education at Saint Thomas and even had good grades in Religion, but, after this episode, I regarded the required, religious instructions the same way that someone might regard Greek mythology. You hear what they are telling you and you can pass tests on the subject, but you are not swallowing it. There was no other way that I could cope with the situation. I would have preferred to go to a Public school, but I was trapped where I was. The Nuns of Saint Thomas had their chance to sell the Catholic religion to me.

They lost me by their reactions to my innocent, and to me, perfectly logical question. After all, the entire focus of the school was to turn young children into devout Catholics. In my case, the way they handled this incident, actually turned me into a Doubting Thomas, a self-fulfilling prophecy.

Since I did not have any close friends at school, my real friends became the kids I met in my own neighborhood. I did not belong to a "gang" as such, however, about fifteen or more of us associated together and formed athletic teams during the normal seasons for each different sport; baseball, basketball, football and sometimes ice hockey. We also did a lot of swimming in Lake Michigan during the summer months. Since I either walked, ran or rode a bike, wherever I went, I was in excellent physical condition. We competed against kids in adjoining neighborhoods, in sports only. There were never any gang wars or fights that you hear about these days. I was a happy-go-lucky kid, except at school.

My mother made me wear knickers and that became my nickname for awhile, "Knickers Nowatzki." That name finally died out after I got old enough to wear long pants. Then they called me Richie. Occasionally, even now, the name of Knickers crops up when I meet an old friend.

There was an element of lawlessness that I was exposed to. On more than one occasion, after a ball game for example, I was approached by some of the older boys who asked me if I wanted to go with them to break into a house or apartment, or act as a lookout for them. It is flattering to a young boy's ego to be asked to join an older group, but I had absolutely no desire or inclination to break the law and I always turned them down. Eventually, they quit asking me.

I discovered that certain individuals behave

normally in all respects except that they have a
kind of criminal mentality that totally lacks a
conscience. To obtain money or material things,
they never consider honest work or saving up for
it, they only consider how to forcibly take what
they desire. All of these, few, outlaws of my
youth, continued on their errant paths during
their lives until they eventually were caught.
Several of them even went to prison for extended
periods. My feelings toward them were mixed. I
enjoyed their company and playing sports with
them, but, I hated their casual way of breaking
the law. I still considered them as friends, but
could not condone their anti-social behavior.

The friendships I formed at that early age have
remained as lifetime friendships. Chicago has a
reputation for having ethnic neighborhoods that
are dominated by one particular nationality. In
my neighborhood, however, we were a multi-
national group. I lived near the University of
Chicago at 55th Street and University Avenue. My
circle of friends was composed of Germans,
Prussians, Polish, Jewish, Greek, Turkish, Irish,
Spanish, Mexican, Italian, Swedish, English,
Japanese and Dutch. We even had regional
representation from the South, one of my friends
was named Binnie-Bob. There were a few black
families in the area, but none of them were on
our teams. We did compete against black teams,
though, in those days, we did not call them
black, we called them, colored.

I considered myself fortunate in having been
raised in such a varied mixture of races and
creeds and finding out at an early age that there
is basically no major difference between races,
only their cultures are unique.

As far as the different religions went, we
ignored that we were raised with different
beliefs. At school one day we were asked to write
Down the name of our best friend. I wrote Melvin

Larson. The Nun said she did not know any Larsons at Saint Thomas.

I told her that he went to Ray School. She asked me, "Is he Catholic?" I can still recall her horrified look when I told her he was Lutheran. I had absolutely no idea that there was so much enmity and bad blood between the Catholics and Lutherans. I was told, later, that Martin Luther had been a Catholic priest who turned against the Catholic religion, for what he considered good reasons, and his actions became the basis of the Lutheran religion. She was flabbergasted that I could associate with anyone, especially as best friends, who was going to go to "Hell" when he died. At one time, I probably would have worried about her reaction. However, since my earlier religious experience as a Doubting Thomas, her comments rolled off me like water off a duck's back.

I can also recall the only instance of sex education that I ever received at Saint Thomas. I was probably in Second or Third Grade when someone in the class asked the Nun, "Where do children come from?". With the whole class looking at her, the Nun explained that when your mother wants to have a baby, she goes to the hospital and sits on a bench, waiting for her doctor. Eventually, he comes out of his room, hands her the baby and she goes home. I had heard that babies come from the hospital, but I had never known all the details before. I promptly filed that knowledge away and forgot about it.

One day, while playing with my neighborhood buddies, I evidently said something that revealed my lack of sexual knowledge because one of my friends asked me, curiously, if I knew how babies were born. When I promptly responded with the fairy tale that the Nun had told us, they rolled around the ground in hysterical laughter. They

15

thought I was trying to be funny. When they realized that I was serious, they wasted no time in explaining to me, in clinical detail, the difference between boys and girls. I was amazed and slightly skeptical as they explained life to me, but the information they gave to me, on that occasion, turned out to be very accurate. Thank goodness I had no desire to straighten out the Nun. I knew better than to pass on my new knowledge to her. However, my neighborhood pals kidded me for years about how babies are born.

Each year, as I went through the grades at Saint Thomas, our teachers gave us punch boards to sell. These are devices that you had to sell 100 chances on. For a dime, you got to punch out a chance. If you were lucky, you won a small prize. If your parents could afford the Punch Board, there was no problem. They bought it for $10. You returned to school the next day with your money, got a pat on the head and a gold star by your name for being prompt.

If your parents could not afford it, you had to go door-to-door, each afternoon after school, trying to sell the chances to your neighbors who were also trying to struggle through the Depression.

With four children in school, it would cost my parents $40 to buy our punch boards, about a month's pay in those days.

A dime would buy a large bag of sweet rolls at the Day Old surplus bakery store. This is where the bakery drivers left their unsold bakery goods at the end of each day's run.

Day after day at school, I was constantly harangued by the Nun for not getting my money turned in, in a timely fashion. When the final deadline arrived for turning in the Punch Boards and cash, I would turn in my best results. I was never able to sell all the chances. On one occasion, I spent a frantic two days looking for the money I collected before I remembered where I had hidden it. From these experiences, to this day, I detest the thought of door-to-door selling. I hated the unfairness of being badgered by the Nuns who simply chose to believe that I was a difficult and uncooperative child. They did not have the slightest understanding of the tremendous effort I put forward.

My mother kept my report card for Seventh Grade. It showed that I had an "A" average for that year. I remember the Nun, Sister Doloretta. She was very considerate and fair and the only one that I ever liked in that school. I can still recall her telling us to develop our imaginations so that we could realize our full potentials.

Eighth Grade was a different matter. The Nun was another tough one who constantly threatened to not graduate me. I finally found a way to get her to ease up on me. One day we had to write down what type of career we intended to pursue. On a wild impulse, I wrote that I wanted to become a priest. It worked like a charm, the Nun thought that she had me brain-washed and no longer threatened to flunk me. I believe that she thought she was going to get credit for producing a prospective priest.

It almost back-fired though when one evening my father grabbed me and wanted to know what the hell I was up to. He said a priest came to see him about my ambition to become a priest. I explained to him that it was a trick I had made up to ensure I graduated. He thought I was nuts but he began to believe me when I told him I wanted to go to a Public High School, no more Catholic schools.

In June 1937, I graduated from Saint Thomas. In seven years, I had managed to make friends with about 3 boys in my class, but I had received a good, basic, education. I felt that there was something, somewhere, that controlled the universe we lived in, but I was not convinced that the Catholics had the answer. The seven years of religious instructions had not taken root in me. Little did I realize that in a few short years, my beliefs, or non-beliefs, would be given several, severe tests.

3
THE TEEN YEARS

For the first time, since Second Grade, I was going to be in a class room, on the same level as my peers. No more would I have the feeling of being the class outcast. Whether real, or imagined, that feeling had definitely stayed with me all through my years at Saint Thomas. Based on a recommendation from Vince Treacy, one of my neighborhood friends, I attended Tilden Technical High School as a Freshman.

Tilden was located next to the Chicago Stock Yards, where they slaughtered the cows, pigs, and lambs. There was always a terrible stench from this operation and, if the wind was blowing in the wrong direction, the odor was almost unbearable. I took the normal high school subjects, plus Mechanical Drawing and Wood Shop. I was a satisfactory student, but Tilden was a long street car ride from home and the Stock Yards were always there. I decided to transfer to Hyde Park High, much nearer to the house and coed. Tilden was an all boys school.

To make use of the Shop credits that I had earned at Tilden, I had to register for a modified Business course at Hyde Park, in lieu of a normal College Preparatory course. It did not seem important to me. I knew that, with the "Great Depression," still on, and with the limited financial resources of my family, I would not be going to college anyway. Growing up near the University of Chicago and seeing the institution, right there, I really had a strong desire to go to college, but I knew there was no hope.

I had various, part time, after school jobs to make a little spending money. I worked in grocery stores, jewelry stores, delicatessens and had paper routes. In the jewelry store, my job was to

19

transport, watches, rings and other valuables, needing repair, to the Downtown area, called the "Loop," in Chicago. I would drop off the items and pick up any repaired work. I commuted on the Illinois Central train. One day, one of my older acquaintances, with a criminal outlook on life, asked me what I carried in the satchel that I used in the jewelry store job. I explained that it was "only junk" to be repaired. He asked me to let him know if I ever had anything really valuable. He said he would meet me at the train station, punch me in the eye to make it look good and we would split the profit. I told him I would let him know, but I had no intention of ever cooperating with him. About a week later, I noticed him and one of his friends at the train station and I knew it was only a matter of time before they would rob me. A few days later, I quit the jewelry job and went to work in a grocery store.

I liked working in groceries, though they did not pay very much. One summer, I worked in an IGA store (Independent Grocers Association). The independent stores got together to form an association. This way they could buy their products in large quantities and get much better discounts on their purchases than they could as individual stores. At the IGA, I received $1 a day, for twelve hours work. From 7AM to 7 PM, Monday through Saturday. We were closed on Sundays, but, we had to take inventory each Sunday from 7 to 7. That day had to be donated no salary. So I wound up working 84 hours a week for $6, a little over seven cents per hour.

In those days, the stores were operated, just like auto parts stores are operated now. Each customer came up to the counter, usually with a shopping list. The clerks would go get each item and bring it to the counter. You would bag the groceries and carry it out to their car or carry it to their house, whatever the manager told you to do. I do not remember ever receiving a tip for helping a customer. I was a hard worker, but, the store owner insisted that I wipe off cans, straighten shelves or do anything else to look busy whenever there were no customers in the store. That was the hardest part of the job, trying to look busy when I really was not.

After about two months, I had an offer of a better job at an A&P Store, (Atlantic & Pacific). It was 1936. President Roosevelt had just signed the Social Security Act into law. I had to get my Social Security card before I could go to work at my new job.

The man, who hired me, said we were going to change the store into a "Super Market." Then he explained to me how we would lay out the shelves, aisles and cash registers so that the customers would collect their own grocery items and bring them to the registers, exactly as they do now. In 1936 however, it was a revolutionary idea.

When I told my boss, at the IGA store, that I was leaving, he said, "I've been carrying you for two months, now when you can do me some good, you are quitting." I guess he thought that I was not worth the seven cents an hour he had been paying me. In any case, I left for the A&P and a small pay raise. I worked there until school started in the Fall.

I believe that my home life was average for those times in the Thirties. Newspapers and radio were the main communications media. Movies were inexpensive and fun to go to, though sometimes the ticket price was hard to raise. Most families were still struggling to get by.

My mother was a good woman and we children all loved her very much. She was a Dutch lady. Her maiden name was Izora Van Horn. I believe she was born in Martintown, Wisconsin, in 1889. She died of a heart attack in 1976, in Monroe, Wisconsin.

Her father, John Van Horn, died before I was old
enough to remember him, but my mother told me he
was a happy-go-lucky, hard working, Dutchman. Her
mother, Ella Howder Van Horn, lived to be 96,
out-living two husbands. She had several children
from Mr. Heckman, her first husband, and two
girls, my mother and her sister Lola with John
Van Horn, her second husband. Therefore, my
mother had several half-brothers and sisters
named Heckman, but I never was able to keep them
all straight in my memory. There was also an
Oscar Van Horn who I believe was a half-brother
to my mother. Possibly, her father, John Van
Horn, had been married previously.

My mother was very petite, about five feet tall
and she did her best to raise a family during
difficult times while living with a very trying
husband.

My father was also a hard worker, but he was an
unpleasant person to live with, primarily due to
his unpredictable and short fused temper. He was
Prussian and could speak German. I was told that
his ancestors came from Posen, in Prussia. Since
the end of World War Two, in 1945, Prussia no
longer exists as a country. Posen is now part of
Poland.

I understood that my dad was born in Gogebic,
Michigan, in 1889, but that is all I ever heard
about his early life. He died in Hot Springs,
Arkansas in 1960, eighteen months after suffering
a stroke. I heard my mother mention once that he
had a sister, but I never heard any details. My
sister Marian told me that she remembered
Grandmother Nowatzki visiting the family, before
I was born. It was the Christmas season and she
was teaching the children to sing Christmas
carols in German. Marian said that our mother put
a stop to it, saying, "There will be no German
spoken in this house." It was probably, shortly

after the end of World War One and the Germans were in great disfavor. In any case, Marian said that she did not recall that Grandmother Nowatzki ever came back to our house after that event.

I never knew, or heard anything, about my Grandfather on my father's side.

My dad was a large man, over six feet, about 240 pounds and, as I previously mentioned, had a violent temper. I do not know if he was always that way, but that is the only way I ever knew him. It could have been the stress of raising a large family during the Depression that made him so hard to live with, but, since he could fly off the handle for no apparent reason, I always steered clear of him. My mother did her best to protect us from his periodic rampages. However, at five feet tall and 100 pounds, she was no match for him. When he decided we needed a whipping, nothing could stop him, and he always used his belt.

I recall asking my mother once, "Why did you ever marry him?". She told me that they met at a church social in a small Wisconsin town. It was an affair where the single girls would prepare a box supper and hide their name inside it. The eligible bachelors would bid on the various box suppers and, once they opened the box and discovered the name, would invite the girl to share the supper with them. In that way, the ice was broken and it was an acceptable way for young people to become acquainted in 1910.

I do not know what she saw in him, but they were eventually married. He may have been a good prospect as a husband, at least he was a good provider. I imagine he kept his temper under control until after they had been married for awhile. I do not know if my mother ever wanted to leave him, but, in those days, divorce was not a normal solution to problem marriages. If you made a mistake, you lived with it for the sake of the children. I would have been happy to see him go.

Fortunately for me, I inherited most of my traits from my mother's side of the family. I have always been hard working, cheerful and enjoy making people laugh. I am sure I got my sense of humor from my Dutch grandfather. I know that I could not have gotten it from my own father.

Besides school, one major influence during my formative years was my love of books. I enjoyed reading. I would virtually live the experiences as I read about them. I have always had a strong sense of adventure and I think it started when I first read Robinson Crusoe. Of course I read all the Tom Swift books and other stories of that type when I was young. As I matured, I began reading biographies, Jack London stories, Mutiny on the Bounty and tales of the great explorers. I read all the aviation books I could find and developed a desire to become a pilot.
Whatever the future held for me, I was determined to lead an adventuresome life.

My sister Dorothy married in 1937 to Charley O'Kane. Charley emigrated from Ireland at the age of eighteen. I always liked to talk to him. He was fun and knew a lot of things. One time we were discussing my future and he recommended that I sail in the Merchant Marine, possibly as a radio operator. Now Charley was my kind of a guy. He had a sense of adventure.

I had a lot of success in playing football with the neighborhood teams and was an above average player. I dreamed about becoming a famous player, maybe getting a scholarship to make my remote hope of attending college come true. I confidently went out for the football team at Hyde Park. The coach sent me for a physical exam and gave me a permission slip for my parents to sign

I was totally surprised and bitterly disappointed when my father immediately tore up the permission slip and threw it away. When I asked him why, his response was, "I did not raise you to get all crippled up, so some damn coach can keep his job. Then I would have you on my hands for the rest of my life because you would not be able to work." There was no appeal to one of his decisions and I had to admit, he had a point. I was five foot, six and weighed about one hundred twenty pounds. My scholarship dreams vanished into thin air.

I was a good student in high school and enjoyed attending classes. The studies were easy, in my opinion, and I was able to breeze through the required courses without working too hard. I was not lazy, it was just that the subject matter was not the least bit difficult for me. I could easily complete my homework assignments during study periods at school. There was no interference with my after school jobs or fun.

I took Bookkeeping as part of my overall Business course. After my final exam, my teacher called me aside and told me that I was skilled enough that she could guarantee me a job as a bookkeeper after graduation. She told me that with my present ability, I was better than some bookkeepers she had seen, working in offices. She stressed to me that I had a knack for the subject and could do well in it if I followed it as a career. However, when I pictured a bookkeeper, I envisioned Scrooge and his clerk Bob Cratchit, perched on a high stool, entering figures in a large account book. It did not square with my growing desire to lead a life of adventure. She had kindly, opened a door for me, but I refused to walk through it.

I not only became eighteen in June 1941, I also graduated from High School. The Depression was still on but I started walking around to all the

employment offices that I could find, whether
they were hiring or not. Within a week, I located
a job as an Apprentice, Stationary Engineer
working for the University of Chicago. I just
happened to be there at the Personnel Office,
just as the job was going to be advertised. I did
not consider that, luck. If I had not been out
there, beating the bushes, I would never have
found the job.

The University generated their own electric
power and had a plant located a few miles from my
home. Despite the nice title, I found myself with
a shovel in my hands. I was either digging holes
or shoveling coal, but I did not mind. I had a
job. I also knew that I could work my way up to a
good position. One thing I never lacked was self
confidence.

I believe that I started working at about thirty
cents per hour, an average starting wage in those
days. I paid room and board at home, kept a
minimal amount for pocket change and gave any
remainder to my mother to save for me. One
evening after supper, my father looked at me and
said, "I will never understand how you managed to
find such a great job by yourself. You have
located a lifetime job. All you have to do is
keep your nose clean, do as your told and you're
set for life." I am sure that his intentions were
friendly and he meant well, but, I was not about
to take his advice at this late date. From force
of habit, I did not reveal my true feelings to
him. His words painted a dismal future for me. I
did not intend to spend my life in the first job
I found and continue living with him. His comments though, were the catalysts I needed to
remind myself that it was time to leave the nest
and get out on my own. Time to start the big
adventure, the question was, how to go about it?

In 1933, when I was ten, Hitler had become
Dictator of Germany. We used to hear him on the

short wave radio stations as he preached to the
German people. I did not speak or understand
German, but there was no mistaking the hate,
anger and violence in his voice as he raged
through his political speeches.

Within a few years of taking over, he re-
occupied the Rhineland which Germany had lost, in
1918, after being defeated in World War One.
Neither France nor England protested. He then
took over Austria with the approval of Italy. He
became partners with Italy. He and Mussolini, the
Italian Dictator, signed a "Pact of Steel" and
called their organization the Axis. Hitler next
declared that a Czechoslovakian problem existed.
According to Hitler, German citizens, living in
that country, were being terrorized. France and
England had treaties with Czechoslovakia and both
had been on the winning side in 1918, when
Germany was defeated. However, twenty years had
passed, it was now 1938. Germany had re-armed and
re-mobilized and was becoming a very strong
power. France and England had never recovered
their former strength after the tremendous
manpower and economic losses of World War One and
were in no condition to challenge Germany. As a
result of this situation, France and England
abandoned Czechoslovakia to German actions. They
hoped that this would appease Hitler and prevent
another war. The Prime Minister of Britain,
Neville Chamberlain, returned to England and
declared that his actions had "Guaranteed peace
in our time."

On September 30, 1938, Hitler took over a large
portion of Czechoslovakia. In March of 1939,
despite promises to the contrary, he took over
the rest of the country and Czechoslovakia ceased
to exist as a separate nation.

In that same year, 1939, Hitler declared that
there was a "Polish problem." According to him,

27

German citizens living in that country were being terrorized by the Poles. This was becoming a familiar refrain and always ended up as a reason for attacking one of his neighbors. In this case, there were a few complications. Communist Russia was the country that lived next to Poland and was a mortal enemy of Fascist Germany. Also, France and England had a signed Defense Treaty with Poland and would either have to live up to it or sacrifice their national honor. They could not abandon it as they had done to Czechoslovakia.

England and France were trying to get Russia to also help guarantee Poland's safety, when Hitler in Germany and Stalin in Russia stunned the world by signing a "Non-aggression Pact." They both agreed not to go to war against each other. There were secret provisions in this pact that allowed Russia to take over half of Poland, among other things. This Pact, turned Germany loose, making World War Two, not only possible, but inevitable.

On September 1,1939, eight days after Russia signed the Pact, Germany attacked Poland. On 3 September, France and England declared war on Germany, honoring their treaty with Poland. They obviously were not prepared for this action. They had gained twelve months of time by sacrificing Czechoslovakia, but this was not long enough for them to match Hitler's war machine.

France pinned her hopes on the Maginot Line. An expensive system of concrete and steel under-ground bunkers, designed to re-fight World War One. It was built opposite a similar German defense line called the Siegfried Line.

Hitler's troops defeated Poland in three weeks and then the war stood still. France waited behind the Maginot Line. England sent an Expeditionary Force of about 350,000 troops to France and the Germans divided up Poland with Russia.

On November 30, 1939, Russia attacked tiny
Finland, after making territorial demands on her.
Hitler favored the Finns, but his Pact with
Russia made him keep his nose out of this affair.
The Finns thrilled the world by fighting the huge
Russian army to a standstill, though being
outnumbered about five to one. Finland caused
massive casualties to the Russians, but, in the
end, she had to lose to the superior Russian
strength. Finland surrendered on 12 March 1940.
That Russia had such a hard time defeating
tiny Finland, reinforced Hitler's belief that
Russia could not withstand an attack by Germany.

On 9 April 1940, Germany occupied Denmark and
Norway. On 10 May, she attacked the Netherlands,
Belgium and Luxembourg. These countries were
quickly defeated. Belgium collapsed on 28 May and
the British Expeditionary Force retreated to
Dunkirk where they were heroically rescued by
British military and civilians and brought back
to England, minus their weapons and equipment.
Germany continued attacking toward France until,
to the utter dismay of the free world, France
surrendered on 17 June 1940.

Hitler tried to get England to sign a peace
treaty. When that failed, he attempted to bomb
her into submission, but he did not succeed.
Britain, now being led by a new Prime Minister,
Winston Churchill, stubbornly held on.

On 22 June 1941, one year after France's
surrender, Hitler revealed his true intentions of
world domination by attacking his partner,
Russia. Six days later, I reached my eighteenth
birthday. I did not realize it at the time, but
due to the insane ambitions of Hitler of Germany,
Stalin of Russia, Mussolini of Italy and Tojo of
Japan, I was prime "cannon fodder" just as I was
entering early adulthood. An adventuresome life
was not only possible, it was un-avoidable.

4

BOOT CAMP

In 1940, due to the war in Europe, the United
States had decided to start drafting men into the
Army. It was to be for one year, as a preparedness measure. They drafted men between the ages
of 21 and 35.

At that moment in time, among the armies of the
world, the U.S. Army was 7th in size. Portugal had
a larger army than the U.S.

My oldest brother Bill, had been drafted into
the Army from his job as a streetcar motorman. He
was among the first group to go. A popular singing trio, The Andrews Sisters, had a hit song
called, "Good-bye Dear, I'll be back in a year",
which referred to the one year draft.

America was still officially neutral regarding
the war, except for some of our Navy Destroyers
that were helping escort ship convoys in the
North Atlantic. We were supporting Russia and
England with war material as they struggled with
Hitler's forces. The American people were not
united in this aid to the Allies. There were some
who advocated helping the Germans. The majority
though, appeared to be in favor of staying out of
the fighting war.

In the meantime, manufacturing the desperately
required, huge amount of war material for England
and Russia, was priming the economic pump in the
U.S. We were gradually beginning to come out of
the "Great Depression".

With the on-going draft and the European War, it
was only natural to think about joining the
Armed Forces as a way of getting out on my own. I
considered them all and eventually settled on the
Navy. The more I thought about it, the more I was
sure I was making the right decision for me. It
appealed to my desire for adventure and I would

Be out of the nest.

An older friend of mine, Ollie Hamilton, had previously joined the Navy. I had talked to him when he returned home on leave. He was stationed aboard a Cruiser at Pearl Harbor and seemed to really enjoy the life. I finally made up my mind and decided to enlist in the Navy.

I took a day off from work and went downtown to the Navy Recruiter's office, located in the Chicago "Loop." They welcomed me with open arms. After listening to their pitch, I signed up for six years instead of the normal four. There was one hitch, at eighteen, I needed my parent's signature to join.

I brought the enlistment papers home and tried to get my mother to sign them. She said I would have to have my father do that. She said, "It will be up to him."

That evening, I handed the papers to him, hoping that he would sign them. I repeated all the good things the recruiter had told me and hoped for the best. He told me to leave the papers and he would think it over that night. I left without any real confidence that he would let me go. As far as I knew, he had never been in the service and I still remembered how he had refused to let me play football.

The next morning, I was totally surprised when my mother told me that my father had signed the papers. I was on my own at last. I was eighteen, with a decent education, excellent health, no ethnic hang-ups, with nothing or no one to tie me down. I could keep my own counsel and had a great eagerness for adventure. The door I had been searching for was open and I leaped through it.

I was sent to the Naval Training Center at Great Lakes, Illinois on 19 August 1941, for six weeks of "Boot" camp. I believe they called it that because all the trainees wore leggings that resembled boots. I had enlisted as an Apprentice

Seaman.

At the Boot Camp, we were given another, more thorough, physical exam and administered a series of shots. We were issued uniforms and a sea-bag to keep them in. Then they gave us a regulation, military style haircut and marched us to an "Isolation" camp for one week. This effectively separated us from the main training center to prevent the new recruits from bringing any contagious disease into the entire camp. If any disease broke out among us during our first week, it would be restricted to the 100 recruits in my training company.

During the first few days, when everything was new and strange and we were being ordered around like robots, I felt as if I had lost my own identity. I realized for the first time that by enlisting, I had voluntarily surrendered my personal freedom to the government and had lost control over my destiny for at least the next six years. It was a very sobering thought and I made up my mind, for better or worse, I would make the best of it.

The first order of business was to stencil our names on our uniforms. Then we learned to wash our clothes in a bucket, tie them onto clothes lines to dry and finally roll them, into small, sausage shaped bundles so they would all fit into our sea-bags.

The ends of each sausage were tied, using the same, small cord, that secured them to the clothes line for drying. The theory was that if you rolled your clothes properly, they would appear as if pressed when they were un-rolled. I have never met a sailor yet who could make that theory work. Whenever I saw anyone wearing a freshly un-rolled uniform, it looked rumpled, or slept in.

We were also issued hammocks and blankets. Many navy ships did not have bunks or cots for enlisted men and we could be required to sleep in hammocks. The barracks were constructed without beds and we had to use our hammocks to sleep in. At first glance, it would appear an easy matter to sleep in one, but, like most things, there is a trick to it. First, you learn not to roll over as you do in a normal bed. If you do, you can find yourself on the floor after a sudden drop.

During the first few nights, we were constantly being awakened by sleepers who fell from their hammocks. Dropping over three feet, from a sound sleep, is guaranteed to start a loud commotion.

We were assigned guard duties at night to assist those who fell, back into their hammocks. On the first night that I had guard duty, I heard several people fall, but when I shined my light on the deck to find the victims, sometimes, there was no one there. After this happened several times, it was getting kind of spooky, until I realized that I was on the ground floor of a two story building and I was also hearing the ones who were falling on the second floor, above me. Fortunately, they had their own guard.

Incidentally, standing night watches was extremely hard for me to get used to. I have always been a very sound sleeper and had a hard time getting up to standing the night and early morning watches. It was one of those annoyances that every job in this life has in abundance. I was to discover that night watches were a normal way of life in the Navy and I learned to adjust to them. I never learned to like them, but I learned to accept them.

We had to use Navy terminology for everything. Floors were decks, walls were bulkheads and ceilings were overheads. The bath room was the head, drinking fountains were scuttle-butts, candy became pogey-bait, ice cream was a gedunk, after shave lotion was foo-foo juice and our underwear was called skivvies.

33

Wherever we went, we had to march there in formation. I quickly discovered that I did not like to march and drill. I was very glad that I had not joined the Army or Marines. I was also pleased to hear our instructor say that we would have few occasions to march, once boot camp was over.

We were also taught how to salute properly. We were told of all the dire things that could happen to us if we neglected to salute anyone that we were required to salute. As a result, we saluted everyone, just to be on the safe side.

At the end of our week of isolation, we marched into the main training center for five weeks of instruction. We attended classes on a wide variety of naval subjects, practiced marching and close order drill, learned to shoot on the rifle range and dreamed about what we would do during our one week "boot" leave after graduation.

During the entire six weeks of training, we were not allowed to leave the camp, or go on liberty as the Navy termed it. We were grounded. We looked with envy at the instructors and others who were free to leave every night. It is strange how you do not realize how precious freedom of movement is, until you have it taken from you. Even though, in our case, we had voluntarily surrendered our freedom to the Navy, the restrictions on our movements were tough to endure.

One thing I gained in boot camp was a nickname. Anyone in the military with a last name, ending in a ski sound, is automatically called "Ski." They do not even bother trying to pronounce your name, they just say "Ski."

With my own brand of humor, I had a lot of fun with this development, by running the words together. For example, if someone asked, "Are you going to the mess hall, Ski?" I would give them a puzzled look and ask, "Messhallski, what the hell

34

language is that, are you trying to speak Polish?" I got a lot of blank looks from my unwitting straight men. My Dutch Grandfather, John Van Horn, would have been proud of me.

Our six weeks of training finally ended and we graduated from Boot Camp. I got on the train and headed for Chicago, on leave for one whole week. We were still required to wear our leggings, but I wanted to look like a real sailor. I took them off as soon as I got on the train.

I had six weeks pay, which, at $21 a month, did not add up to very much. I had signed up for a five thousand dollar insurance policy that took several dollars each month for the premium. They also deducted a few dollars, monthly, for a book we were required to have called, "The Bluejacket's Manual." In addition, during our six weeks training, they had issued us coupons that we could spend in the Navy Canteen for toilet articles, cigarettes and similar items. On payday, they collected for these coupons. All together, I had about $18 for my leave. To a young man, raised in the Depression, the money was adequate. I was happy to be free again, if only for a short time.

My first stop was to go home and see my mother. Then I went out to find my friends. I soon located some of them and began telling them of my boot camp experiences. It was enjoyable to be with them again and the conversation soon turned to girls. One of my buddies said I should not go in the Navy as a virgin. I would be a laughing stock aboard ship if they found out.

I did not see the connection and said, "You guys are virgins too." That is when I discovered that life had not stopped when I joined the Navy.

My friends had been busy and were anxious to ensure that my sex education was completed by having a "hands on" experience. They had found a

35

"red light district" in a town called Indiana
Harbor, a short drive South of Chicago. They were
all veterans of this place and were eager to take
me there. I was tempted, curious and nervous, and
I went with them, knowing it would cost me two
dollars of my leave money.

To me, it was a very un-satisfactory experience.
In the brothel, the madam lined up several, hard
looking women, I had to pick one, and I knew I
was blushing. I pointed at the nearest one to get
on with it. The entire episode was a disappointment. The woman was much older and bored. Now, I
was certifiably experienced and, according to my
friends, could hold my head up in the Navy.

As we drove back to Chicago, they told me that
the first time they went there, one of the
prostitutes saw them and called out, "Hey Mable,
look at the infants." They told me that they had
been embarrassed but they had stayed.

I had been attracted to different girls that
grew up with us in our neighborhood, but I
respected them too much, to ever attempt anything
sexual with them. I knew the facts of life,
having learned them from my contemporaries, but I
never wanted to be the one who might ruin a
girl's reputation by going too far with her. A
few, tame, kisses were all that had ever happened
before in my young life, and now, I was technically no longer innocent.

My friends informed me that none of the
neighborhood girls knew of their visits to
Indiana Harbor. I assured them that their secret
was safe with me. I was willing to forget that it
had ever happened.

5
THE HORNET

My leave went swiftly and I was soon back at the Receiving Station of the Great Lakes Naval Station. I had to stay there while awaiting assignment to my first ship or shore station. It was early October 1941. I impatiently wanted to find out where fate would be sending me.

While still in Boot Camp, I had been interviewed concerning my future in the Navy. The sailor, who talked to me, informed me that I had scored very high on my entrance exams and could even go to Yeoman's school if I wanted to. I asked him what a Yeoman's job was. He said, "I'm a Yeoman." He became insulted when I told him that I did not want to become a secretary or a clerk. He said I would wind up going to sea as a plain sailor. I told him that I had joined the Navy to become a plain sailor.

I envied my shipmates who had received orders to report to various ships at Pearl Harbor, Hawaii. I would have enjoyed surprising my friend Ollie Hamilton if I had been sent there. However, within a few days, I finally received my orders to report aboard the USS Hornet (CV-8), an aircraft carrier, at Portsmouth, Virginia.

We traveled by train from Chicago to Norfolk, Virginia. Early one morning in Norfolk, we shouldered our sea-bags and boarded a ferry boat for the short ride to Portsmouth, where the Hornet was tied up to a pier. Incidentally, this was my very first boat ride and I enjoyed the brisk, invigorating sea breeze as we stood on the Deck of the ferry boat.

We soon arrived at the shipyaed and I saw the
Hornet for the first time. She was a brand new,
20,000 ton, aircraft carrier and had not yet been
commissioned, or accepted, into the US Navy.

She had recently been completed by the Newport
News Shipyard and they had some final work to
finish before the Navy would accept her.

We stood on the pier, gaping at the immense size
of her. They lined up, all of us newly arrived,
Apprentice Seamen, on the pier. They asked for
volunteers to be in the engineering force. Most
of us stepped forward. They arbitrarily split the
line of volunteers in half. I was in the half
that was not accepted. We were told that we would
be temporarily in the deck force and I was
assigned to the Third Division, a group of about
seventy men.

I again shouldered my sea-bag and followed our
guide, up the gangway and on to the Hangar Deck.
We walked Aft (towards the rear of the ship)
until we came to a set of steps, called a ladder,
which led down. We descended one deck and found
ourselves in a large compartment filled with
bunks, three high, and a large number of very
small lockers. We discovered that we were
fortunate and would be sleeping in bunks instead
of hammocks and could live out of a locker
instead of a sea-bag. This compartment became my
home for the next year.

I soon became aware that the Third Division was
responsible for the upkeep of the Main Deck at
the extreme rear of the ship. This deck was
called the Fantail. The name was evidently due to
the fact that the deck was above the propellers
that moved the ship through the water. The
propellers could be considered as huge fans.

Besides this area, we operated several motor
launches, whale boats, a fifty foot officer's
motorboat and the Captain's Gig. We kept the

boats cleaned and ready to go and maintained the boat pockets where the boats were nested when aboard ship.

We kept the decks clean, shined brass, chipped paint, wire brushed rust and re-painted as necessary to keep our areas of responsibility in first class condition. We also maintained our berthing area and rest room facilities, which were called, "the head." We were part of the ship's force, who were responsible for the operation of the ship itself. This included manning the ship's guns during battle.

The Air Department was separate from us. They were responsible for everything that pertained to the handling of aircraft. This included the maintenance of the Flight Deck and Hangar Deck.

A typical day would start with a bugler blowing Reveille over the ship's loud speaker at 6:30 AM. Some ships used recorded bugle calls but the Hornet had live buglers on board.

We would rise, make up our bunks, shower, shave, dress in the prescribed uniform of the day and report to our assigned cleaning station. We would sweep and swab the deck. Then we would shine all the brass or bright work in the area. When we heard the Boatswain Mate, (pronounced Bosun Mate) pipe down chow, we would go to the mess deck and have breakfast.

The Boatswain Mate had a slender, silver whistle on a lanyard around his neck. It was called a "pipe" or a "call." He blew it in a distinctive fashion for different evolutions; to go eat; to turn to; to knock off; to call away a boat; and for various other events. We soon became familiar with this sound and knew what was happening when we heard it. The Boatswain Pipe was also a badge, or symbol, of his station aboard ship.

There was never any doubt about the menu. Every week was the same. For example, every Wednesday and Saturday you knew you were having beans and corn bread for breakfast. Certain days we had chipped beef on toast. There were never any surprises. The food was good and well prepared.

At 0800, we lined up for muster, either on the Hangar Deck or at our cleaning stations, wherever we were told to go. This was done to ensure that everyone was either present or accounted for. We would be given any special instructions or information regarding the events planned for that day and then we would do about fifteen minutes of calisthenics.

When we heard the Boatswain Mate pipe turn to, we went to our assigned work area and proceeded doing the ship's work.

The most senior petty officers in the deck force were the Chiefs. Then came the Boatswain Mate First class, then Second class and finally the Third class who was called a Coxswain (pronounced coxsun). Under these petty officers, in order of rank, were the Seaman First class, Second class and finally us lowly Apprentice seamen.

The primary difference between the deck force and engineering force was that they had Firemen instead of Seamen in their rating descriptions. In the Air Department they had Airmen instead of Seamen. They called us "deck apes" and "swab jockeys" and we called the engineers "snipes." Anyone in the Air Department was called an "airdale".

Each evening, a mimeographed sheet of paper, called the "Plan of the Day" (POD), was distributed to all Divisions and posted on the bulletin boards. It was put out by the Executive Officer who was next in line to the ship's Commanding Officer. This POD listed all the events, such as drills and exercises, planned for the following day. It listed all pertinent information, including ship movements. If in port, it stated which sections had liberty, which

40

sections had the duty and other vital information. The POD was read by all hands each
evening, otherwise you would not know what was
going on from day to day.

When we originally were assigned to the Third
Division, our names were placed on a Watch,
Quarter and Station Bill. This document was
posted on our bulletin board and showed exactly
where we were placed in the organization. It
listed our bunk and locker assignment, where we
worked, where our battle station was, where we
went in case of fire or other emergency and where
we stood watch. There was one category that was
listed as Salvage and Rescue Party. It said that
I was to report to my battle station in case this
team was called for. I asked my petty officer
what this category was for. He said that normally
it meant that this group would be called to
salvage or rescue someone. Since no one could
predict events, this team was an emergency group
for special circumstances.

In any case, by referring to the Watch, Quarter
and Station Bill, you would always know where to
go and what to bring, during any drill, exercise
or actual emergency. All you had to remember was
your own assignment.

On 20 October 1941, the Secretary of the Navy,
Frank Knox, came aboard for the Hornet's
Commissioning ceremonies. We all assembled on the
Flight Deck, in formation, according to each
Division. There were several speeches made, then
Captain Marc Mitscher, the Hornet's first
Commanding Officer, read his orders, assuming
command. Then he had his Executive Officer set
the first watch and the Hornet was officially in
the Navy.

The Navy had some tough commanding officers.
Mitscher, a noted Naval aviator, was one of the
nice ones, a real gentleman. After I learned to

steer the ship and became a qualified helmsman, I
often saw him and became very fond of him. At
sea, he wore a long billed blue cap, a type of
baseball cap. His face was weather beaten with
bright piercing eyes. He invariably wore a kindly
expression. I have since met other fine officers
in the service, but I do not recall ever knowing
another Navy officer that I respected more than
Mitscher.

Many of our petty officers had spent lengthy
tours in the Navy and were old salts. I enjoyed
hearing them tell sea stories about their
experiences in China and other exotic places. I
was interested in learning all I could about
seamanship since I was a sailor and in the deck
force. They could see I was eager and they soon
taught me all the marlinspike seamanship I would
need to know. They showed me how to tie knots and
splice manila rope and wire, how to sew canvas
and how to worm, parcel and serve standing
rigging to protect it from the elements. In
addition, I studied all the available seamanship
manuals until I was confident that I understood
the basic principles of handling a small boat at
sea.

I was assigned as part of a boat crew on a fifty
foot motor launch. The coxswain of the launch
trained me until I became a qualified boat
handler. Before long, I was as adept as he was in
maneuvering the large motor launch. This was
quite a responsibility since the launches could
carry up to 150 passengers. Of course, since I
was still an Apprentice Seaman, I could not be
designated as coxswain of the boat. However, I
was getting prepared for my future advancements.

If you stayed aboard the ship at night, when you
rated liberty, you were considered as fair game
for working parties, fire watches or any other
temporary assignments that would occur suddenly.

As a result of this policy, I went ashore whenever I could, to avoid these extra duties. I normally went ashore alone to one of the local bars in Norfolk.

It was the winter of 1941 and we wore our dress blues ashore, with a flat blue hat instead of the normal white hat. This flat hat had a ribbon with the name of our ship on it. After we got into the war, these ribbons were replaced with one marked, "US Navy," so that people would not know which ships were in port. However, on this particular night, the Hornet ribbon was on my hat.

An English sailor, seated next to me at the bar, said, in his thick British accent, "The Hornet is a carrier, one of those flattops, isn't that right Yank?" When I said yes it was a carrier, he continued on, "Get yourself transferred off that ship matey, them flattops are always being bombed."

Since England had been at war since 1939, I assumed he knew what he was talking about, but, if the Hornet was ever in a battle, I wanted to be there with it.

I also knew that even if I wanted to, I could not be transferred. Shortly after reporting to the Hornet, I and another apprentice, Jim Anderson, who had been in Boot Camp with me, applied for Submarine duty. We had found out that they received more pay than a surface ship sailor. The Yeoman in the Personnel Office told us that we could not be transferred until we became Seaman First Class.

The Hornet was soon underway for our "shakedown" cruise. We operated for several weeks off the coast of Cuba. We went through a series of tests that all new or over-hauled ships go through to check them out before they join the Fleet. Everything is tested to ensure that it works. Also, the crew is trained, night and day, until

43

they know how to operate the ship in all respects.

My Division was assigned to the 20 millimeter, antiaircraft, machine guns as our battle station. My job was to prepare the shells by loading them into a spring loaded magazine and then placing them on the gun as the gunner fired it.

Our battle station was alongside the Flight Deck and I watched as the very first planes flew off the Hornet. It was a thrill to be there seeing it, but I was really surprised to see that the Navy was still flying the Hell Diver biplanes at that late date. I had always been interested in aviation and read many articles about the progress in aircraft development. I knew that the planes I saw taking off from the Hornet were already obsolete and no match for the German air-force. I hoped we had more advanced planes than this available.

During flight operations, the Hornet turned into the wind and increased speed until a minimum of 30 knots of wind was blowing straight down the deck. Then she could launch or recover aircraft. To take off, the pilot would rev up his engine to top speed, when everything sounded right to the Launch Control Officer, he would signal with his flag and the pilot would take off.

When landing, the Landing Control Officer stood at the extreme, after end of the Flight Deck on the Port (left) side. He held a large visible paddle in each hand. The incoming pilot watched the paddles. He would raise or lower each wing in response to the paddle movements. When he was lined up correctly, at the right speed, the Control Officer would give the signal to cut the engine and the plane would land. If things were not right, he would wave him off and the pilot had to go around again.

When the plane landed, there were a number of

arresting gear wires that were stretched across
the deck in the landing path, each about twenty
feet apart and raised about six or eight inches
off the deck. The plane that was landing had a
long tail hook that would eventually snag one of
these wires. This would bring the plane to a
halt. As soon as the plane stopped, a tail-hook
man would run out, unhook the plane and it would
taxi forward.

All the arresting gear wires would drop to the
deck during the taxi operation. Half way up the
flight deck, there was a set of barricade wires,
about eight feet high. This barricade would also
be lowered so that the plane that just landed
could taxi to the forward part of the Flight
Deck. As soon as the plane passed this barricade,
it would again be raised and set in position. If
a plane that was landing, missed all the
arresting gear wires and continued on up the
Flight Deck, the barricade would prevent it from
crashing into the planes that were waiting to be
taken down to the Hangar Deck. In this fashion,
the Flight Deck was separated into two sections,
landing operations were going on aft while planes
were being taken below by the large, forward
elevator.

It was interesting to watch the air-dales work.
Each man wore a distinctively colored hat and
"T" shirt that indicated at a glance, to the
informed observer, what his function was. Each
task had its own color.

I thoroughly enjoyed the sights and sensations
of sailing through the blue Atlantic seas and I
knew I had made an excellent choice by joining
the Navy. I felt I could watch the ocean for
hours and marveled at the different ways it would
appear. Usually it had small waves, sometimes
larger ones, but, the strangest times of all were
when it was flat calm, like glass. I tried to

imagine myself aboard a sailing ship with
Columbus or Magellan when they sailed the sea.
The ocean had to look exactly the same to
them, regardless of how many years had gone by.
My daydreams would end when suddenly one of our
accompanying ships would come into view and bring
me back to reality.

At sea, I rapidly became qualified to stand
helmsman watches on the Bridge, steering the ship
and operating the engine order telegraph to
control the ship's speed and direction. Of
course, you only do whatever the OOD (Officer of
the Deck) orders you to do. However, you have to
do it instantly and correctly.

During a normal four hour watch, I would spend
two hours steering and two hours on the speed
control. I was able to master the job and soon
gained a reputation of being able to steer an
exceptionally straight course. This was easily
determined by the OOD by glancing back at our
wake. The wake remains visible for a very long
time as a ship sails on. A straight course not
only saves fuel but was a sign of professionalism
to the adjoining ships that always accompanied
the Hornet. We never sailed alone.

One afternoon, the OOD complimented me on my
steering as I left the helm. Captain Mitscher
happened to be on the Bridge. He looked at me,
asked my age and how long I had been in the Navy.
I told him I was eighteen and had enlisted on 19
August 1941, not quite three months earlier. He
was amazed that I had progressed rapidly enough
to become a qualified helmsman in such a short
time. He told me that I was off to an excellent
start in the Navy. He also mentioned that the
Navy was expanding and there would be great
opportunities for anyone with the foresight and
ambition to prepare themselves. After that
episode, Captain Mitscher always said hello to me

and seemed to take a personal interest in my progress in the NAVY..

We were tied up to a pier in Norfolk when I received word about a good friend of mine, Johnny Sotos. He had died in a freak accident in a garage in Chicago.

He had his father's car jacked up in his garage and the car started to slip, sideways, off the jacks. Johnny was on the outside of the car, on the driver's side. He evidently tried to grab the emergency brake by opening the front door and reaching in to set the brake. The car slid sideways, against the garage wall. The door closed on his neck, strangling him.

I thought back to a strange incident that had occurred just a year before, in that same garage, before I joined the Navy. I was with Johnny and another friend of ours, Sam Blair. It was the only time I had ever been in that particular garage. The three of us were in there for some reason or other.

Just as we started to leave, Sam stopped us. He said, "Here we are, three young men, healthy, seventeen or eighteen years old, just starting life." We looked at each other and looked at Sam and said, "So what? What's your point?" Sam said, "Do you ever wonder which one of us is going to die first?" Johnny and I both looked at Sam in astonishment. Johnny said, "Are you nuts? Why would you ask a question like that?" Sam said, "It just occurred to me, one of us has to be the first to die." It was a very strange and unusual comment to make and here, one year later, Johnny died tragically in that very garage. For whatever reason, Sam had a strange premonition of death that day in Johnny's garage.

6

WORLD WAR TWO

On Sunday, 7 December 1941, the Japanese attacked our Naval Base at Pearl Harbor, Hawaii. It was about 0800, Hawaiian time. There had been no "Declaration of War". Forever after, this event would be called a "sneak attack."

In Norfolk, Virginia, aboard the Hornet, it would have been around 1300 (1 PM), due to the time differential.

The war that had been raging in Europe, since 1939, was a European war. Once Japan attacked us, the conflict truly became a World War.

Everyone who was alive then, remembers where they were when they heard about the Pearl Harbor attack. The Hornet was alongside a pier in Norfolk that week-end. I rated liberty and had gone ashore on Saturday, December 6. Rather than return to the ship on Saturday night, I stayed at the YMCA. Sunday, I had breakfast and went to an early movie. It was probably about 3:30 PM when I got out of the theater. I stopped at a cafe for a sandwich and the waitress asked me, "Aren't you supposed to be back on your ship?" I told her I had liberty until 7 AM Monday morning. She asked me if I knew about the Japanese attack. When I told her no, she gave me all the details. She told me that the radio broadcasts were notifying all the service men to report to their units. She also said that the Shore Patrol and Military Police had been rounding up the service men.

I immediately returned to the Norfolk Naval Base and was stopped at the gate by an FBI. Agent. He examined my ID and Liberty cards. He then began interrogating me about my whereabouts since 1 PM.

He wanted to know why I had not returned as soon as the attack happened. I explained that I had been in a movie and had no knowledge of the event. He could not believe that the theater would not stop the film and make an announcement. All I could do was repeat exactly what I had done that day and he finally allowed me to proceed to my ship, I could never understand why he was so suspicious of me.

When I got to the Hornet, it was like a bee hive. Practice ammunition was being off-loaded and all sorts of supplies were being brought aboard. It seemed as if everyone was running to wherever they were going. When I had gone ashore on Saturday, everything was moving at a natural pace. Now, since the attack, everyone was in high gear.

I reported to my Division and was sent on a working party, loading supplies aboard. The Navy got their money's worth out of me that night. I did not get to sleep until 0400.

On December 8th. President Roosevelt announced that we were at War with the Japanese Empire.

He did not declare war against Germany. Three days later Hitler declared war against the United States and this brought us into the European War.

That morning, the Bugler sounded General Quarters and we all raced to our battle stations. This was the last time my Division manned the 20 millimeter machine guns. A short time later, we traded battle stations with the Marines that were stationed on board. They took over the 20 millimeters and we manned the large, five inch, 38 caliber, dual purpose, anti-aircraft guns.

They were called dual purpose because they could be used for surface firing or aircraft defense. They were slightly larger than the 90 millimeter guns used by the Army. There were eight of these large guns on the ship. My Division took over

49

four of them, two on each side, aft. When we
manned the machine guns, that were located
alongside of the Flight Deck, we exposed the
upper part of our bodies. The five inch guns were
in open gun tubs, but the Flight Deck was several
feet over our heads. This change of battle
stations meant little to us at the time, but, in
less than a year, it would become a significant
factor in our lives.

I was on gun number seven. The gun farthest aft
on the starboard (right) side of the ship. I was
a "sight setter." If you can imagine yourself
shooting at a flying target, you have to offset
your aim to hit it. If you aim at where the
target is when you pull the trigger, it will be
gone from that spot when your shot gets there. If
you aim ahead of a flying target, you have a
chance of hitting it. My job was to offset the
sights so that when the Pointer and Trainer
looked through them to aim the gun, the gun was
actually pointing to where the target was going
to be.

In actual practice, this information was being
sent to us from a Gun Director. All I had to do
was match my dials with the dials being
controlled by the Gun Director. When matched up,
I placed the sights into automatic and they
followed the Director's dials. I was there as a
manual back-up, in case something happened to the
automatic system.

On 19 December, I had been in the Navy for four
months. I was advanced to Seaman Second Class and
my pay leaped from $21 to $36 a month. It was a
thrill to have that second white mark sewn onto
the cuffs of my dress blue jumper, indicating to
one and all that I was no longer on the bottom of
the totem pole. I went ashore to celebrate and
ended up having a small tattoo placed on my right
shoulder.

Around this time, in early February, we loaded Two Army Air Force B-25 bombers on board and sailed out into the Atlantic. These large planes took off and flew away, then the word was passed that what we had just done was a military secret and could not be divulged to anyone. We then returned to the Portsmouth area.

That weekend I decided to do some sight-seeing. With my extra pay, I took a bus ride to Washington, D.C. I got a room at an inexpensive hotel and asked for directions to the White House. By the time I got there, it was dark. The weather was cold and it was snowing slightly. I walked entirely around the fence that guarded it and finally came to a spot where I could see a few lighted windows. I let my imagination roam, visualizing President Roosevelt inside the building, probably working at his desk. He may not have been in the city for all I knew, but, in my imagination, he was there. After awhile I left, found a small restaurant, had dinner and returned to the hotel. The next day, I rode the bus back to Norfolk. I do not know what impelled me to go to D.C. but I am glad I did. The trip was interesting and I had visited it during a very historic time in our nation's life.

Eventually, we left the Norfolk area and sailed to Panama. We were on the alert for submarine attacks during the entire trip. We transited the canal and then went to San Diego.

Sailing through the canal was a fascinating experience. The trip is a little over 50 miles in length. The Hornet was so wide that we had to remove the nests of life rafts that were hanging on her sides. We placed them on the decks. When we reached the Pacific side of the canal, we re-hung them on the sides.

We entered the canal at Colon, on the Atlantic side, tying up to a pier. I went ashore with a working party to remove the rafts. It was the very first time I had ever stepped onto foreign soil. I looked around and noticed signs that said, "No Fuma." I found out later that this was Spanish for "No Smoking." This was an un-welcome sign to me. My one bad habit was that I smoked. In those days, we really did not know of the great health risks we ran by smoking and I could buy cigarettes aboard ship for fifty cents a carton.

For a ship to pass through the canal, she has to be raised about 85 feet to reach the level of Gatun Lake, a freshwater lake that makes up a large part of the canal.

In going from the Atlantic to the Pacific as the Hornet did, the raising is accomplished by the ship first going through a series of locks, named Gatun Locks. The ship enters a large walled area, called a lock. A watertight gate is closed behind the ship that is now enclosed on all four sides by high walls. Additional water is pumped into the lock area and the ship rises with the water. This continues until the ship is at the same level as the water in the next lock. The wall in front of the ship opens and the vessel moves forward to the next lock. The gate again closes behind the ship and water is again pumped in, repeating the same process as before. The ship must go through a third lock before it reaches the level of Gatun Lake.

After sailing across Gatun Lake, the ship enters Miraflores Lock to descend about 30 feet to Miraflores Lake. After crossing this lake, the ship goes through the two Pedro Miguel Locks that lower it to Balboa Harbor and the entrance to the Pacific Ocean.

The Hornet was under her own power while transiting the lakes, but we were towed by electric locomotives, called mules, while moving through the locks. The canal workers would row out to the ship with heavy tow lines that were attached to the mules. The ship would throw a heaving line to the row boat, the worker would secure it to the tow line and we would haul it aboard.

A heaving line consists of an eighty foot sash cord with a heavy, lead filled, knot, called a monkey's fist, on one end.

You throw it by first dividing it into two equal coils, one in each hand. You then throw the coil, with the weighted end, toward the target. You let the second coil feed freely from your hand. It takes a lot of practice to become proficient with this line.

I was on the Fantail when my Division officer ordered me to throw a line to an on-coming row boat. I picked up a heaving line and tried to separate it into two coils. Unfortunately, it had become snarled. I looked around for another heaving line but did not see any. The Bridge passed the word, via our phone talker, to expedite getting the tow rope aboard. My Division officer became impatient as I tried to untangle the line and hollered, "Throw it now." In disgust, I threw the single, snarled coil, expecting to see it end up as a tangled mess. To my great surprise, it straightened out beauty-fully and dropped across the rowboat, precisely between the man rowing and the man holding the eye of the tow rope.

It was a magnificent throw. We were the first station aboard the Hornet to get our tow rope secured and my Division officer received a "well done" from the Bridge. He patted me on the back and said he had never seen such accuracy with a heaving line. I kept my mouth shut and accepted the compliments. I was the only who knew that it had been a lucky shot. My reputation in the

53

Division was going up.

We were not allowed to go ashore on liberty in Panama but headed directly for San Diego. When we arrived, we anchored out and started running liberty boats into port. We were there several days and after a few trips, I became qualified as the coxswain of a 50 foot motor launch.

I was enchanted to discover that a large dolphin would accompany us to the boat landing, wait while we unloaded and then travel back with us to the ship. The dolphin was always there, waiting for us. I had never heard of anything like that before and asked the older sailors about it. They told me that dolphins frequently became very friendly. It was almost like having a pet fish.

Having grown up in grimy, sooty, Chicago, it was a real pleasure to see the clean streets, bright colorful houses and palm trees in San Diego. I soon discovered that the bars were much more elegant than they were in Norfolk, but, they checked your ID card at the door. You had to be 21 to enter. So naturally, I altered the age on my ID card to indicate I was 21 instead of 18.

The day before we were to leave San Diego, I was working on the Fantail. My petty officer came over and asked for my ID card. I took out my wallet and was removing the card when I asked him why he wanted it. He said the Executive Officer was going to check them out for "altered" birth dates. If the card was altered, it meant 30 days restriction to the ship. I asked what would happen if you lost your card. He told me that it was two weeks restriction if that happened. I was standing by the lifeline and I flicked my ID card over the side, into San Diego Bay. He looked at me in astonishment and asked, "Did you just throw your ID card over the side?" I said, "No, that was an old cleaning ticket for my dress blue uniform." Then he said, "Well, give me your ID

Card." I looked at him with a straight face and told him, "I can't, I lost it."

He stared at me for a few minutes and realized that I had out foxed him. He said, "You're a wise bastard, be careful you don't out smart yourself someday."

Since we were scheduled to get underway the next day, I did not mind two weeks restriction to the ship, it beat having 30 days restriction plus a black mark for altering an ID card.

We operated off the coast of southern California for a few days, qualifying Marine pilots for carrier landings. I was relieved to see that the Navy was now flying modern, single wing aircraft. They had Grumman Wildcat fighters, Douglas SBD dive-bombers and Douglas TBD torpedo planes. The torpedo planes were slow and vulnerable, but the fighters and dive-bombers were first rate.

We eventually passed under San Francisco's Golden Gate Bridge and put into port at Alameda, California. We tied up to a pier at the Naval Air Station. We noticed a group of Army Air Force B-25 bombers on the pier. To our surprise, they began loading them onto our flight deck with a huge crane. They spread sixteen B-25s across the length of our Flight Deck, taking up most of the available room. Another American carrier, the USS Wasp, had recently ferried some British fighter planes to the Island of Malta in the Mediter-ranean Sea. A rumor was soon going around the Hornet that we were going to ferry these bombers to Alaska. Nothing could have been farther from the truth.

We were granted liberty that evening and I had a chance to briefly explore San Francisco. The next morning we got under way and again passed under the Golden Gate Bridge, heading out into the Pacific Ocean. I had absolutely no idea of where we were headed, but I knew it would be interesting

7
DOOLITTLE'S TOKYO RAID

It was the first of April, 1942 and I was
pleased to learn that I had just been advanced to
Seaman First Class. It came as the result of a
recent test I had taken. I had studied and worked
hard for this promotion. It not only raised my
pay to $54 a month, it improved my status in the
Division by exempting me from routine working
parties and other onerous duties. I was starting
to rise above my peers and I was ambitious.

The United States had been in the war for about
four months. It should be noted that the U.S. had
not been prepared for war. There had been a lot
of public support for "neutralism, letting Europe
fight her own battles" and similar sentiments.
President Roosevelt had tried to aid England and
Russia, but the Congress did not always side with
him. The original one year preparedness draft had
barely passed the vote in Congress. When the year
was almost up and Congress was asked to extend it
to keep the draftees in a little longer, it
passed by one vote. The draftees started holding
up signs that read "OHIO." It did not mean the
State of Ohio, it meant, "Over the hill in
October." We were short of trained troops,
pilots, sailors, and most of all, equipment, when
we were attacked.

The Japanese attack at Pearl Harbor sank a large
number of ships, including six Battleships and
killed about 3,000 sailors. They also wiped out
our air power in Hawaii. They attacked Hong Kong,
Malaya and the Philippines, eliminating our air
power there also. In January 1942, Manila fell.
Our forces, led by General MacArthur, retreated
into the Bataan Peninsula.

56

The British were also in extremely bad shape in
the Pacific. Hong Kong fell on Christmas Day. The
Malaya Peninsula was rapidly overrun by Japanese
infantry and Singapore fell in mid February,
surrendering about 70,000 British troops.

Off the coast of Malaya, Japanese planes sank
the British Battleship, HMS Prince of Wales and
the Heavy Cruiser, HMS Repulse. Prime Minister
Winston Churchill commented later on, that the
loss of these two ship were "bitter pills to
swallow."

The Japanese moved to capture the Dutch East
Indies by landing troops near Borneo. In late
February, in a three day sea battle in the Java
Sea, they sank an entire force of American, Dutch
and Australian ships. By March, all the Dutch
East Indies were gone and an additional 100,000
prisoners captured.

The Japanese landed on New Guinea and were
bombing Darwin, Australia. Australia was in a
desperate situation because they had sent their
own troops to North Africa to help the British
out. Now they faced invasion of their own country
without any troops to defend it.

Guam and Wake Islands had been captured early in
the war. In March, General MacArthur escaped by
PT (Patrol Torpedo) Boat from the Philippines and
was sent to Australia. At about the same time
that the Hornet left Alameda with the sixteen B-
25 bombers, the Philippine defenders, surrendered
Bataan and retreated to the island fort of
Corregidor for their final stand.

In short, we and our allies were losing ground
on all fronts. Germany was still winning in
Europe and Africa. Their "U" Boats were steadily
sinking our shipping in the Atlantic. America,
England and Russia were concentrating their
resources in the European Theater. They reasoned
that Hitler had to be defeated first.

In the meantime, Japan was whipping everyone she

met in the Pacific, taking thousands of prisoners
and conquering all the territory that she set her
sights on. Those of us in the service and in the
Pacific area, at this moment in our nation's
history, had to try and hold off this onslaught
until the US had time to get her industrial
capacity in gear and train the troops needed to
defeat Germany and Japan. The issue was very much
in doubt and we were all expendable.

With the preceding situation in mind, you can
imagine our total surprise, the day we left
Alameda, to hear an announcement, by Captain
Mitscher, over the ship's public address system
after we were at sea; "This ship will carry the
Army bombers to the coast of Japan for the
bombing of Tokyo."

There was a stunned silence and a then terrific
roar of approval rang out from the crew of the
Hornet. We were finally going to strike back at
Japan and the Hornet was going to help to do the
striking.

We were to rendezvous with the Enterprise to
provide air cover since we could not bring our
own planes to the flight deck with the bombers
there.

Admiral "Bull" Halsey was aboard the Enterprise
and was in charge of the operation. Lieutenant
Colonel Jimmy Doolittle of the Army Air Force
would lead the raid. At that time, the U.S. did
not have a separate Air Force.

It was exciting to stand helm watches during
this trip. When going on watch, I could check our
latest position on the Quartermasters chart. The
Japanese had secretly sailed through the North
Pacific to a point near the Hawaiian Islands.
From there, they launched their 7 December
attack. We were turning the tables on them by
reversing the process. We were sailing through
the same waters, to a point near Japan. If all

went well, we would soon be launching our attack
against them.

The air crews moved the bombers as far aft as
they could. Then they painted a large white
stripe, the length of the Flight Deck. This was
to guide the nose wheel of the B-25s to ensure
that their right wing tip did not strike the
ship's Island structure during takeoff.

As the Hornet steamed steadily through the cold,
gray, North Pacific, I spent most of my spare
time walking around the Flight Deck. I enjoyed
looking the Army planes over and talking to their
crews.

One day, I was with a shipmate of mine, also
from Chicago, Charley Pellinat. I happened to
look at the underside of a B-25 and thought I saw
a wooden machine gun. I took a closer look and
discovered that the guns were indeed made of
wood, black painted broom sticks. I pointed it
out to Charley and we asked one of the Army
pilots why they were going into combat with fake
guns. He told us that they had removed the normal
guns to reduce weight. They also mounted a camera
at that position, to record the bombing mission.
They had placed the wooden guns there to possibly
fool any plane that might attack them from that
position.

We started to leave and I asked the pilot how
they managed to operate the camera at that
location. In those days, we did not have all the
remote technology we now have.

He told us that they were supposed to get Navy
volunteers to do this task. Charley and I looked
at each other and asked him who was going to
select the volunteers. He told us, "Colonel
Doolittle."

Charley and I wasted no time in locating the
Colonel. He was at the ship's gedunk stand,
eating a dish of ice cream.

Now Jimmy Doolittle was a world famous man. He held many speed and distance flying records. He was the first man to fly on instruments and pioneered blind flying. He was always in the headlines of the news papers or in the news reels at the movies. It was very intimidating to me to approach any high ranking officer, especially such a famous man. However, I could not chicken out in front of Charley. I gathered up my courage and walked up to him.

I asked him if I could speak to him. He graciously said yes. And stood up, I was surprised to see that I was taller than he. I was only five feet six inches tall. He must have been at least two inches shorter than I was. I explained about seeing the wooden guns and related the information the pilot had given us. I told him that Charley and I wanted to volunteer to operate the cameras. To our astonishment, Doolittle doubled over with laughter. He really cracked up. When he regained his composure, he told us that the pilot operated the camera by remote control from the cockpit.

He thanked us for offering to go with them, but he had no need for additional volunteers. We apologized for bothering him and quickly walked away. We had very red faces and felt like two country bumpkins. He was still chuckling as we left. When we were safely on deck, we looked at each other and busted out laughing. We had really been taken in by that Army pilot. We agreed not to let the Division know how we had made asses out of ourselves and we promptly forgot about the entire episode.

Despite that embarrassment, I still spent time, roaming about the Flight Deck. I noticed that they were loading conventional bombs and some long, rectangular shaped, crates. They appeared to be slightly larger and longer than orange

crates. I asked about them and one of the crewmen
informed me that they were incendiary bombs. Each
incendiary bomb was about three feet long and two
or three inches square. I believe he said that
they were bundled together in groups of fifty.
When they were clustered together they had the
appearance of a large box. When dropped over the
target, they would separate and spread out over a
large area, causing many fires. I think that each
plane was loaded with both regular and incendiary
bombs.

One day a special ceremony was performed on the
Flight Deck. Mitscher, who would soon be promoted
to Rear Admiral, and Doolittle, attached some
Japanese medals to the fins of one of the bombs.
Several Japanese medals had been received over
the years, by various personnel and they were
taking this occasion to return them.

In 1942, for an aircraft carrier, with Navy
planes, to attack a land target, it had to be
within 200 miles of the target. With the longer
ranged Army bombers we planned to launch at 400
miles.

We could launch them, as we had proven off
Norfolk, but we could not recover them. The
planes were much too large and were not equipped
with tail hooks which were needed for landing
purposes. The planes were to bomb their targets
and continue on to China. They were supposed to
land at Chunking, a town that was under Chinese
control. Since the 1930s, the Japanese had been
fighting the Chinese and held many areas in
China.

A day or so before we were to launch the attack,
we refueled the Task Force while underway and
then sent our oil tankers, with a destroyer
escort, racing back to Hawaii.

On 18 April, at about 0600, our bugler sounded
general quarters. We ran to our battle stations

and learned that we had encountered a Japanese patrol ship. It was about the size of a large fishing trawler. One of our cruisers, I believe the Nashville, opened up on the ship and blew it out of the water. No one knew whether the patrol ship had gotten a message off or not. We were about 600 miles from Japan as we steamed through the wreckage of the ship that we had sunk.

Aboard the Enterprise, Admiral Halsey had to make a decision. If we launched early, the bombers would have to fly farther than planned. The fuel capacity of the planes was marginal at best. If we continued on course, we would be getting closer to a, possibly, alerted enemy. We might be sailing into overwhelming odds. At the time, the US had only four operational carriers in the Pacific Ocean. The Navy could not afford to lose two of them on this mission. The decision was made to launch the aircraft.

Colonel Doolittle was the first one off. He roared over the Hornet one time, waggled his wings and then headed for Japan. Gas was going to be the critical factor. As each plane took off, it headed immediately for its target. They did not wait to form up and fly in formation.

The seas were rough that day and the Hornet was pitching fore and aft. Occasionally, we would take heavy spray over the bow of the Flight Deck. The pilots tried to time their takeoff so that they would reach the end of the Flight Deck, just as it pitched up.

Navy Flight Deck personnel were releasing the tie down ropes from the wings of the last plane. The ship pitched up, causing the plane to roll backwards. One of the plane's propellers hit a Navy crewman, cutting off his arm. I don't know if the pilot was even aware of the accident.

As the last plane departed, the Hornet swung around and headed for Hawaii at Flank speed.

Flank is a term used for maximum speed possible.
The Bridge tuned the ship's radio to a Japanese
broadcast station. Our thoughts and prayers went
with the Doolittle group. We hoped that they
would not be intercepted by the Japanese. We
still did not know if the patrol ship had sent
off a warning or not.

Listeners, fluent in Japanese, intently
monitored the programs. After about two hours,
they could determine, by the excited announce-
ments, that something unusual was happening in
Japan. It had to be that the raid was a success.
The planes had evidently reached Japan and
carried off the raid.

An announcement was made on the Hornet that the
raid had apparently succeeded. We were then
cautioned that the entire episode was a military
secret and we were forbidden to disclose our part
in the raid to anyone. We had to keep the story
to ourselves, but we had helped make history.

When President Roosevelt announced the bombing
of Japan to the American public, it boosted the
nation's morale tremendously. After four months
of constant defeats, the U.S. had something to
cheer about. It was a psychological shot in the
arm for the entire country.

8

HAWAIIAN OPERATIONS

It took several days to reach Hawaii. In those days Hawaii was not a State, it was a Territory. Regardless of what the designation was, it was a beautiful and exotic land and I was anxious to get there.

About two days before we arrived, one of the seamen in my Division fell dead of a heart attack. He was a young fellow, apparently healthy. My petty officer told me that the seaman had been in the hospital for a heart problem, but they thought he had recovered.

They normally bury dead sailors at sea. Since we were due to be in port, shortly, they decided to bury him in Hawaii. I was picked as part of the burial detail. I was anxious to experience Hawaii, but my first day there was a sad event as we buried our young shipmate. We returned to the ship after the funeral and I contemplated how quickly and unexpectedly a life can end. I was disappointed in the delay before I could go ashore in Hawaii, but I reflected that the young man we buried that day would have gladly traded places with me.

The air-crewman, who had lost his arm when the last B-25 took off, was transferred to the Naval Hospital. The Hornet took up a cash collection and presented it to him before he left, our first casualty of the war.

I went ashore the following day. Liberty ran from 1000 to 1700. There were no overnight passes. Hawaii and Honolulu were fascinating. The mixtures of Oriental, Hawaiian and Caucasian races had produced some un-believably beautiful and attractive girls. Unfortunately, they evidently had all been warned against sailors. It was extremely difficult to become acquainted with anyone.

Hawaii was under Martial Law, ever since the war began. The military ran everything. In Honolulu, they allowed brothels to operate. They even set the rates. Since there were so many on liberty, long lines of servicemen would extend from the brothels and wind around the block. It was an amazing sight when you realized what the lines were for.

Whenever I heard the word prostitute, I would remember the VD films we were shown periodically. They displayed some terrible diseases, in living color. I remember one old salty sailor telling me that he was approached by a working girl in Norfolk. She tried to tempt him by saying, "Come with me and you'll get something you never had before." He asked her, "My God, what have you got, leprosy?"

After the war, one of the prostitutes that worked in Honolulu, wrote a book about her experiences there. I believe it was called, "The Revolt of Mamie Stover". I never read it but I am sure it accurately described the conditions that existed in Honolulu in those days.

It had been four months since the Pearl Harbor attack. They still worried about another raid. We all had to carry gas masks while on liberty.

The majority of the sunk and damaged ships were still resting where they were when the attack ended. The shipyard was working around the clock but there was so much damage that it was hard to see any headway.

I operated one of the Hornet's 50 foot motor launches. Whenever I had the opportunity, I would circle Ford Island to view the sunk and damaged hips. On occasion, I would be detailed to operate the 50 foot officer's motorboat. Invariably, they wanted to view the destruction also and I would take them on a tour. The amount of damage caused by that attack was truly awesome.

On my duty days, I operated a liberty boat. I took liberty parties ashore at 1000 and brought them back at 1700. I would travel between the Hornet and the Fleet Landing. There was always a traffic jam of boats at the landing. The Navy had a Beach Master there. He controlled the traffic by determining which boat could land. He did this by use of an amplified loud speaker.

I remember one occasion when I picked up 150 inebriated sailors and started back to the Hornet. Part way there, several of the passengers decided to smoke, a definite violation of regulations in a Navy boat. I tried to get them to put out the cigarettes but they ignored me.

I operated the launch from a small platform at the rear of the boat. It was surrounded by a railing, called a taffrail, and I used a tiller to steer with. I regulated the speed by pulling a cord to ring a bell. The engineer, who was some distance from me, would respond to the bell. One bell for forward, two for neutral, three for reverse and four bells for full speed in which ever direction we were traveling.

My immediate problem was, how to gain control of my passengers. A five foot, six inch 130 pound seaman cannot physically coerce 150 drunks, I had to use my brain. Suddenly I had the answer. I rang two bells. The engineer put the engine in neutral and we lay to, in the middle of Pearl Harbor.

My passengers began to ask me why I stopped. I told them that we would not move until all the cigarettes were extinguished. They all wanted to get back in time for the evening meal and they made the smokers throw their cigarettes over the side. When all the cigarettes were out, I started up again. There were no more incidents on that trip. I felt good about the way I had handled the situation.

I was getting a reputation of being an excellent boat handler. However, I found out that the pendulum swings both ways. One day I was coming into a landing, alongside a float that extended out from the Hornet's gangway. A 50 foot launch has a crew of four, a bow hook, stern hook, coxswain and engineer. As I approached the float, I sounded two bells for neutral. I rang the bell by pulling on a rope lanyard. The engineer put it in neutral and we coasted gently in. The bow hook stepped onto the float and I rang three bells to go into reverse and stop my forward motion. As we were facing, the bow of the launch was heading straight at the side of the Hornet. That is when everything went to hell.

When I attempted to ring the bell three times to reverse the engine, the rope lanyard broke after the first ring. The engineer heard one bell only so he put it in forward gear. We were heading straight into the side of the Hornet. The bow hook was hollering at the engineer and so was I but he could not hear us due to the sound of the diesel engine. I finally threw my hat at him and he looked at me. I pointed at the Hornet. He looked up and threw the engine into reverse. It was too late, the bow hit the side of the ship, just as we started backwards.

By this time the Officer of the Deck and my bow hook were both hollering at me and pointing behind me. I looked around and discovered that my stern hook, a short red headed kid, had been pulled off the float and was frantically trying to swim away as I was now backing down on him. I got the engineer to put it in neutral. We tied up the launch and rescued the stern hook from the water. He was as mad as a wet hen. I tried to explain to him what had happened, but he did not

67

want to talk. He angrily went aboard ship to change clothes. The entire Quarter Deck had thoroughly enjoyed the spectacle and I kept hearing comments about Laurel and Hardy and the four stooges.

I repaired the broken lanyard and finally went aboard. The Officer of the Deck did not help when he told me, "That was the funniest thing I ever witnessed." I could picture him telling the story in the wardroom during the evening meal. By the time I reached the Third Division compartment, they all had heard the story. I was the butt of a good many jokes for the rest of the day. My ego was definitely deflated. I had to admit though, it was funny.

When I had joined the Navy, I did not have any particular girl friend. But there was a girl I knew back in Chicago that I was very fond of. It happened to be near her birthday so I shopped around in Honolulu for a present. I finally found just the right thing, a small, musical, jewelry box. I thought that it was very attractive, though it was expensive.

I went ahead and bought it and mailed it to her. I hoped that she would enjoy receiving it and maybe this would inspire her to write to me.

After a week or so, we got under way for the South Pacific. On the way to bomb Japan, we had crossed the 180th Meridian, the International Date Line. According to Navy tradition, by crossing that line, we were now official members of the Golden Dragon Society. Some ships make a big deal out of it and issue certificates attesting to your new status, though the Hornet did not.

On the voyage we were now on, we were heading for the Coral Sea, located Northeast of Australia. We would be crossing the Equator. Almost all ships mark this event by holding some type of ceremony. Before you cross the line, you

are a "pollywog." After you once cross the line,
you are, forever more, a "shellback."

Ceremonies were set up on the Hornet. A sailor
was dressed up as King Neptune and placed on a
throne on the Flight Deck. The word was passed
that the King was aboard and holding court. All
the pollywogs were to assemble before him.

The King's assistant would bring each pollywog
before him. They would charge him with invading
the King's domain. They would then carry out the
sentence pronounced by the King. The sentences
ranged from wild haircuts to wearing your uniform
backwards for several hours. It was all good fun
and passed rapidly. We were now, all shellbacks.

We arrived early in May. The "Battle of the
Coral Sea" had just ended and we missed the
action. This was the first time that two opposing
fleets had fought without actually being in sight
of each other. The entire battle was fought by
planes from the aircraft carriers. The U.S. lost
the carrier Lexington and the carrier Yorktown
was damaged.

The Japanese had lost one small carrier, had
another one damaged, and lost most of the pilots
on the third carrier. The fight was deemed a
draw, with the exception that the Japanese had
intended to land troops at Port Moresby on New
Guinea, a large island near Australia. They were
prevented from doing so.

From that perspective, we and the Australians,
who would have been threatened by having enemy
troops on Port Moresby considered the outcome of
the battle as a success.

We were soon ordered back to Pearl Harbor. We
heard rumors that the Doolittle raid had been a
success and all but one plane, crashed in China.
The one exception had landed in Russia.

We also learned that the Japanese had captured
some of the crews and executed a large number of

Chinese civilians who were suspected of aiding the Doolittle fliers.

We had hoped that they would all come through in good shape, but wars do not usually work out that way. In any case, we had helped to give the Japanese something to think about.

During each sea battle, the Navy learned many new and valuable lessons that they immediately applied. They learned to off-load any item that they could do without. This was done to reduce the number of "missile hazards" that were generated when ships were hit by a high explosive bomb or shell.

Following this new policy, the Navy ships removed a large number of their motor launches and whaleboats. They sent them to a boat pool in Pearl Harbor. The ship's kept a minimum number of boats aboard. When in port, a ship could request that the boat pool loan them boats, and coxswains, if required.

My Division's leading petty officer, BM1 Crook, told me I was being transferred to the boat pool, along with some of the Hornet's boats. It was very tempting to remain in Hawaii, a real paradise, but I did not want to leave the ship. I wanted to stay aboard and share the Hornet's adventures with my shipmates.

I talked Crook into letting me remain on board. I think he was pleased that I was loyal to my ship. He told me that he would have no problem finding a replacement. He said it was a sought after job. He did tell me though, that he thought I was making a big mistake. He said, "There is an old saying in the Navy, the worst shore duty is better than the best sea duty." He may have been right. He had opened a door for me, but I declined to walk through it.

I was pleasantly surprised to receive a letter from Vince Treacy, one of my Chicago buddies. He was the one who recommended that I attend high school at Tilden Tech. He told me that he had attended a birthday party at the home of a mutual friend of ours, the girl who I had sent the musical jewelry box to. He said that she had received a present of a very expensive portable radio from one of her admirers. When she later un-wrapped the jewelry box that I had sent, they made fun of it, as if it were a cheap gift.

He said he thought it was an attractive present and it made him angry to see them using the jewelry box as an ash tray.

I wondered why I had never received a letter from her, acknowledging receipt of my gift. Now I knew why. It had not been appreciated.

Portable radios were expensive, but I had taken quite a few hours shopping for an appropriate present for her and spent a large part of my meager salary to purchase the jewelry box.

I was disappointed, but I also now knew, what her true feelings were, towards me. I discovered that it really did not bother me. For me, she simply ceased to exist.

I wrote back to Vince and thanked him for the letter and the information.

I believe it was on this visit to Hawaii that we lost our Junior Division Officer, a very pleasant man. The air squadrons were always training and it was possible to arrange to take a joy ride during a training flight. The joy riders would take the rear gunner's place. In this particular instance, the junior officer from our division, went with a dive bomber pilot. They went into a dive, with a 1,000 pound bomb, and never pulled out. The plane dove straight into the ocean. They never found either one of them. The word was put out, "No more joy rides".

9

THE BATTLE OF MIDWAY

It was the latter part of May when we again
sailed. After we were at sea, we were issued, fur
lined, foul weather jackets and gloves. The
rumors were that we were headed for Alaska.

Within a few hours, the word was passed, over
the loud speaker, to turn in the foul weather
gear. I never did find out if we were originally
scheduled to go to Alaska, or if some one thought
we were. In any case, issuing the foul weather
equipment had been someone's mistake.

The Hornet headed North-West where we eventually
joined forces with the Enterprise and the
Yorktown. The Yorktown had been damaged at the
Coral Sea Battle. She had been hastily repaired
in time to join us. We were not sure what we were
in for, but we knew we were headed for the
vicinity of Midway Island. Mitscher, who was now
a Rear Admiral, was still aboard as Captain of
the Hornet. He announced over the Public Address
System, "This is the Captain. We are going to
intercept a Jap attack on Midway." With Mitscher,
we always knew what we were doing.

I believe it was on this trip that an incident
occurred that always comes to mind, whenever I
think of Admiral Mitscher.

One afternoon, during a four hour watch on the
Bridge, the Quartermaster relieved me at the helm
for a short break. I walked out on the wing of
the Bridge to smoke a cigarette. Mitscher was
seated in his Captain's chair, facing aft, as he
habitually did. On this trip, we had some news
correspondents aboard. One of them approached
Admiral Mitscher. He had his notebook and pen out

and he asked Mitscher why he always looked backwards, where we came from, instead of looking forward, where we were headed.

He was searching for a possible hidden meaning in the Admiral's actions. I was curious myself, now that someone brought it up. I was only a few feet away and I listened intently for the answer. Mitscher looked at him and with a serious expression said, "No big mystery about it, when I face the other way, the wind blows in my face."

The writer put his pen away and left. Mitscher knew I had overheard the conversation. He turned toward me with a big smile and nodded at me. I always remembered sharing this private moment with him.

I saw Mitscher frequently on the Bridge when I stood my watches. Whenever General Quarters sounded, the Quartermasters took over the helm. I would run to my battle station on the gun mount. As a result, I never had an opportunity to observe him during any of the battles we were in. He was to become a very famous Admiral before the war ended.

We were operating to the North-East of Midway Island. The Japanese were expected to approach from the North-West. The ship was keyed up in anticipation of a big fight. We were at our battle stations each morning and each evening. From a half hour before sundown or sunrise until a half hour after. The theory was that this was the expected time for an attack. If an air raid or submarine attack occurred at these times, we would be ready.

On 4 June, at sunrise, while we were at our battle stations, the Hornet turned into the wind and began launching aircraft. We knew the battle was on. We remained at our gun positions all day. Whenever this would occur, at meal time, we would send a detail to the mess deck to pick up our battle rations. They consisted of bologna with cheese sandwiches, coffee and doughnuts.

Eventually, some of our planes returned, with the exception of Torpedo Squadron Eight. A squadron of fifteen planes.

We assumed that they might have landed at Midway. We found out later that they had all been shot down, by enemy planes, while attacking the Japanese carriers. They had been flying the slow, obsolete Douglas TBD Devastators. They were no match for the swift Zero fighters and the heavy anti-aircraft fire they encountered. Only one man, Ensign Gay, would survive from this group.

Early in the afternoon, I was at my sight setter position on the open gun mount. I happened to look over at the Yorktown which was about 14 miles away. I thought I saw a large swarm of aircraft. Then I realized that I was seeing anti-aircraft bursts. When the shells exploded, they would leave a dark smudge in the sky that lingered for several minutes before dissipating. The Yorktown was under attack and the sky above her was full of these shell bursts.

One of her fighter planes, that was shot up trying to defend her, attempted to land on the Hornet. It crashed on our Flight Deck and the plane's 50 caliber machine guns began firing, killing five Hornet crewmen and wounding twenty others.

One of those killed was Lieutenant Royal Ingersoll. His father was Admiral Ingersoll, one of the top men in the Navy Department at that time. He was the head of the Atlantic Fleet.

Late that night, about one in the morning, I had come off watch and was on the Hanger deck talking to one of the air-crewman. I was trying to get any information I could about the battle.

We heard a voice call out, "Attention on deck,

funeral party is passing." We came to attention as a burial party passed slowly by. They were taking the five dead sailors to the Fantail. When they got there, they held a brief ceremony and buried them at sea.

The way this is done, the bodies are sewn in a large canvas bag. The bag is weighted on one end. It is then laid on a flat board and a large flag is placed over it, covering the entire body. Several men hold the board up to the lifeline. A prayer is said, commending the body to the deep.

Then, at a signal, one end of the board is raised, causing the body to slide under the flag and over the side. All you actually see is a sudden flutter of the flag and then it flattens out onto the board. The ceremony is ended.

Later on, in my bunk, I had a hard time going to sleep. I kept seeing the five bodies sinking deep into the ocean. I thought about the families of the five men killed that day. They were still blissfully unaware of the tragedies and the grief they were going to face. Of course I realized that a lot more men had died that day, on both sides. However, I had seen these five and their deaths were close to me.

The battle lasted for three days. We were continually launching and recovering aircraft as the battle progressed. The pilots were very excited and animated when they returned to the Hornet. The sense of a huge victory hung over the ship.

When it finally ended, we had lost the carrier Yorktown and one destroyer. The Japanese had lost four carriers and a cruiser. Most importantly, they had been forced to abandon their planned invasion of Midway Island.

The Japanese had launched a diversionary attack at Dutch Harbor, located on Unalaska Island in the Aleutians. Their main force was brought to a

75

position near Midway. They had launched air attacks to soften up the Midway defenses before they invaded. To their great surprise, three American carriers ambushed them, sinking four carriers. It was the first naval defeat in Japanese history. I had only a minor part in these historic events, but I was there when they were happening.

Much later, we heard more about Ensign Gay, the only survivor of Torpedo Squadron Eight. After he was shot down, he avoided being picked up by the Japanese by hiding under a floating seat cushion.

He had a ringside seat to the rest of the battle on 4 June as our planes continued to attack. He saw the sinking of three of the enemy carriers.

He was rescued by a Navy PBY Seaplane on the following day. He was flown to Hawaii and gave a personal eyewitness account of the battle to Fleet Admiral Nimitz. The man who had planned and launched the Battle of Midway.

Years later, I discovered that Ensign Gay had undoubtedly saved his life by not letting the Japanese pick him up. I read a story concerning a dive bomber, from the Enterprise, that was shot down at the same time as Ensign Gay. The pilot and rear gunner were picked up by a Japanese destroyer. They were interrogated for a day or so. Then they were taken up on deck where water cans were filled with water and tied to both men. Then, they were thrown over the side, alive. We knew the Japanese were brutal, but I never realized that they were capable of this type of cold blooded murder.

10
SOUTH PACIFIC OPERATIONS

The Hornet returned to Pearl Harbor for supplies and ammunition. Rear Admiral Mitscher was relieved as Commanding Officer by Captain Mason and left for new duties. I decided to try my hand at surf boarding.

I would see the Hawaiians, standing on their surfboards, gracefully speeding along with the waves. I wanted to try it. Today, surfers have small, light weight, fiber glass boards. In 1942, all they had was heavy, six foot long, redwood boards.

One morning at about 1100, I went to Waikiki beach and rented one of these monster surfboards. The fellow that rented it to me told me to swim with the board until I caught a wave. Then, all I had to do was to stand up. I spent the entire day trying to do just that. I paddled out into the surf and tried to swim fast enough with that heavy board to catch a wave. I could lie on it and eventually, kneel on it. However, I only stood up on it once, for about one minute. It promptly threw me off. Then the board conked me on the head. Once the board got away from you, it became a hazard to you in the surf. I gave up on my surfing career. When I dressed to return to the ship, I found out that I had received a severe sunburn on my back and legs.

When I returned to the Hornet that evening, I discovered that the entire deck force was hanging over the sides, on wooden stages, repainting the ship's camouflage design. My petty officer told me to change into dungarees and start painting. He said that we had to change the camouflage pattern that night. I was soon over the side

77

working. My sunburned back and legs were very painful. I wished I had never seen a surfboard. We eventually finished the job and I thankfully crawled into my bunk.

The Hornet began automatically advancing certain Seamen Second to Seaman First, without requiring them to take the examination for it. They picked the ones who had been Seaman Second for a long time. I did not resent it except for the fact that it meant I would no longer have that small edge over my peers.

At about this time, one of the Yeomen told Jim Andersen and me, that we could now transfer to Submarine duty. I told him "no thanks." I said that I had put in that request in peacetime, not wartime. I had no desire to spend the war under the seas. Jim took him up on it and he transferred to submarines.

A few days later, I was told that I had been selected to be interviewed as a possible Radar-man striker. Whenever you go after a certain specialty in the Navy, you are said to be striking for that rate. Radar was totally new. It was on the cutting edge of the electronics field. I went up to the Bridge and located the Radar room. I entered a dark compartment and saw several sailors staring at two or three, round, illuminated, dials. Each dial was about twelve inches in diameter. I asked one of the sailors, "What does a Radar-man do?" Without taking his eyes from the screen, he said, "We watch the screen for bogies, enemy aircraft, then we report them." I asked him, "What do you do when you're not on watch"? He said, "We clean this place up."

I compared my job of operating a boat in the fresh air and sunshine with cleaning that Radar compartment. I thought about my battle station on the open gun mount and compared it with the Radar-man's lot. He spent his time in a dimly lit room, staring at a greenish looking screen. It was no contest. I turned down the offer to become a Radar striker.

The engineer on my launch told me that his Division had an opening for an Engineman striker. He said that he had recommended me. If I took this job, I would have to transfer from the Deck force to the Engineer force. I would be a Fireman instead of a Seaman. I checked into the offer a little further and discovered a small detail that the engineer had not mentioned to me. All the Firemen in his Division had each served their three month mess cooking requirement. If they did not get some new Firemen into the Division, they would each have to start serving a second three month tour as a mess cook. If I transferred, my first assignment would be to go mess cooking in the galley. I turned down the chance that they had offered to me.

The Deck force had the same mess cooking requirements. Since I had qualified for helmsman watches and then became a qualified boat handler, I was too useful to the Division to be sent mess cooking. They always needed my services as they did not have enough qualified seamen to fill the required slots. I never did go mess cooking.

Things did not always go my way. There are two incidents that stick in my mind. On one occasion, my petty officer, BM2 Amundson, decided to go over the side in a boatswain chair while the ship was underway. He had some work he wanted to do to the ship's side. A boatswain chair is a flat piece of hardwood, about two feet long and ten inches wide. It is used as a seat. The wood is secured inside of a large eye at the end of a heavy, two inch diameter, line.

The petty officer designated another seaman and me, to lower him over the side, using a boatswain chair. He also wore a separate life line. It was called a twenty-one thread line. It was about three-quarters of an inch thick. We were working at an opening off the Starboard side of the Hangar Deck. When we refueled at sea, this opening was where my Division brought the fuel hose aboard from the tanker. We wrapped both lines around a cleat and lowered him down. He was a few feet above the water as the ship sailed on.

She was doing about twenty knots on a straight course when we heard two short blasts on the ship's whistle. It meant the ship was going to turn to Port, to the left. It did not register with me at that moment, but when a ship turns, it heels over to the side away from the turn. That meant that our petty officer would automatically be lowered much closer to the water that was racing by at 20 knots.

As the ship began turning, we heard a shout, we looked down and the sea had caught his legs. The life line became as taut as a wire and then parted. This allowed him to drop lower and he was engulfed. He submerged completely under water and trailed Aft.

The boatswain chair line held. The line strained, quivered, then he popped out of the top of a wave. The seat had slid up his back and he had a death grip on the line. We were unable to pull him up. I shouted to the other Seaman to get help and he ran onto the Hangar Deck hollering "Man overboard." The petty officer had at least three more dunkings before we were able to get enough people around to pull him up. Each time the sea caught him, he looked up at me with a heart rending, pleading look before he again submerged. He was receiving tremendous punishment each time he went under water. If he should slip off the line, we might never find him. In the meantime, the man overboard alarm had reached the Bridge and the ship slowed down.

80

When we got him on board, he was alive but was unable to speak. We placed him on a stretcher and rushed him to the sick bay.

The incident was investigated. Since it had interrupted a planned maneuver of the ship, it reflected upon the professionalism of the Hornet and her Commanding Officer. This in turn embarrassed the Deck force and finally the Third Division. Someone's head had to roll.

Since I was the leading Seaman on the scene, I was on the spot. That night I was assigned to incinerator duty until further notice.

I did not even know that we had an incinerator until I found myself working there. There were two of us assigned to it. We stood eight hour watches and relieved each other, around the clock. All burnable trash, generated by the ship, was brought there to be disposed of. Trash would arrive night and day.

The incinerator was designed so that the smoke and ashes were routed up through the ships funnel. The Chief Master at Arms, who is similar to a sheriff in civilian life, explained my duties to me. He told me that the most vital thing to remember, before starting a fire, was to turn on a water spray. This unit was mounted within the ship's funnel. The smoke and ashes had to go through this spray to extinguish any burning embers before they could reach the flight Deck. He said, "If you forget to turn on the spray and you manage to catch any of our planes on fire, let me know right away. Then we will both jump over the side."

It was a terrible job. The incinerator area always had that sickening, sweet, garbage smell. The work was filthy, hot and boring. I was spending twelve hours there each day.

I visited Amundson, the injured petty officer in sick bay. He was bruised all over his body, but

81

he was recovering. He told me that he had
defended me to the Division Officer. He knew that
we had saved his life by holding on to the heavy
boatswain chair line. I admitted that I had not
realized the significance of the two short blasts
until it was too late.

He told me that since I had never gone mess
cooking, I could look at this incinerator detail
as being in place of working in the galley. I
only hoped it would not last for three months.

After several weeks in purgatory, I was relieved
of the incinerator job and restored to my normal
duties.

The second time I goofed up, we were returning
to Pearl Harbor from sea operations. It was in
the afternoon and I fell asleep in my bunk.
General Quarters sounded and I did not hear it. I
did not man my battle station. I slept through
the entire event. I was reported as "missing"
from my battle station.

After they secured from General Quarters, they
searched and found me, still sleeping in my bunk.
I was placed on report. When this happens, you
are immediately placed on Restriction. You cannot
leave the ship until your case is disposed of.
The Executive Officer reviews the charge and
either dismisses it or sends you to Captain's
Mast. If you go there, the Captain hears the
charge, listens to your story and decides your
fate. For more serious offenses, the Navy had
Summary Court-martials. If they wanted
to authorize more severe punishment, up to and
including death, they would try you by General
Court-martial. I did not envision anything that
serious, but I hated to go before our new Captain
and admit I had fouled up.

The next day we arrived in Hawaii. I rated
liberty, but since I was on report and
restricted, I could not go. The Division PO

(Petty Officer) took advantage of the situation and told me that I was assigned to operate one of the liberty launches.

I changed into the white sneakers that all the boat crews wore. In this way we did not mark up the varnished boat decks. We also were better able to maintain our footing while we walked along the narrow boat boom that extended out from the side of the ship about 25 feet above the boats that were tethered there to bow lines.

When we reached our boat, we descended via a rope ladder to the boat itself.

When my boat was called away, I walked toward the boat boom to reach the launch, the Chief Master at Arms saw me. He noticed the sneakers and told me that I could not leave the ship for any reason while I was restricted. I told him I was just following orders.

He took me back to my compartment. He found the Division PO and chewed him out for trying to use a restricted man for boat duty. An argument ensued and I found out that my Division was in a spot. Evidently, they had allowed all the other qualified boat coxswains to go ashore. I was the only one available.

They contacted the Division Officer. He came to the compartment and was told the problem. He argued, but the Chief, who worked directly for the Executive Officer, would not budge. The Division Officer then went to see the Exec. In the meantime, the Officer of the Deck had passed the word over the loud speaker again to bring my launch to the gangway.

My Division Officer returned about ten minutes later. He gave me a short lecture about not missing any more General Quarters alarms. Then he informed me that he had torn up my report slip. He notified the Chief that I was no longer restricted. Then he left the compartment.

The Officer of the Deck was passing the word for

83

the third time to bring my launch to the gangway.
My PO told me to hurry up and get the boat going.
The devil must have made me do it. I could not
resist the impulse. I said, "Hell no, if I'm not
restricted, I rate liberty, I'm going ashore."
The Chief Master at Arms started laughing and I
thought the leading PO was going to bust a blood
vessel.
Before he could speak, I said, "OK, I'll make a
deal with you, I'll run the boat today, but I get
liberty tomorrow." He did not trust himself to
speak. He just nodded. I ran to the boat as the
ship's loud speaker was calling for my launch for
the fourth time. I felt pretty good about the way
everything had turned out.
While operating off Hawaii, we were continually
undergoing training, especially the air department. The Hornet had a large, wooden sled that we
would sometimes tow behind the ship. The planes
would try to drop bombs and depth charges on it.
The tow line was a ten inch (circumference)
mooring line. It was over several hundred feet in
length. The line was stowed on a large, vertical
reel on the Fantail. To stream the sled, we would
take several turns around an electric powered
capstan. Then we would attach the eye of the line
to the sled. We could then lower the sled to the
ocean and let it trail behind us. The line fed
through a small chock in the stern of the ship as
we let it out. Due to the tremendous strain on
the line, the Hornet had to slow to about twelve
knots while towing the raft. Whenever we were
towing the sled, we had a phone talker on the
Fantail who was connected to the Bridge.
On this particular, sunny day, we had been
watching our planes practice bombing our tow. The
Bridge sent down word to retrieve the sled. I was
standing between the capstan and the vertical
stowage reel. There was about five turns of line
around the capstan. My job was to keep a manual

strain on the line as it fed from the capstan.
Two other seamen took the line from me and
wrapped it neatly around the vertical stowage
reel. The operation was going smoothly until the
Bridge sent the word down to expedite the operation. They wanted to speed up and turn into the
wind to land the planes. The only way to speed up
the operation was to speed up the capstan. It had
a low speed, neutral and a high speed. We were
operating in low speed.

Whenever we used the capstan, an Electrician was
there to actually operate it. The Division PO in
charge told the Electrician to shift to high
speed. He tried to and that is when everything
went wrong. As he shifted from low to high, he
had to go through neutral.

With the heavy strain on the tow line, when he
reached neutral, the capstan began free wheeling.
The proper method would have been to stop the
capstan and place straps, called stoppers, on the
tow line. Then shift the capstan to high speed,
cast off the stoppers and continue the operation.

As the capstan began free wheeling, the line was
going back out the chock at the speed of our
ship, twelve knots. The line was also feeding
back out from the vertical stowage reel at twelve
knots. Three of us were trapped into a narrow
pocket of space between the reel and the capstan.
I was horrified to see several blurred, whirling
loops in the air, directly above the spinning
capstan. It was the ten inch line. If any of us
became entangled in that line we would be
instantly crushed against the capstan and then
dragged through the small, one foot chock
opening. We were in mortal danger of a terrible
death as the capstan spun madly before us, the
vertical reel clanged behind us and the whirling
line snaked past us. The line barely brushed me
several times, each time it tore my shirt and
left burn marks on my skin. Finally the hurtling

tow line came to the end. As the end went by, it tapped me on the back of my shoulders. Just that small tap was enough to knock me to my knees. My shirt was in shreds and I had a bruised shoulder, but I was thankful to be alive and in one piece.

The phone talker notified the bridge that we had lost the raft. I do not know if any of our escort ships recovered it. I never saw it again. At least I was not in charge of that operation. I did not have to worry about any repercussions.

On August 7, the Marine First Division landed at Guadalcanal in the Solomon Islands. These islands are located North-East of Australia, on the North side of the Coral Sea. The Japanese had been constructing an air base on Guadalcanal that would threaten Australia and New Guinea. This was our first ground action against the Japanese and became a definite turning point in our war in the Pacific.

Japanese warships and planes responded immediately. The troops had landed, but the Japanese drove off our ships before they could complete unloading their cargo. The marines were forced to fight with only a small portion of their expected supplies and equipment.

The Hornet began operating in the Coral Sea area as we supported this campaign. It would eventually take six months of bitter, air, sea and ground fighting before Guadalcanal could be captured. It was not a fore-ordained decision. It could have gone either way on several occasions. It was a very brutal struggle.

When I first heard the name, Guadalcanal, I immediately thought of a canal, like the Suez or Panama. I had to look up its location before I realized where it was situated. At the start of this particular fight, I was not aware of how significant it was.

As the weeks went by, some of our planes would land there and operate from that airstrip for a time. When they returned to the ship, they brought back stories of the primitive living conditions that the marines were living under.

The name, Guadalcanal, became more and more a part of our lives. I had no idea that within a few short weeks, I also would be living there, under primitive conditions.

One evening, we were steaming in a Task Force that included the carriers Wasp and Saratoga. It was August 31. The Wasp had been transferred from the Atlantic in June and the Saratoga had recently been damaged and repaired. We were operating in an area known as "torpedo junction" due to the large number of submarine attacks there. The words were a take-off on a popular song titled, "Tuxedo Junction."

It was early evening when, suddenly, a Japanese submarine fired a torpedo into our force and struck the Saratoga. The damage was not too severe, but she had to return to port for repairs. That night as we watched her depart with her escort, one of my shipmates on our gun commented, "I'll bet that they are already, scrubbing their dress blues, getting ready for liberty. While here we are, holding down the fort."

Two weeks later, in the early afternoon of September 15, our Bugler blew General Quarters. I raced to my gun and discovered we were under submarine attack. We had evidently encountered a submarine Wolf Pack. The Wasp had already been hit and was ablaze off our Starboard side. Two torpedoes were then fired at our Port side. A destroyer, the O'Brien, cut in front of one torpedo and intercepted it. It blew her bow off. The battleship, North Carolina intercepted the second torpedo. It struck her on the Port side. We later heard that the O'Brien had some wounded

87

but no fatalities. The North Carolina suffered five dead.

I watched the Wasp through my gun's telescopic sights. She had just finished launching aircraft before she was torpedoed. Her aviation gas lines were still charged with fuel, helping to spread the fire. She was heeled over and blazing furiously as bombs exploded from her own burning planes. To my horror, I could see crowds of sailors trying to escape the flames and explosions. Some who were trapped by flames, on the edges of the Flight Deck, were leaping into the sea. As the Hornet turned away, leaving her with an escort of destroyers, I felt she was doomed. She sank that night. She lost almost two hundred men and had another four hundred wounded.

The Enterprise had recently suffered bomb damage while operating off Guadalcanal and was in Hawaii being repaired. The Saratoga was undergoing repairs for her torpedo damage.

The Hornet was now the only operational carrier in the Pacific.

We did not know it, but, having already been to sea for a month, the Hornet had only forty-one days left to live.

11

CONDITION TWO

The ship's personnel were in four sections. One
and three were the Starboard sections. Two and
four were the Port sections. Ordinarily, we
steamed in Condition Three. This meant that one
of the ship's four sections would be on watch at
any one time. We also had a "modified" Condition
Three that caused us to be on watch four hours
and off for eight hours. Of course, you still did
your normal ships work when you were not on
watch.

Under the present circumstances, being the only
operational carrier in the Pacific, we went into
Condition Two. Four hours on watch and four hours
off, night and day half of the ship was at their
battle stations.

I will describe a typical day in Condition Two.
Starting at 0800 in the morning, if my watch goes
on at noon, I perform the ship's work from 0800
to 1130. I eat lunch and relieve the watch at
1200. I stay at my battle station until relieved
at 1600.

I write letters or whatever and eat supper at
1645 because I have to relieve the watch at 1700
so that they can eat. One half hour before
sunset, General Quarters sounds, (Condition One).
We all stay at our battle stations until one half
hour past sunset.

To rotate the watches so that we have different
watches on the following day, we 'dog' the
watches. We stand two hour watches between 1600
and 2000. After the evening General Quarters
ends at one half hour past sunset, I stay on
watch until 2000. I sleep until 2330. I get up
and relieve the watch at 2400. after, at

most, three hours sleep. At 0400 I am relieved but there is no chance of sleeping because General Quarters will sound at one half hour before sunrise. It will end at one half hour after sunrise. Then I eat breakfast and relieve the watch for their breakfast. Then it is about 0800 and I have the first day watch. When I get off watch at 1200, I eat lunch and perform the ship's work in the afternoon.

Keep up a routine like this for a few weeks and it is easy to see how a ship's crew can become totally exhausted. You are never able to sleep more than about three hours in any one stretch.

I can recall stopping for a cup of coffee in the mess hall after about three weeks in Condition Two. I had just come off watch. I dozed off for a moment as I was sitting there. I woke up with a start, not knowing if I had just come off watch or if I was just going on watch. There was another sailor sitting there. I asked him if he was going on watch or coming off. Then I had to ask him what watch he was in, Port or Starboard. Then I had to remember which watch I was in. It is hard to keep things straight when you do not get enough sleep.

One of the old salts told me that sometimes people go a little mad under such pressure. I thought at the time that he was exaggerating, I soon discovered otherwise.

Several of my friends on the Hornet had been passing the time, and boredom of the watches, by imagining what it would be like to be out of the Navy and sailing their own schooner in the South Seas. I joined in these conversations, enjoying the flights of fancy. It was fun to plan a life of never ending adventure with like minded companions. We had discussed working in the islands after the war and saving up for our sailing ship. I believe that originally we thought it might take as long as four years to save enough if we

all worked. There were about six of us all
together. As the Condition Two watches dragged on
and on, our idealistic ideas began to be revised.
Eventually it became a half baked plan to go over
the hill and get a sail boat by hook or crook. No
one wanted to wait for four years after the war.
It was still fun to talk about it. Since we had
been steaming out of sight of land for several
weeks, I considered it as an academic discussion.

One evening, I was told that the ship was
expected to pass very near the French Island of
New Caledonia on the following night. The group
decided to go over the side in life jackets and
swim to the island. Then they could carry out
their plan to get a sailing ship.

It was as if I had been splashed in the face
with cold water. These guys were serious. I tried
to talk sense to them. I had no intention of
ruining my life by deserting the Navy, especially
in wartime.

I reminded them of their oath of allegiance. I
told them that I had thought they were having
idle discussions to pass the time away. I had no
idea that they were actually intending to go
through with it. I said that I thought they had a
good chance of drowning since the currents and
wind could keep them from reaching the island,
not to mention the sharks.

They were not happy that I had rejected the plan
and insisted that I not tell anyone else. That
ended the conversations that night. I reflected
back on the older sailor's comments about people
going a little mad under pressure. I thought that
maybe he was right after all.

The next morning, I was happy to see that they
were all still onboard. It turned out that their
information was almost right. We were not going
to pass near the island. We were going to stop
there for a short visit.

Before we had gotten into the Condition Two

91

routine, I had decided to strike for the Boatswain Mate rating. I had finished all the
required "practical factors" and had studied very
diligently for the test. I had also put in an
application to be allowed to take the next test
for the Coxswain rating. If I passed it and was
selected, I would be a Petty Officer Third Class.

In the peacetime Navy, some seamen spent twenty
years or more without ever making it to the Petty
Officer level. Four years of service entitled you
to sew a diagonal stripe on the left sleeve of
your uniform It was called a "hash mark." Until
you had your first four years in, you were called
a slick arm. Few of the Deck Force Seaman and
none of the Petty Officers were slick arms.

The ship's POD came out the evening before we
were to enter the French Island of New Caledonia.
It detailed our arrival and said that liberty
would be granted for three percent of the ship's
crew. Since there were seventy-one men in my
Division, two people would be allowed to go
ashore each day. The Division Officer would pick
the men to go.

There was one other notice in the POD. the test
for Coxswain was going to be held shortly after
our arrival. In those days you could only go up
for a rating if there was an opening on your own
ship.

As fortune would have it, my Division Officer
informed me that I was one of the two men
selected for liberty upon arrival. I was
flattered because it was really an honor to be
considered as one of the most deserving men in
the group. I thanked him for selecting me and
told him I would have to turn it down as I was
going to take the test for Coxswain. Turning down
liberty for a possible career advancement really
impressed him. He told me that I could go ashore
the following day. I had the best of both worlds.
I could take the test and still go on liberty.

In the morning, I found out that several men had gone over the hill by swimming ashore from our anchorage. I was not surprised to learn the missing men included my discussion group.

We were in Noumea, the capitol of New Caledonia for about three or four days. Fortunately, they returned to the ship before we left port. If they had not, they would have automatically been termed deserters for missing a ships movement. Not only that, they did it in a war zone. That opened them up to a possible death penalty. I was relieved that they had not actually deserted. they just had a little French leave.

They told me later on, that they had located a brothel, known as the Pink House, surrounded by a high wall. They climbed over the wall and discovered that there was broken glass cemented into the top of it. That did not stop them and they managed to get in. They stayed there until their money ran out, then they returned to the ship. I guess there is some truth in the old saying, "The best laid plans of mice and men often go astray."

I took the test for Coxswain and was confident that I had scored very high. I had recently been designated to operate the fifty foot officer's motorboat and since I was aboard the first day in port, I started making runs from the anchorage to the dock at Noumea. It was called the Nickel dock. New Caledonia is noted for exporting nickel from their mines.

Instead of bells, the motorboat was controlled directly by me from the cockpit. I had a gear shift, throttle and helm. The cockpit was located between the two large cabins,

There was only one long pier for landing boats. Noumea was not set up for the volume of shipping that was in her harbor during the war. Loading and unloading ships was always a bottleneck. As I

approached the pier with my first load of
officers, I found boats lying three deep, waiting
for a spot to land. There was no beach-master
there. They sure could have used one. My officer
passengers were really disgusted as they
envisioned a lengthy wait to go ashore.

The Nickel pier was a long wharf with about ten
boats tied up to it. I looked it over and noticed
that where the dock ended, there was just enough
room to tie up around the corner of the pier. I
intended to pass directly by it and then make a
sharp left turn as I backed down full speed. I
figured that this would get my stern into
position to off load my passengers. I could see
that the boat presently at that spot was getting
ready to cast off.

I had eased the motorboat through the other
waiting boats and I made a dash for the spot that
I had seen. As I came racing in, another boat, a
landing craft, much faster than my boat, saw this
same opening and shot in ahead of me. He crossed
my bow and stopped. I had to throw it into
reverse and back down full to keep from hitting
him. Now I was not worried about landing the
boat. I was worried about avoiding a collision.

Luckily for me, the boat on my right side that
I had just passed alongside of, during my wild
maneuver, pulled away from the pier. As I backed
down frantically to avoid the boat in front of
me, the torque from my propeller moved my boat to
the right and I slid alongside the pier, into the
spot just vacated by the other boat.

I kicked it into neutral and tied up. The
Officer passengers were ecstatic that I had
managed to land them so quickly and skillfully. I
acted as if I had intended to land at that spot
from the beginning. I humbly accepted their kind
words and pats on the back. My boat handling
reputation was secure. It reminded me of the time

and the episode with the heaving line when I made the lucky throw in the Panama Canal.

I went on liberty the following day and enjoyed myself exploring the quaint little French shops. They did not have bars as such, but some cafes sold a heavy, sweet liqueur.

I soon discovered that the Army troops stationed there, came from the Illinois 124th Field Artillery, a National Guard outfit from Chicago. The same unit that my brother Bill used to belong to when it was a cavalry outfit, with horses.

It was located in an Armory, just a few blocks from where I grew up in Chicago. To my total surprise I met an Army acquaintance of mine from Chicago. He was several years older than me but we knew each other. We talked for awhile and he asked me what ship I was on. I pointed out the Hornet to him at its anchorage. Liberty expired early. I said good-bye and returned to the ship.

We got underway the next day. Feeling somewhat refreshed, we resumed our Condition Two existence. On October 1, I was advanced to Coxswain, (BM3. I was now a Petty Officer Third Class. In those days, the Navy had right arm and left arm rates. There were six rates that put their insignias on the right arm. All the rest put their insignia on the left arm. All right arm rates were militarily senior to all left arm rates of the same level, first, second or third class. Among the six right arm rates, Boatswain Mate was senior to all of them.

As an example, I was senior to any other petty officer third class in the Navy, except another Coxswain with a date of rank before mine. It was quite a pecking order and it gave the old ego a boost. Of course, I was a slick arm Third Class, but I was now more of a supervisor than a worker. I also received a pay raise. I already had my boatswain pipe with lanyard and had become adept at blowing it. I was enjoying the Navy more and

95

more as I moved ahead of my fellow seamen.

Recent sea battles and ship sinking's had provided more hard won lessons. They found that sailors were dying from bomb flash burns. They issued us flash suits to wear at the exposed battle stations. These were loose, hooded, parkas and trousers to wear over our other clothing.

They found that smoke from paint and deck coverings hampered damage control actions during fires. We scraped all the paint off of our interior bulkheads, down to bare metal. We ripped up all the heavy battleship linoleum from our decks and threw it over the side.

We had heavy rubber matting's around our gun tubs. We took them up, scrubbed the decks, cleaned the mats and then replaced them. This was to help prevent infections to wounded men in the gun tubs.

The familiar Navy white hats were dyed blue so that we would not be so obvious to enemy planes as they strafed the ship with their machine guns. The Navy was doing everything they could think of to give an additional edge to their only carrier.

Even though we always fired our guns in the automatic mode, we spent one day firing in manual operation, with the power off, just in case.

12

THE END OF THE HORNET

The Enterprise joined us on 25 October. We were
very happy to see her. For 41 days we had been
holding down the fort all alone. We hoped that
with two carriers, we might be able to return to
a modified Condition Three.

Before anything could happen, we were told that
at least two enemy carriers were in our vicinity
and we were to get ready for the first night
carrier action of the war. We went to our battle
stations, but, for some reason or other, the
night action was canceled. We returned to
Condition Two.

After breakfast the following day, 26 October, I
washed my flash clothing by tying it to a heaving
line and letting it drag over the side for a few
minutes. The sea pounded it clean in short order.
It reminded me of Amundson, the petty officer,
who was dragged over the side in the boatswain
chair.

I was at my gun station, letting my flash
clothing dry in the sun, when General Quarters
sounded. I put on the trousers but the top was
still damp. I left it off for awhile as I
strapped on my phones and reported in to the
director. I normally would have put the parka on
first and then the phones. A few minutes later, I
slipped the parka on, over the phones.

We launched aircraft at about 0730 and settled
down at our battle stations to await develop-
ments. We happened to be operating near the
island of Santa Cruz.

Around 0830, I overheard some partial conversations on the phones that indicated that our

overhead fighter protection was engaging enemy
planes. I searched the skies but saw nothing in
our immediate vicinity. I did see some slight
smoke in the sky at quite a distance away, but I
did not see any aircraft. I passed the comments,
that I had overheard, to our Gun Captain. The
tension began to mount at our battle station.
  Whenever one of our planes wanted to pass a
message to the Hornet without breaking radio
silence, he would fly the length of the Flight
Deck and drop a small, hand held cylinder, with
the message inside it. An air-dale would run it
up to the Bridge. The ship would always pass the
word, "Stand by for message drop."
  On this particular morning, around 0900, I heard
over my phones, someone say, "Stand by for message drop." Immediately, another talker said, "If
he is going to drop a message, why are his wheels
down?"
  When I heard the phrase, "wheels down", I
quickly looked up. In those days, some of the
Japanese planes did not have retractable landing
gear.
  I looked toward my right and saw a Japanese Val
dive bomber heading straight for our gun tub. His
wing guns were winking brightly as he fired at
us. I shouted at the Gun Captain and our gun spun
around to fire back at him. I locked the sights
into automatic and looked again at the plane. I
could hear the machine gun bullets strafing the
Flight Deck and our gun tub as he dove at us. It
was my "moment of truth." My first gut reaction
was to seek cover, but my training had kicked in
and I had automatically performed my job
  I realized at that moment that my life could end
in the next fleeting second. It was a terrifying
thought as I watched the plane's tracer bullets
converging straight at us.
I saw his bomb release. It headed for our wildly

careening ship and struck our Flight Deck. It hit
near my station, but slightly forward of our
guns. We heard the bomb hit and the plinking
sound as it continued through several decks
before exploding with a tremendous force. We lost
all power to our gun mount as soon as the bomb
exploded. All of our automatic circuits were
disrupted. Our struggle had just started and we
were completely on our own, in "manual"
operation.

Dive bombers were plunging at us from all
directions as we put up a screen of anti-aircraft
fire. Then I saw enemy torpedo planes, low on the
horizon on the Starboard side. I pointed them out
to the Gun Captain and he trained the mount
around to take them under fire. The dive bombers
were tremendously distracting, but we had to
ignore them and concentrate on this new threat.
The bombers could cripple us. The torpedo planes
could sink us.

I manually zeroed the sights since the torpedo
planes were heading straight into us. We put up a
wall of shrapnel and the planes kept coming. We
fired as rapidly as we could in manual, but we
could not stop them all.

Other ships were firing at them also but there
were just too many planes. The torpedo planes
began making a very erratic approach, jerking
themselves up and down to spoil our aim. When
they were within range, they straightened out
into level flight, just long enough to release
their torpedoes. They flew right through our
defensive fire and zoomed over us. We could hear
bombs ripping into the Hornet as we watched the
rapidly approaching torpedo wakes.

On the gun mount, I had to stand while at my
battle station. A bomb exploded near us and I
felt a sudden, sharp pain in my right thigh
muscle. I shifted my weight to my left leg. I had

heard stories of men in battle who lost an arm or leg and only felt a small pain at first. I was afraid to look down as I cautiously felt for my right leg with my right hand. It was still there, but so was something else. I felt a sharp pain in my right hand. I looked down and discovered that a burning wooden splinter from our wooden flight deck had stuck in my thigh. It was about twelve inches long and was still smoldering. I jerked it out, relieved that I still had both legs.

Suddenly the first torpedo exploded against our Star-board side. It shook the Hornet like a rag doll. A second later, another torpedo struck the same side and we began to roll to Starboard. Heavy smoke started coming out of our powder and shell hoists. We had to quickly empty them before they exploded in our gun tub. A plane dived into our stack area and plunged to the Flight Deck, detonating his bombs. Another plane circled our bow and then crashed into the forward part of our ship. He continued on, through the officers' compartments and into the hangar area. He finally crashed into the steel shaft in the center of the forward elevator. The wreckage fell into the elevator pit and started a tremedous fire.

When the first attack ended, the Hornet was seriously wounded. We had been hit by two torpedoes, four or more bombs and two planes had crashed into us. We were dead in the water, no power, listing about twelve degrees to Starboard and had numerous fires raging aboard the ship. We later discovered that we had run into four enemy carriers. Their planes had simply overwhelmed us.

The bombs that had exploded on the Flight Deck had cut down many of the marines at their exposed, 20 millimeter gun stations. The same battle stations that we used to have before we traded for the five inch guns. At our present battle station, we were all still alive.

Destroyers came alongside and used their fire hoses and foam to help us fight the fires. I could smell the sickening stench of human bodies burning, a smell that I can still recall. Our Damage Control parties had the fires under control in about an hour. The destroyers started removing the wounded and excess personnel of the air department.

The heavy cruiser, Northampton, attempted to take us in tow. We were suddenly attacked by more dive bombers. The Northampton and the destroyers moved away from us so they could maneuver. The dive bombers missed and the rescue efforts resumed. The Northampton managed to secure a tow line to us. As she took a strain, the tow line parted.

It was early in the afternoon. The ship's side ladder was lowered to the water's edge on the Starboard side. I was ordered to try and launch the motor whaleboat and bring it to the ladder.

I quickly went down to the Hangar Deck and walked over to the boat pocket on the Starboard side. Wherever I looked, I saw a slaughter house. Evidently at least one bomb had exploded in the Hangar Deck area. Dead and mutilated bodies were lying all about, even in the boat pocket.

The boats were launched by means of an electric crane, located in the boat pocket. I would have to climb a ladder to get to the operating controls. I met the boat engineer as I entered the pocket. I told him we were going to try and launch the whaleboat. As he threw off the boat gripes, I went up the ladder to the crane controls. I tried to start the crane, but the electric power was off. The crane was equipped with an emergency power source, supplied by a huge battery. To engage it, I had to go back down the ladder and throw a large lever from the Normal to the Emergency power position. It took quite a bit of strength to throw the lever. As I

got in position, I saw the body of a young
sailor, lying right where I had to stand. I did
not want to shove him aside, so I spread my legs
to straddle him as I threw the lever.

I glanced down at the sailor and noticed that
his left cheek was twitching. I thought to
myself, "This guy may still be alive."

I reached down and caught him by the shoulders
to set him up. Then, to my absolute horror, I saw
that he was gone, from the waist down. He had
been blown in half. I could see only a thin strip
of flesh hanging from his waist.

I lowered him to the deck as gently as I could
and turned away from him. I leaned against the
bulkhead for a few seconds to compose myself
before I could again go back up the ladder.

When I got back to the controls, I pressed the
power button. This time, I heard the crane motors
start up. I raised the hook, taking the slack out
of the boat slings. Just as I was taking a
strain, the emergency power went off. The battery
was dead. There was no way to launch the boat. I
told the engineer to forget it and I headed back
to my battle station.

I tried not to look at the dead and mangled
bodies as I again passed through the Hangar Deck.
Walking through that scene was a mind boggling,
traumatic, experience.

Suddenly a young sailor came up to me. In a
bright, cheerful voice, he asked me, "Did you see
all these dead sailors lying on the deck?" I
looked at him and could see that he had "gone
around the bend". He showed me his arm, he said
that it had been broken but he had fixed it
himself. The arm looked normal to me. I tried to
gently get away from him. He was insisting that I
go with him to look at more bodies. He was
completely fascinated by the slaughtered people
lying about. I told him I had to return to my
gun, but I would look for him later. The last I

saw of him, he was walking rapidly down the deck, talking loudly to himself.

I kept a tight mental grip on myself as I walked back to the gun. I reported that launching the boat was hopeless without electric power.

The Hornet had been listing to Starboard for several hours. The blood from the dead sailors had been steadily running over the side of the ship through the scuppers. Charley Pellinat called me over to the edge of the gun tub and pointed down into the water. I saw at least three, huge, white sharks. They were rolling wildly in the human blood that was chumming the area. They were searching frantically for the meat. Charley said, "If we abandon ship, don't go over this side."

A short while later, I was given another order to, "Report to the Fantail." I went there and discovered it was completely covered with dead and dying sailors. I tried to find out what I was to do there, but no one seemed to know. The Medical people seemed to be in charge, so I asked several of them if they had sent for me. They had no idea of why I was there. I returned to the gun and reported that no one needed me there. I never did find out why I was sent there.

About the middle of the afternoon, the Northampton finally got a tow line rigged and slowly got us in motion. We had a faint glimmer of hope that we might be able to save the Hornet after all.

I was exhausted as I lay on the deck of the gun tub with my head pillowed in my helmet. I tried not to think of my slaughtered and mutilated shipmates. We all knew the enemy would return, our only hope was to be gone from this location when they got here. I re-played the morning's events in my mind. I realized that the coordinated attack of dive bombers and torpedo planes had been extremely well executed by the Japanese. We had been attacked by professionals. I hoped our own planes would prove to be as effective when they reached the enemy carriers.

I wondered if I could possibly survive this battle. The present chances of being killed or crippled were very high. I realized that I had not really experienced life. I had never had the opportunity for a meaningful sexual relationship. I might never have a chance to marry or raise a family. I was nineteen. It seemed to me that nineteen would be an awfully young age to die.

Then my thoughts turned to God. I wondered if there really was a "spiritual" being who could bail us out in our hour of need. I thought about my experiences at Saint Thomas and came up with the same rationale I had formed at school. I still did not believe that the Catholic religion had the answer. I really wished that they had been able to convince me because it would have really helped if I had something within me to turn to in my hour of need. However, I could not lie to myself and pretend to believe, especially at this moment when I was face to face with death or life as a cripple.

The thought crossed my mind that possibly there was something beyond us, maybe some force, maybe the Devil himself. There could be something or someone that we were unable to understand. I said to myself, if there is something or someone, somewhere, who can control these things, get me out of this tight spot this time, and I will never, ever, ask for help again.

As an after thought, I said I want to survive in one piece, I don't want to be a basket case.

Then, as a true "Doubting Thomas" would do, I asked for some sort of a sign, that my message had gotten through.

At that very moment, when I asked for a sign

while I was lying there, one of my shipmates, named White, came over and sat next to me. He handed me his address and asked me to write to his parents and tell them what happened in case he did not make it. I told him I would. Then I asked him, "Wait a minute, we are in the same spot together, what makes you think that I'm going to survive and you are not?"

He was very sincere as he said, "You look to me like you will make it." That was the only conversation we had that day. He was assigned to the other gun in my tub, gun 5.

I wondered if that could possibly have been the "sign," that I had just that instant asked for. If it was not the sign, it had been an almost unbelievable coincidence.

After an hour or so, a little after 1600 (4PM), we saw another flight of enemy torpedo planes on the horizon. They headed in towards us, again using their now familiar, erratic movements. The Northampton cut the tow line so she could maneuver and we were again dead in the water. We fired our remaining shells at the planes but we were ineffective. We watched as they straightened their planes to level flight. Two planes, flying wing tip to wing tip, dropped their torpedoes simultaneously. I saw the two torpedoes heading for our Starboard side. They struck together with a tremendous explosion. The blast caused the Hornet to actually lift up until she was on an even keel. Then, she started to swiftly roll back down to Starboard. We watched helplessly as she rolled, watching the water come closer to us. The roll stopped once and then started again. When it finally stopped, we were listing about twenty degrees.

We were next attacked by dive bombers but I did not feel any hits. There were several near misses. At about that time, the word was passed to, "Abandon ship, abandon ship, all hands abandon ship, except for the Salvage and Rescue Party." That was when I found out what that particular team was really for, to salvage and rescue our own ship.

In my case, my salvage and rescue station was on the gun. I was already there. I stayed at my battle station and watched my shipmates abandoning the Hornet. The powder and shell hoists were inoperative. The ammunition magazines were probably flooded anyway. We had only five shells in our ready box and no powder. I called around with my sound powered phones to the other guns. I located four powder cans. My gun could now fire, at most, four shells if we had to. We could not afford to waste any of them.

It was late in the afternoon. We felt awfully lonely on the slowly sinking ship, still manning our battle stations. The wind was blowing us further away from the other ships. A destroyer began circling us, over his loud speaker he announced, "On the Hornet, all hands abandon ship, we are leaving the area. All hands abandon ship."

As far as I was concerned, that officially released the salvage and rescue party. I picked up a kapok life jacket and headed quickly to the Fantail area. Since I had put my flash jumper over my phone set that morning, I still wore my phones.

When I reached the Fantail, the decks were slippery with oil and blood. The Medical department had been bringing the dying and wounded to that area and there was a large group of corpses lying there. I tried not to think about them. I concentrated on making my escape from an obviously 'doomed' ship.

I remembered the sharks on the Starboard side and my only concern at the moment was to go over the Port side, the high side. I tried three times to reach the high side. Each time, just before I

106

could reach the lifeline, I would slide back down the steeply slanted deck. The oil and blood were everywhere, making the decks very slick. I had the maddening thought that it was just like one of those dreams when you try to run but cannot. I fought off a feeling of panic and focused on the effort at hand. By using various bulkhead fittings, I slowly managed to pull myself up to the Port side life line.

I saw that there were many monkey lines hanging over the side. These were ropes with knots tied in them about eighteen inches apart. I straddled the life line and took off the flash jumper to remove the phones. Now that I was safely at the lifeline, I glanced over at the pile of corpses. There were about twenty or thirty bodies, jumbled together. I was struck by the sight of the bottoms of so many bare feet. You normally do not see the bottoms of anyone's feet. I dropped my phones onto the deck. They made a sharp sound as they hit and slid down the Fantail. I put the flash jumper back on and then the life jacket. I started to lower myself on the monkey line.

Suddenly, I thought I heard someone call out. I stopped and hollered out, asking if anyone was there. I stared at the jumble of bodies and hollered again. I was not sure if I saw a movement or not. I pulled myself back up and re-straddled the life line. I called out for the third time. I did not see any movement. I thought about going over to the pile of bodies but I was not sure what I could possibly do for a badly wounded or dying man. I called out one more time, I decided that if anyone answered, I would get them a life jacket and help them get over the side. I called for the last time and got no response. I also did not see any movement among the bodies lying there.

I lowered myself over the side and down to the water. To this day, I still have a feeling of

guilt, because I did not go over to the pile of
bodies and ensure that they were all dead. I
dreaded the thought of trying to crawl up that
slippery deck to the high side again. Possibly
that was the real reason that I did not go back
down there.

When I reached the water, I was relieved to find
out that the life jacket would actually keep me
afloat. I started to swim away from the Hornet. I
had gone about twenty feet when I felt the monkey
line pull on my right leg. I had become entangled
in it.

I was gently pulled back to the side of the
ship. I had visions of the ship sinking with me
trailing along on the line. I tried to reach it
but it was impossible with the life jacket on. I
forced myself to remain calm. I removed the life
jacket and tied it to the monkey line. I ducked
under water to free my leg. Something struck me
painfully in the head. I surfaced and saw a
marine. He had come down the line next to me and
had happened to kick me as he splashed away. I
ducked under a second time and managed to untangle myself from the line. In the process, I
lost my right shoe. I got back into my lifejacket
and swam away from the ship, into the wind. I
knew that the wind would help blow the Hornet and
her sharks away from me.

As I swam, I lost the sock from my right foot. I
could visualize my bare, white foot, fluttering
in the water. It would act like a lure to any
nearby shark. I tried to keep such maddening
thoughts out of my mind. I knew with a certainty
that my survival depended solely on my ability to
remain completely calm and rational. I could not
afford to let my imagination have free rein.

Though there were many sailors in the water, a
lone swimmer is so physically low in the water,
he has a hard time seeing anyone. I had a very

lonely feeling as I continued putting distance between the Hornet and myself.

I suddenly came upon a shipmate of mine named Morelock. We had been on the same gun together. We teamed up, just as we saw a flight of horizontal bombers. They were at a high altitude, in a "V" formation, as they released their bombs on the Hornet. Most of the bombs missed but the ones that hit appeared to land in the gun tub that Morelock and I had just abandoned. We had not left any too soon.

We heard the bombs explode. I asked Morelock if we were supposed to be on our backs or stomachs when being bombed in the water. He said that he did not know, he had missed that lecture. I had missed it also, however, fortunately for us, the bombs that missed the ship, landed on the side of the ship that was away from us. This gave us a little protection.

To understand what happened next, you have to realize that you cannot compress, or squeeze, water. In the case of a bomb going off in the water, it causes a shock wave to travel rapidly through it. It will crush or penetrate any openings in its path. That is why a near miss sometimes does more damage to a ship than an actual hit. A torpedo uses the same principle. It explodes on contact and uses the sea water to push a much larger hole into the ship than the torpedo alone would cause.

In our situation, we heard the bombs explode. A few seconds later, to our complete, unexpected, surprise, a tremendous shock wave, traveling through the water, reached us. The water crushed my sides and testicles in an agonizing iron grip while simultaneously being brutally forced into my anus and lower intestines. At the same time, my spine felt as if I had been struck on the tail bone by a large hammer, it really jarred me. We

109

both involuntarily cried out in agony. It only lasted for a moment, but the unexpected pain was excruciating. If we had been much closer to the ship, the shock could have easily killed us. Whether we should have been on our backs or stomachs was not important. We should have been one or the other, not neck deep and upright as we were when the shock wave hit.

We were both groaning and gasping for breath and surprised to have weathered this latest, un-expected, onslaught. After a quick, desperate discussion, we decided to try for a raft to get out of the water.

We spotted a raft. About the time we started for it, dive bombers were again attacking the Hornet. We debated whether or not the planes would strafe the rafts. We also considered the sharks. We knew it would soon be dark. Darkness falls quickly at sea. We did not want to spend the night in the water in case those sharks decided to fan out to find their dinner. The sharks were constantly on our minds.

It appeared that the destroyers who were rescuing survivors, were stopping at the rafts and not for individual swimmers. We decided to take a chance on being strafed and join a raft. The one we reached was full of men. We held onto the sides and kept a weather eye peeled for strafing planes.

A destroyer, the USS Barton, stopped near us. I let go of the raft and swam quickly to the ship. I expected to climb up by myself. About amid-ships, I grabbed a line and tried to climb up. I found out that I did not have enough strength left to climb out of the water. Normally, I would have been able to climb up that rope like a monkey. Until that moment, I had not realized how totally exhausted I was. Being bombed in the water had taken a lot out of me also.

A Filipino sailor looked over at me and tried to pull me up. He got me about half way up and then let go, dropping me back into the water. I was too heavy for him. He hollered down that he was going to get help. Then he left. I had a death grip on the line and hung on for dear life.

In the meantime, the raft had reached the Barton and the wave action was slamming it heavily against the ship. The raft was a large, sturdy one, made of Kapok that had been painted over many times. It was very solid and it was moving toward me as it continually crashed against the ship's steel side. I had no doubt that if I got caught between the raft and the ship, I would be crushed. I had to make a decision. If I let go of the line, I might be too weak to again reach any ship. If I stayed where I was, I could be crushed. I was truly between the Devil and the deep blue sea.

The raft slammed against the ship about a foot away from me. I had to make a life or death decision to release the rope or not. At that moment, I felt the line that I was gripping start to move. Suddenly I was being pulled up. The Filipino had indeed gotten another man to help. Between the two of them, they hoisted me aboard as the raft slammed into the ship's side below me. I hugged and thanked my rescuers profusely. They then directed me to go into their mess hall to be given a quick medical check. As I walked away, I realized that I had also lost my other shoe. I was barefooted, but I was saved.

There was a Pharmacists Mate in the mess hall, examining survivors. When he got to me, he asked me if I was wounded or bleeding. After what I had seen on the Hornet, I did not consider myself as being wounded. I told him about being bombed in the water and I was not sure if I had any internal damage. He had me strip and checked me

111

over quickly, I had deep cuts on both hands and
he found the wound on my right thigh where the
splinter had struck me. I had completely
forgotten about it. He bandaged my cuts and I
dressed. I was elated to have been rescued, still
alive and in one piece. I already felt as if I
was regaining some of my strength.

A Barton sailor gave me a cigarette but he did
not have a match. I went out on deck to find a
light. I thought I might also be useful in
helping bring other survivors aboard. Before I
could do either, the ship's General Alarm
sounded. The loud speaker announced, "Enemy
aircraft approaching, all survivors get clear of
the weather decks". As the Barton got underway,
I opened the nearest water tight door and jumped
inside. I slammed the hatch shut and spun the
locking mechanism, dogging down the door. When
the door closed, the compartment lights automatically came on. I turned around to discover
that I was in an ammunition space, directly
beneath an antiaircraft gun. If a bomb hit in
this space, I would be obliterated.

I started to leave, when a sudden wave of anger
surged through me. I thought to myself, to hell
with it. All day long I have had the crap scared
out of me. It had been one damn thing after
another. The bombs, torpedoes and sharks had not
been enough. Then, when I thought I was safe, the
raft almost crushed me against the side of the
ship. I said to myself, "If anyone is going to
kill me, do it here and now, in one big blast, I
don't give a damn".

I sat down in the ammunition space and waited
patiently for the ship to secure from General
Quarters. Strangely enough, after my mental Dutch
Uncle talk to myself, I was very calm and relaxed. I had lost the fear that had accompanied me
all day, since that first plane had strafed my

battle station.

We could still see the crippled Hornet blazing from numerous fires as we steamed away from her. There were two destroyers circling her as we left. We were told that Japanese surface ships, including battleships, were heading towards us. The Barton and the rest of our group were scattering like quail, in all different directions, before this formidable force. The largest American ship present was the North-ampton, a cruiser. A battleship could stay out of range and leisurely blow us out of the water. Our only possible protection was to avoid being caught by them.

Years later, I found out that the destroyers who stayed with the Hornet, were the Mustin and Anderson. They fired five inch shells and torpedoes into her but were unable to finish sinking her before leaving. They had to escape to save themselves when they saw the Japanese searchlights on the horizon.

The Japanese fleet arrived to find the fiercely blazing Hornet, still afloat but slowly sinking. They fired two more torpedoes into her and she sank at 0130 (1:30AM) on 27 October. Ironically, this is the date that the Navy celebrates as Navy Day. The Hornet had been in commission for a year and seven days.

It could have been much worse. If the Japanese had managed to salvage the Hornet and tow her to Japan, it would have been a humiliating turn of events. Japan knew by then that the Hornet was the ship that bombed Tokyo. When reporters had asked President Roosevelt where the bombers came from, he told them, "From Shangri-La" This was the name of a mythical Himalayan kingdom in the novel, Lost Horizon. Though he hated to lose a carrier, I am sure that Fleet Admiral Chester Nimitz was relieved to learn that the Hornet was sunk and had not been captured.

13

NEW CALEDONIA

That first night aboard the Barton was dark and
stormy. The weather was welcome because it
helped conceal us from the enemy forces. The rain
was extremely heavy as I searched for somewhere
to lie down. Every bunk and interior deck space
was filled with sleeping men. The Barton had a
crew of over 300 men. We 275 survivors almost
equaled them.

I was desperate to find a place to sleep as I
went out onto the weather decks. There was no
place to even lie down inside the ship. I crawled
under the torpedo tubes and soon fell sound
asleep. I was lying on an exposed steel deck, in
the rain. When I awoke in the morning, I was as
stiff as a board, but I felt much refreshed. I
was thrilled to have been rescued.

We were en-route to the French island of New
Caledonia. It took about seven days to reach it.
I was pleasantly surprised to run into a Barton
crew member whom I had previously known on the
Hornet. He was a large fellow, over six feet
tall. He had been in my Division on the Hornet.
He was later transferred to the Barton and was
presently striking for Gunners Mate.

Unfortunately, I can no longer recall his name.
He saw I was barefooted and let me have a pair of
his white, Navy, sneakers to wear. He had cut
numerous air holes in them for use in the
tropics. They were also size eleven. I wear size
nine. However, I was glad to no longer be
barefooted.

One day he told me that he had talked to the
Executive Officer about me and the Exec had told

him that I could stay aboard the Barton if I wished to. They had an opening for a Coxswain rating.

It was tempting and I thought about it for some time. However, I finally decided to stay with the Hornet survivors and share their fate. A door had been opened. Fortunately for me, as I would soon discover, I had declined to walk through it.

During our trip, we stopped and rescued the crew and passengers of a downed Army transport plane and two Navy PBY seaplanes that had tried to rescue the Army plane.

The Barton launched her whaleboat to effect the rescues. Then, she destroyed the planes by gunfire before we sailed on.

At least one of the survivors had gone into mental shock as a result of the battle we had experienced. He was an older petty officer. I noticed him on the Barton, standing rigidly on the Main weather deck, leaning against a bulkhead. He would not enter any of the compartments or speak to anyone during the entire week it took us to reach the island. Some of the survivors brought him food but I never saw him eat any of it. I do not know if he slept or not. I happened to look at him when the Barton tried to destroy the sea planes. Even during the firing of the ship's heavy guns, his expression never changed. His eyes kept their same vacant stare. The shock of our ordeal had evidently caused his mind to deny what he was seeing. He had retreated somewhere, deep within it. I felt very sorry for him. Through no fault of his own, he was condemned to many years of therapy to try and find his way back from wherever he had gone, or, failing that, to life in an institution. I thanked my lucky stars that I had managed to keep my sanity.

Years before, while a student studying about Columbus and other explorers, I had read that sailors, after extended voyages, could smell land, long before they actually saw it. I found out that this is really true. The day before we reached New Caledonia, long before it was in sight, I could smell a wonderful aroma of earth and vegetation. The next day as we entered port, that same green earth smell was intoxicating. I felt a great sense of relief at having been saved. I looked forward eagerly to going ashore.

The harbor contained several troop ships and a large Navy hospital ship. It was painted completely white and had huge red crosses painted on her sides and decks. At night the ship was illuminated with searchlights to show her red cross markings. The wor was passed that any survivor with cuts or wounds was to be transferred to the hospital ship. A couple of my friends asked me if I was going to the hospital ship because of my hands and leg. I told them no. My cuts were healing nicely and I wanted to stay with my shipmates. I put my hands in my pockets and ignored the white motor launches that came alongside the Barton. Another door had opened for me and I refused to enter it.

We said our good-byes to our rescuers and were taken ashore to Noumea. We were lined up and marched through the streets to an Army assembly point. Several citizens appeared on the streets to watch the parade go by. One old Frenchman was smiling and vigorously waving an American flag. I wondered what he would have thought if he knew he was cheering a group of sailors who had managed to lose their ship.

After passing through most of the town, we were loaded aboard Army trucks. We rode into the interior for several miles, finally coming to an open area. The Army gave us tents and showed us how to erect them. We soon were established in a survivor's camp. We ate in the open and the wood, cooking fires, smelled heavenly to me. I believe that my brush with death had made me extremely more sensitive to my surroundings. We had absolutely no idea of what the future held in store for us, but, we were alive and safe, for the time being.

After dinner, that first night, we heard that we were near a native village. Several of us decided to do some exploring and walked over to it. I had no idea if they had any type of stores there or not. I had a five dollar bill in my wallet. The rest of my money, forty dollars was in another wallet, along with my ID card, in my locker on the Hornet.

Following directions from a soldier, we strolled over to the village. We did not find any stores, but we discovered that they did have a brothel. It was located in one of their grass huts. We all entered and I discovered that I was not qualified to participate.

It turned out that the price for a visit with one of the native girls was a pair of shoes. The mamasahn, the old madam, took one look at my air-holed, sneakers and busted out laughing. She had black, betel nut stained teeth and was still giggling as she shoved me outside. In the South Pacific, the natives chew betel nut as a light narcotic. I waited for my buddies. I was the only one wearing shoes when we walked back to our camp. They had fun teasing me on the way back. They pretended that I had been turned down because I was too ugly.

I slept like a log, that first night in my Army cot. In the morning, I could smell those wonderful wood burning, cook fires going. I ate a huge breakfast. I was enjoying the opportunity to be camping out. Several of us wandered over to a near-by river and decided to go swimming. In a short time, a Melanesian native ran over to the shore and began hollering at us. He kept it up until one of our group went over to see what he

wanted. Then our shipmate got out of the water
and started hollering at us also. We could
understand him. He was shouting, "There are
barracuda in that river".

We got out of the water in record time. We
thanked the native for warning us. We managed to
carry on a conversation with him in Pidgin
English. We asked him about his hair. He was
black, but his hair was dyed a reddish color. He
told us that the males let the females know their
marital status by the color of their hair. When
it was dyed red, it meant he was single, eligible
and looking for a bride.

As we walked back to camp, I noticed two Army
men. They were standing off to the side of the
road, engaged in conversation. I saw that one of
them was the older acquaintance of mine from
Chicago, the same one I had previously met while
on liberty in Noumea. He was a Sergeant and was
talking to a Second Lieutenant. I pointed him
out to my friends, saying, "There is a guy from
my hometown."

We all walked over to him. I called out his name
and he turned towards me. The officer frowned at
being interrupted by several ragged looking
enlisted men. The Sergeant asked me, "What are
you doing here?" I told him that we had been sunk
in a sea battle. He looked at me and sarcastic-
ally said, "You didn't last long, did you?" Then
he turned his back on me and resumed talking to
the officer.

I felt as if he had slapped me. I was flabbergasted at his response. While he had been sitting
on a peaceful island, we had gone through a
savage fight that had cost us about two hundred
dead and at least four hundred wounded. He had
acted as if it was of little or no consequence. I
was humiliated in front of my shipmates. They
were totally outraged at his reaction, as we
walked away, at least two of them wanted to go

118

back and beat him up. They asked me, "What kind
of a hometown did you come from?" I told them to
forget it. I explained that this particular
individual was considered as a jerk by my
hometown buddies and he had just proven it. I
said that someday I may get a chance to pay him
back for his kind compassion. At the time, it was
an idle statement, but, my opportunity to re-pay
him would actualy eventually happen.

14

GUADALCANAL

That evening, after supper, an Army band came to our camp and serenaded us with popular, Glen Miller type, music. I remembered particularly that they played, "As Time Goes By." It made me think of home and being on leave.

Finally, an Army Major approached the microphone and made a patriotic speech. The essence of it was that the Marines on Guadalcanal had to be reinforced immediately. The battle had reached a critical stage. They were not sure if they could hold the island. They were certain it could not be held without additional troops and supplies. It also had to be accomplished before the Japanese could get there with their own rein-forcements. They had military intelligence that an enemy convoy was getting ready to sail in a few day's time.

Time was running out and Admiral Halsey had authorized the Army to take any available men they could find, including survivors from Navy ships. The Army was presently being loaded onto the Troop ships that we had seen in the harbor at Noumea. They were going to place us, temporarily into the Army. We were going with them to Guadalcanal.

Ten percent of the survivors were to be allowed to return to the U.S. The rest of us were in the Army. In my Division of seventy-one men, that meant seven would get to go home. They drew names from my hat. My name was not drawn.

We were taken to an Army warehouse and marched through it. I came out the other end wearing a khaki shirt, khaki pants and Army shoes. I was carrying an Enfield rifle that had been packed away in a preservative grease, in 1919, at the end of World War One. I had one hundred rounds of ammunition and a cartridge belt. I also had a canteen, a mess kit and a World War One helmet. The flat type, that air raid wardens wear. Our final item was a three day supply of canned C-rations. We were warned to save them for an absolute emergency. They were considered as our Iron Rations, to be consumed only if faced with starvation.

After being outfitted, we were loaded aboard a troop transport ship, the Crescent City. Within a short time, our convoy sailed for Guadalcanal. We were with five other troop ships, two cruisers and four destroyers. The Hospital ship sailed the same day. However, she headed for either Hawaii, New Zealand or the States.

I spent the entire four day voyage trying to remove the preservative from my rifle. It was called Cosmoline. It had been on the gun for about twenty years and had hardened into a type of plastic. I finally removed most of it and got my rifle in operating condition. I reflected on my boot camp training on the rifle range. I had gotten by, but I was no marksman. I knew I might be soon shooting at the enemy and it was too late now to worry about more training.

Reveille sounded at 0400 on the morning of September 12. Just seventeen days after the Hornet sank. We ate quickly and went up on deck. Our ship was anchored off the coast of Guadal-canal.

As the dawn came up, we stared at the beach and the heavy, green forbidding looking jungle behind it. The day was already quite warm and I could see where the writers got the phrase, "The steaming jungle." I could see the steam rising from the vegetation. The area we were in, about ten degrees below the Equator, has some of the heaviest annual rainfalls in the world.

We waited on the open decks, near the cargo nets that hung over the sides. We were to use these nets to get into the landing craft. We heard the word passed, "Away, the landing force." Before we could start over the side, we saw a huge water spout erupt next to our ship and heard the sound of a large caliber gun firing. Then a second spout erupted and we realized we were being shelled. Our cruisers and destroyers began firing back, but every few minutes, the Japanese gun would fire a couple of rounds. Our ships were never able to silence this particular enemy gun. I found out later that it was an eight inch gun and the Marines had nick named it, Pistol Pete.

I went down the cargo net and got into the landing craft. It seemed like we had not gone too far when the boat stopped and we were ordered out. The boat did not have a bow ramp and we had to crawl over the sides. When we got into the surf, the water was up to my eyes. I had to bounce on my toes to see which way to go. I finally got into shallower water and reached the beach. If that boat coxswain had gone just a little bit farther, the landing would have been much easier on us. It all depended on how brave the coxswain was.

I found out that we would also have to unload the ship we had just left. I placed my rifle and pack near a palm tree. I waded back into the surf to help unload the boats as they returned with supplies. I refused to go farther out than neck deep. I made the boat operators come at least that close to shore. Most of them would come in close, but some of them had to really be coaxed in.

It was getting near noon. I had been dragging supplies and ammunition ashore for almost six hours. It was thirsty work and I had finished my canteen of water. I asked a Marine where I could

go to refill my canteen. He pointed to a long
line of men standing near a vehicle with a large
tank mounted on it. They were in line to get
water. There were several thousand men on the
beach as I walked over to the water wagon. There
were about twenty people ahead of me and the line
went quickly. I filled my canteen
and decided to take a drink while still there.
Then I would top off the canteen again, before I
left the wagon. I tilted the canteen up and took
a long swallow. I refilled it and turned to go.
To my utter astonishment, the line behind me and
every person on the beach had vanished. I could
not believe my eyes, How could several thousand
people disappear? Had I lost my mind like that
poor sailor that I saw on the Barton?

As I stood there, perplexed, I heard and then
saw, a low flying plane coming straight up the
beach. It was a Japanese Zero Fighter plane. He
was heading directly at me and I saw his wing
guns winking as he strafed the beach. I was the
only person standing on it. I instinctively ran
toward the jungle for cover. As I ran I could see
people lying in small depressions in the ground.
That is where they had all disappeared to. I
found out later that they were called foxholes.
As I raced frantically for the protection of the
jungle, I glanced back and saw the plane bank
towards me. His guns winked brightly as he
continued strafing. Just at that moment I ran
past a terrible looking, swampy area. I hesitated
and realized I could never reach the jungle in
time. I turned and dove into the swamp. I could
hear the bullets thudding into the beach near me
as I came up sputtering in that putrid, scummy
water. When the plane left, I crawled out of the
swamp and sat on a fallen tree until I had my
self under control.

I asked a passing Marine if they had many air

123

raids. He said that they were bombed and strafed every day. Normally, the raids occurred at the same time each day. He said the plane, that had just been strafing us, was earlier than usual. Then he asked me if I was the guy who dove into the swamp. When I told him I was he said, "We have crocodiles on this island."

I believe that even if I had been aware of the crocodiles, I would have still dove into the swamp under similar circumstances.

I returned to my work detail. I was happy to see that there were once again several thousand people on the beach. I resolved to myself to be more alert at all times. One moment of relaxation had resulted in my becoming the main target of a Japanese plane because everyone else had hidden.

Late in the afternoon, sixteen torpedo planes attacked our ships in the harbor. Twelve planes were shot down and none of the torpedo planes scored any hits. One plane dove into the cruiser San Francisco and one destroyer was hit, either by an anti-aircraft shell or by a falling air-plane.

This attack ended the off loading of supplies and all the Navy ships departed. This was one of the major problems at Guadalcanal. The Navy could not provide adequate protection for our cargo and troop ships. Thus, they could never remain long enough to deliver the required amounts of supplies and equipment.

Feeling very much abandoned by the Navy, we were marched over to the airstrip called Henderson Field. It was named in honor of a Marine pilot who had been killed during the Battle of Midway. This airfield was what the Battle of Guadalcanal was all about
. The Japanese started building it, then the Marines landed and took it away from them.

Due to our controlling the airfield on Guadalcanal, our planes kept the Japanese from landing supplies and troops during daylight hours. They tried to solve this problem by making their landings at night, under cover of darkness.

During the march to Henderson Field, we passed a barbed wire enclosure with about twenty Japanese prisoners inside of it. They were emaciated looking and dressed in rags. They looked frightened and desperate. A little farther on, we came to a rough looking wooden building. It had a large sign on it that read, "Tojo's Ice House, under new management". I got a laugh out of that sign, it gave me a morale boost when I needed it most.

We had just arrived at the airfield when I was startled to hear a tremendous cheer go up from the Marines around us. I looked around and saw eight P-38 planes coming in for a landing. Until that very moment, there were only a few outclassed P-39s and Wildcat fighters at the air strip. The twin engine P-38s were newer and a much better airplane. These eight were the very first to arrive. It signaled to the Marines that they were getting some solid support at last.

We were led into some palm trees next to the airstrip. It was a campsite called the "coconut grove" area. We were instructed to remain in the immediate area and our guide headed off somewhere. I believe he was going to find out where we were to be assigned. As we waited for orders, I was concerned about what we were expected to do, as soldiers. I hoped that we would at least be given some instructions or basic information before being sent out on patrols. I wanted at least a fighting chance to survive. We would be going up against experienced enemy troops.

It had started to rain and I noticed a fellow walk by wearing a poncho. It was a type of rain slicker. He also was wearing a Navy Officer's khaki hat. I spoke to him and asked if he was a Navy Officer. He said he was and he was looking for some Navy men who were mixed in with the Army troops. As we talked, I learned that he was looking for replacements for a PT (Patrol Torpedo) Boat squadron on Tulagi Island. After I found out that Tulagi was a small island, about twenty miles North, with no Japanese on it, I told him I was a Navy man.

He chewed me out for not telling him immediately that I was in the Navy. I explained that when you lose your ship, you are like an orphan. You are up for grabs, I said, "It doesn't hurt to be a little careful before you volunteer for something." He admitted that I had a point.

I then helped him round up about thirty Navy men. He asked me who we should check out with. I told him, "Nobody, we did not check in with anyone". I did not want some Army Sergeant stopping my chance to rejoin the Navy. I mentioned to the officer that our names would be reported as joining his squadron. The Navy would eventually know where we were. That seemed to settle it. We marched away to a location called Lunga Point. I had opened my own door this time and had walked through it.

It was already dark and raining intermittently when we reached the pier at Lunga Point. A small ship was there, off loading fifty gallon drums of aviation gas. It was either a sea going Tug or a Mine sweeper. It was hard to tell. In either case, it was named the "Bobolink." We were told that we would be riding on the Bobolink to Tulagi as soon as they finished unloading the gas. It seemed like a long process. We passed the time by questioning the Navy Officer about the area we were in and the PT boats that we were to join. He told us that we would pass near Savo Island, a small island about nine miles from Guadalcanal. A night time sea battle had been fought there on August 9, shortly after the Marines landed on Guadalcanal. The American fleet was badly defeated. The Japanese had sunk four of our cruisers. They were the Vincennes, Quincy, Astoria and the Australian ship, the Canberra. The enemy had received relatively minor damage to their ships in return.

As a result of this battle, with so many ships lying sunk there, the area we were to sail across had been nicknamed "Iron Bottom Sound."

I thought about the recent battle we had experienced. Even though we had damaged two carriers and shot down many planes, the Japanese had sunk the Hornet and one destroyer. I considered it as a defeat. The Japanese were a very formidable and tenacious enemy.

The Navy had brought the PT boats to Tulagi to try and stop the Japanese ships from bombarding and reinforcing at night. The few planes operating from Guadalcanal helped to prevent the Japanese from landing troops and supplies in the day time.

The off-loading of gasoline had not yet been completed when the skipper of the Bobolink dashed out onto the small bridge area, next to his pilot house. He excitedly stopped the unloading of cargo and hollered for all passengers to get aboard, "On the double." He had evidently received an urgent message and was leaving immediately. We scrambled aboard as the crew were casting off and pulling in their lines. We stood on the open decks, next to the remaining gas drums, as we raced away from the wharf at full speed.

On the Bobolink, full speed was probably ten knots at most. I estimated that it would take

about two hours to reach Tulagi. I had lost track
of time, but it must have been after midnight,
Friday, November 13,1942, as we sailed innocently
across 'Iron Bottom Sound.'

We relaxed on the open decks, on a very dark
night. We were being pelted with intermittent
rain showers. Suddenly, all at once, what
appeared to be meteors, or low flying comets,
arched over our heads. Then we heard the
tremendous explosions and saw searchlights snap
on. We realized instantly that we were in the
middle of a sea battle that had erupted around
us. We found out later that there were 30
warships engaged in this battle. The Japanese had
17 ships, including battleships, cruisers and
destroyers. The U.S. had 13 ships, 5 cruisers and
8 destroyers.

Searchlights would snap on and off, followed by
salvos of high explosive shells. Ships were
exploding and burning in all directions. One ship
blew up so furiously that it was almost as if the
sun had come out for a moment. Then the light
slowly decayed. She must have been hit in the
ammunition magazines.

Huge star shells would burst, briefly
illuminating the confused scene before us. The
ships were spread out, firing shells, launching
torpedoes and maneuvering wildly. Wherever we
looked, we could see shells striking ships. We
had no idea of who was who, or which side was
winning. All we could do was to stand there in
amazement as the occasional star shell lit up the
wild scene that held us spellbound. It was more
of a shock to me than the recent Hornet battle.
That is because it was so completely un-expected.

Now we knew why the skipper of the Bobolink had
appeared to be so excited. He had evidently
received a message warning of a possible sea

battle. I wondered if our world on the Bobolink was going to come to a sudden end.

I started to form a request in my mind to somebody or something to help me through this spot, when I remembered my promise on the Hornet. I had promised that if I got out of that mess alive, I would never ask again. Here I was, seventeen days later, ready to break my promise. Of course, my rescue could have been blind luck. If, on the other hand, I had received help, I had to keep my bargain. Then I recalled that I had asked for help, from any one or anything, even if it came from the devil. I had no idea of who to give thanks to. In any case, I realized that I had closed out any possibilities of future requests for help.

If some supernatural power had helped me, I had promised not to ask again. If there exists such a power, I dare not break my bargain.

If there is no such power, asking for help was a waste of time. In either case, Iif I survived this night, it would have to be without any outside assistance.

About an hour after it started, the battle suddenly ended. To our great relief on the tiny Bobolink, we had come through unharmed.

The rest of the trip was uneventful. We soon tied up at the Government Dock on Tulagi Island. It was dawn by the time we arrived at the PT base at a village called Sesapi. I was standing next to a Hornet shipmate of mine, Charley Pellinat. I said, "I know what we saw last night, but I can't believe it actually happened." Charley said that he felt the same way. It had been a mind boggling episode. After that brief comment, I do not recall ever speaking to anyone about that night again. It was if I did not really believe that I had witnessed it.

15

PT BOATS

We had a memorable first breakfast at the PT
Base. The cook was a Marine. He had piled up fire
wood around the bottoms of two fifty gallon
gasoline drums. These drums had their tops
removed and had been cleaned out. They were both
filled with water. The cook dumped some rice in
the first drum of water. Then he placed a cheese
cloth bag of coffee grounds in the second drum of
water. We watched as he saturated the wood with
gasoline. Then, he stepped back, lit a match and
threw it at the base of the drums.

The gas-soaked wood erupted in a large ball of
fire. The flames towered over the drums. After
several minutes, the flames died down. Each drum
of water was boiling. Breakfast was ready.

We lined up with our mess kits. We received a
scoop of rice, a cup of coffee and one piece of
hardtack. The rice was only partially cooked.

We questioned a Marine who was eating with us
and discovered that we were lucky to have any
breakfast. We were eating captured Japanese rice.
Our mess kits, including the coffee cup, were
made of aluminum. The coffee was terrible, but it
was hot. However, it was impossible to drink from
the aluminum cup without burning your lips. We
had to let it cool off before drinking it.

The hardtack was something else. It was a
cracker, about four inches square and one-quarter
inch thick. I had read about sailing ship sailors
living on hardtack in the olden days. I never
expected to be trying to live on them in the
1940s'. Whatever the manufacturing process is, it

results in a cracker that is compressed so solidly, it is almost indestructible. I don't think anything could cause them to deteriorate. I would soak the cracker in my coffee while waiting for it to cool. When I tried to bite into it, I could barely dent the surface. All I could do was scrape a little film from the surface of the cracker, that was all. It took me about an hour to finally eat about one-third of the wafer. Whatever I managed to eat, expanded greatly within my stomach. It helped fill me up.

I supplemented my meals by eating a small portion of my iron rations. I did this each day until they were gone.

We soon heard that a Japanese battleship had been damaged during the battle we had sailed through. It was circling near Savo Island. It could be seen from the top of a three hundred foot ridge on our island. We climbed to the top and watched, through binoculars, as our planes from Guadalcanal attacked her with bombs. There was a destroyer trying to help her but the planes kept coming after the crippled ship. Enemy planes appeared but were either shot down or driven off. Late in the afternoon, she sank. I found out later that her name was the "Hiei."

We began to hear more details about that wild night battle. The Japanese had lost the battleship Hiei and one destroyer. We had lost the cruiser Atlanta and had three cruisers damaged. Admiral Scott was killed on the Atlanta and Admiral Callaghan was killed on the San Francisco. The Portland was torpedoed and the Juneau was severely shot up. The day after the battle, an enemy submarine fired two torpedoes into the Juneau, causing her to explode violently and sink. She had five brothers serving aboard. They were the Sullivan brothers. They all died. This incident caused the Navy to issue an order forbidding brothers to serve together aboard ships.

We also lost two destroyers and had three destroyers disabled. I found out one of the sunken destroyers was the USS Barton (DD-599). She was the ship that had rescued me from the Hornet and had offered me a job on board. She was torpedoed and obviously was one of the huge explosions that we had witnessed. She went down so fast that the only survivors were those with topside battle stations. The ship exploded and immediately sank. The survivors suddenly found themselves in the water. She lost seventy percent of her crew. That meant that she had suffered as many fatalities as the Hornet did. I never did find out if my friend, the Gunners Mate striker, survived or not. I had certainly made the right decision when I declined to stay aboard the Barton.

Numerically, the Japanese had again whipped our Navy. However, they did not bombard Guadalcanal or land reinforcements or supplies. Considering that angle, it was a tactical victory. We had thwarted their plans.

One additional note, we wound up with some of the Atlanta survivors in our squadron. They maintained that during the confused battle, the cruiser San Francisco, mistakenly, fired at least two salvos into the Atlanta. They were very bitter sailors.

few mornings later, I awoke to find a cruiser, I think it was the Portland, tied up alongside our PT Base. The island dropped off steeply and the ship was able to come right against the shore line and tie up to trees. The crew was busy spreading netting over the ship to camouflage it. The Portland had part of her bow blown off by a torpedo. She was there a couple of weeks while they shored up the forward part of the ship with tree trunks so she could return to a shipyard for repairs.

The Marines, that fed us on that first day, had

a machine gun nest at the PT Base. It was located at the end of a pier. It was one-half of a crossfire arrangement set up for defensive purposes. I remember my conversations with the Marine who appeared to be in charge. His name was Grady Gates. He was with the First Division and had been there since the landing on 7 August. He was an interesting guy to talk to. I liked him from the first time I met him.

He told me that the landings on Guadalcanal and Tulagi had initially been un-opposed. However, on Tulagi, they had run into a hornet's nest of Japanese not long after they were ashore. He said the worst fighting occurred on a couple of small islets in the Tulagi Harbor, Gavutu and Tanambogo. They had used Marine Paratroopers as infantrymen and had suffered heavy casualties. Since the beginning of the campaign, all the rest of the ground fighting had been happening on Guadalcanal.

He told me that they would kill Japanese during the daylight hours. At night, they watched helplessly as enemy transports unloaded fresh troops. There was absolutely no Navy to stop them until the PT Boats arrived around the middle of October. This was four weeks before I got there. Grady had a lot of respect for the torpedo boat sailors. I can honestly say that I had a tremendous amount of respect for the Marines. In peace time, sailors and marines are constantly putting each other down. On Guadalcanal, there was none of that bickering. We relied totally on each other's expertise. Every night before hitting the sack, Grady would say, "Have no fear, Gates is near."

A couple of weeks after our arrival, the Marines were pulled out of Tulagi. We began being fed by Navy cooks. The powdered eggs, powdered potatoes and powdered coffee tasted like gourmet food. However, I missed my talks with Grady Gates.

133

My normal weight of 135 pounds had dropped to
under 120 pounds. All I wore was Army shoes and
shorts, no hat. At night I put on a long sleeved
khaki shirt to afford some protection from the
mosquitoes. They came out every evening at
twilight.

There were two PT Squadrons at the Base,
Squadrons Two and Three. Each had eight boats. I
was placed in Ron Three and assigned to the Base
Force. I helped run the Dry-docks. These were
constructed of large, six foot square, steel
pontoons. They had pontoon decks and bulkheads. A
large boat skid, custom made for PT boats, rested
on the deck, between the bulkheads. Four
Continental gasoline engines were installed atop
the bulkheads on one side of the dry dock. These
engines ran air compressors that forced air into
the deck pontoons. Each engine controlled one-
quarter of the deck pontoons. In this way, the
dock could be leveled by use of the air pressure.

In practice, to sink the dock, we would walk
along the deck. There was a long pipe connected
to each individual pontoon. We would shove the
pipe under water and the pontoon would begin
filling up. As soon as all pontoons were
flooding, we went up a ladder to the air
compressor engines. We started the engines and
let the dock sink to the required depth. When it
was deep enough, we forced a small amount of air
into the pontoons and stopped the descent of the
dock. We would then haul the PT boat into the
dock, and position it properly. Then, using the
air compressors, we forced the water out of the
pontoons and the dock would rise, boat and all.
When that operation was completed, we again would
walk the deck and raise each individual pipe so
that it was no longer under water. Then we could
secure the engines and the operation was
completed. It was a simple process and we kept
both dry docks busy.

When I was not actually raising or lowering the docks, I would lend a hand to who ever was working on the hulls of the boats, usually, it was two excellent carpenters. I remember one was named Olsen and I believe the other Archbold. The PTs were constructed of ¾" plywood. There were three layers of wood, each layer was installed at a forty-five degree angle from the adjoining layer. The boats had three shafts and propellers. Each was driven by a Packard, V12, gasoline engine. They ran on 100 octane aviation gas. Each boat could carry 3,000 gallons of gas. There were two basic designs. One was 77 feet in length. The other model was 80 feet long. They were both made by a company named Elco.

For armament, they had four torpedo tubes, two on each side. They had two, twin, fifty caliber machine guns and a 20 millimeter cannon. They also had engine mufflers and a smoke generator mounted on the Fantail. They could also be rigged with depth charges. Some of the boats had a small radar set installed. They normally had a crew of eight men and two officers.

I originally thought that the PT Boats used their high speed to attack the enemy ships. I found out that this would be suicide. The method actually used was to slowly sneak up on an enemy ship, on a dark, moonless night, with their engines muffled. When in position, they would fire their torpedoes, turn on the smoke generator, open the mufflers, reverse course and use their high speed to escape through the smoke screen. That was the plan, but it was a difficult and dangerous task against the tough, competent Japanese Navy.

The enemy only came on dark, moon-less, nights. They were always in a high state of readiness for action. They also were excellent, highly trained, night fighters. It was almost impossible for the PT Boats to see anything on such dark nights as

they would patrol with their engines muffled.
Sometimes they would spot an enemy ship. They
would be sneaking up on it when another ship, one
they had not seen, would spot them and turn a
searchlight on. Everything would hit the fan when
that happened. Both enemy ships would be firing
machine guns and 4.7 inch cannons at them. The PT
Boat would be fortunate to escape, sometimes they
did not.

Since I was part of the Base Force, I was not
detailed to ride the boats as part of the regular
crew. Normally, the boats were split into two
sections. One section patrolled one night and the
other section patrolled the next night. That way
they were off, every second night.

On two different nights, I was ordered to
replace a crew member who was too sick to go out.
In each case, I was assigned to a battle station
on one of the fifty caliber machine guns. They
showed me how to load and cock it and I was
considered trained. I had never actually fired
one.

We patrolled between Savo Island and
Guadalcanal, the same area where the Bobolink had
sailed through the sea battle. The boat would
idle along with the mufflers on. The engine noise
would be a low throb. We would all be straining
our eyes against the dark. We tried to see
anything that might be an enemy ship. Your eyes
and imagination can play strange tricks on you
when you are in a tense, pressure filled,
situation. We had several false alarms, but, we
did not encounter any enemy ships on the nights
that I rode.

I lived in a tent. My normal nightly routine,
before sleeping, was to listen to our 45 RPM
record player. We had two records. One was
called, "Mister Five by Five." The other song was
"Cow Cow Boogie." We had salvaged the player and

the records from the cruiser Portland. For almost
one year, that is the only music we had available. While listening to the record player, I
would check out my cot for anything that might
have crawled into it during the day. There were
deadly coral snakes, poisonous spiders, scorpions
and other insects that grew to huge sizes on
Tulagi. I did not want to sleep with any of them.

After putting up my mosquito netting and tucking
it in, I would slip inside and close the opening
behind me. I always fell asleep quickly. Practically every night, the air raid siren would
wake me up. One blast on the siren meant
Condition Red, Air Raid Imminent.

I would jump up, grab my shirt, shorts and shoes
and race to the nearest fox hole. I would lay
there until the raid was over and the all clear
sounded. This was accomplished by two blasts on
the siren, which meant Condition Green.

When I first got into the foxhole, I would be
completely calm. I would get as comfortable as I
could. Then I would listen to the sound of the
plane's engine droning overhead. The Japanese
engines were easy to discern. They were slightly
un-synchronized and they would have a kind of
pulsing sound to them.

Aboard ship, with all the noise and commotion, I
never heard the bombs as they fell. Ashore, with
no other sounds, I could actually hear the noise
the bombs made while dropping through the air. It
was a strange, shattering noise. The first time I
heard it, I thought that a tree was falling
through the air. Then of course, I would hear the
explosion as the bomb hit.

About that time, my imagination would start in
and I could visualize a bomb actually dropping on
me. I wondered if I would be aware of the moment
of death or would I be blasted instantly into a
thousand pieces of quivering flesh? Maybe I would

137

wind up maimed and be a basket case for the rest
of my life. My imagination would slowly succeed
in terrorizing me as I lay in the foxhole.

I tried to think of other things, but the
reality of my situation always came back to my
thoughts. If I had a battle station or something
to keep me occupied, I would have been all right.
Lying there helplessly, with nothing to do but
think, was very difficult for me. It seemed to me
that anyone who was not frightened when helplessly facing death or being maimed would have to
be totally lacking in imagination. He would have
to be a real "clod."

Besides the air raids, I developed an
intermittent toothache. Some nights it kept me
awake for hours. I heard that the Marines had a
dentist with them. I located him one evening in
his tent on Florida Island.

It was getting dark and he had a kerosene
lantern for a light. The drill he used was
operated by a foot treadle. It was exactly like
an old fashioned sewing machine. Of course, these
were the days before Novacain. Dentists worked on
you with nothing to deaden the pain. He told me
that I had a filling that had developed a cavity
below it. He removed the old filling and drilled
into the cavity until I could no longer stand the
pain. He refilled the tooth and I left. The tooth
seemed to be all right for a few weeks and then
it started to bother me again, intermittently.
The Marine outfit had pulled out and I had no one
else to turn to. I hoped that it would not get
too bad before I could find another dentist.

I recall one night, after an air raid. I
returned to my tent and went through my cot
checking routine. I slipped under the mosquito
net and quickly fell asleep. Something woke me
up. I opened my eyes and could see a shaft of
moonlight coming in through the tent flap. It
fell across my mosquito netting, illuminating a

section of several inches. At that moment, I saw
a huge insect, of some variety, crawling slowly
across the net. It was about four inches in
length and was right about eye level. I knew it
had to be outside the net because I had checked
the cot before going to bed. I hit the net with
the back of my hand to shoo it away. I felt the
bug's clammy body against the back of my hand. It
was inside the net with me. I jumped up with a
shout, scrambling out of my cot. Naturally I woke
up my tent-mates. I spent a fruitless hour trying
to find the insect that had gotten in bed with
me. I never did find it.

We had several men that were stung by scorpions.
Their sting was very potent. It could lay you up
for weeks. I had a hard time getting back to
sleep that night.

The Capital of the Solomon Island Group was
located on Tulagi Island. The Solomons included
Guadalcanal and a number of nearby islands.
Tulagi was extremely small. It lay next to a very
large island named Florida. The local natives
were Malaysians. They were dark skinned and of
average or small stature. The principal peace
time industry around the Guadalcanal area was
coconut plantations. These were owned by the
Lever Brothers Soap Company of Great Britain.

The local tribes were not too far removed from
the days when they actively practiced head
hunting. Their main weapon was a large, knobby,
club, studded with sharp rocks. This was called
their "war club." It was a mean looking weapon.
By talking with the local natives, we found out
that the natives who ruled the roost in the
Solomons lived on Malaita Island. This island was
as large as Guadalcanal and lay about thirty
miles to the Northwest, on the other side of
Florida Island.

The natives told us that the Malaita tribes were
physically much larger and more warlike than the

139

Guadalcanal natives. They said that the Malaita Islanders were head hunters who would raid adjoining islands and capture slaves, even during the time we were there. As far as being head hunters, all the Malaysian tribes had that reputation in their background. The only question was, if they still practiced it or not.

I was not the only one who was getting desperate for a full nights sleep. Several of the Base sailors had gone almost to the top of the 300 foot ridge behind our Base. They had built a shack and dug a fox hole at the bottom of a cliff. They angled it back into the hill so that a bomb could not possibly drop into it. They invited me to move in with them and I gladly took them up on it. For once I felt completely safe during an air raid. I could even doze off in the fox hole.

Every night after supper, we would climb up the ridge to our home. We would start up while it was still light so we could follow the steep trail. After about a week, we started missing things from our shack, little odds and ends, especially mosquito netting. One day I decided to investigate. After lunch, when I knew none of them would be there, I went up alone to the shack. I moved as quietly as I could.

If you will recall, I was a Third Class Boatswain Mate, A right arm rate. I was used to giving orders. Glancing through a net covered window, I thought I saw a movement inside the shack. I pushed the door open and jumped in. At the same instant, I hollered, "Gotcha."

Expecting to find a sailor, I was stunned to see a gigantic, black native, whirl around toward me. He had been bent over, searching through one of our bunks when I jumped in, startling him. The natives I had been used to were of small stature. They were a brownish color. This guy was at least six feet, six inches tall. He probably weighed close to three hundred pounds. He wore only a loin cloth and was all muscle. He was a solid gleaming black, kind of a bluish black, with highlights. He gripped a huge war club in his right hand. There was absolutely no doubt in my mind that I had surprised a Malaita Islander, a headhunter.

I had initially startled him and his eyes were wide open as he stared down at me. We were about two feet apart. I could even see the little red veins in his eyeballs as we silently stared at each other. From the corner of my eye, I could see his grip tighten on the war club.

I was in an extremely bad spot and I knew it. Talk about your moment of truth, I was a five foot, six inch, 120 pound, unarmed sailor. I was challenging a six foot, six inch, 300 pound, savage headhunter, armed with a war club.

We were on a remote hilltop, on a South Sea island, on his turf. I could almost see the gears going around in his mind. He sees that he has been caught. He might be in trouble. He sees a little skinny guy in front of him. All he has to do is swat him with the club and leave. The problem is solved.

Of course, all of these thoughts had been streaking through my mind at the speed of light since the instant that I had stupidly jumped into that shack. I knew I had to do something, fast, before he made his move. I did not dare turn around to leave or he would surely strike me instantly with his club. Then a possible solution came to me.

I forced myself to look as angry and fierce as I possibly could. I pointed my finger close to his nose, without touching him and hollered in a loud angry voice, "Your ass better be out of here before I get back!"

He blinked in astonishment. I know he did not understand what I had said, but I hoped that my

141

fierce tone and loud words would cause him to
hesitate, just for a moment, that was all that I
needed. Still facing him, I backed quickly out of
the door. I turned and streaked down the steep
trail, expecting at any instant to feel that war
club striking me. I was slipping, sliding and
falling, but I made it down safely. I found my
tent-mates and, after I got my breath back, I
told them what I had discovered. I also told them
I was moving. I never went back to that shack
again. I moved back to my regular tent and had to
put up with the lack of sleep once more.

One day I ran into my Hornet shipmate, Charley
Pellinat. When we joined the squadron, I was
assigned to the Base Force because I was a
Boatswain Mate. There was no billet on the boats
for that rating. Charley was a seaman and could
be assigned anywhere.

They put him with one of the crews as a Gunners
Mate striker. He told me that he and the rest of
his crew had recently been awarded Silver Star
Medals and his skipper had received the Navy
Cross. He told me that their boat had been
alerted that an enemy submarine was supposed to
surface one night at a certain area off Guadalcanal. They were waiting there with another PT
Boat. The sub surfaced and his PT fired a torpedo
into it, sinking the sub. This was a tremendous
accomplishment for a small plywood boat.

In February, the fighting on Guadalcanal ended.
The Japanese gave up and evacuated their remaining troops.

The PT Boats had sunk or at least damaged,
thirteen Japanese vessels during the campaign.
They included cruisers, destroyers, transports
and at least one submarine. This was an amazing
record for these small, wooden boats. Of course
there had been a price to pay. We had lost about
thirty men and several boats during the various
battles.

It seemed that as soon as the fighting on Guadalcanal ended, the nightly air raids became more intense. Daylight raids also seemed to have more planes involved. Commander Calvert was in charge of the various PT Squadrons and had established another base on Florida Island. It was called, Calvertville.

The air raids were getting to me and I noticed that the planes seldom bothered Florida Island. One day I suggested to the dry dock crew that it might be a good idea to sleep on Florida Island. No one wanted to go with me. I took the boat to Calvertville and managed to find room in one of the tents. That night, during an air raid, a bomb landed directly on the PT Base at Sesapi.

When I returned in the morning to go to work, one of the dry dock engineers kept eyeing me suspiciously. Finally he came over to me and demanded to know how I knew that the base was going to be bombed that night. I explained that it was a sheer coincidence. However, I could see that he really thought that I had some type of crystal ball. I noticed that he and quite a few others were on the boat to Calvertville that evening.

A few days after moving to Calvertville, three friends of mine discovered a natural cave on a ridge behind the camp. It was quite a hike. It took almost an hour to climb up there, but the rewards were great. We could sleep inside the cave and be completely safe from bombs. A plane would have to drop a bomb exactly in front of the cave to hit us. Of course, in the morning, it took a much shorter time to descend back to camp. It is always faster going downhill.

We packed a few items up the hill to make the cave more comfortable. We had cots, lanterns, flashlights, extra canteens of water and cans of C-rations. Since Florida was such a large island, we knew that there was always the danger of

143

Japanese infiltrators. We always carried rifles
with us when going to and from the cave. It
wasn't only the danger of the Japanese, there
were a variety of poisonous snakes and huge six
foot long monitor lizards in the jungle. I
believe they are related to the Komoda Dragons
that are found around Indonesia or Borneo.

A lot of the sailors said that these giant
lizards were afraid of us and would always run
away. I heard that they were meat eaters and had
been known to attack the natives. I had also told
my friends about my encounter with the Malaita
Island head hunter. To be safe rather than sorry,
we carried the rifles.

I received an unexpected present. Someone gave
me a copy of a book titled, "Studs Lonigan." It
was written by James T. Farrell. The novel was
about this fellow Studs who grew up in Chicago,
in the same area I was raised in. Of course it
was about the generation that preceded mine, but
the locale was exactly the same. Even some of the
happenings in the book were identical to my life
experiences. Every evening, after reaching the
cave, I would read a few chapters. With my ability to become totally engrossed in my reading, it
was almost like a brief visit back home. At that
particular time in my life, that book became a
real treasure to me. I did not want to finish the
book too soon, I wanted to stretch it out.

Since we were so high up, whenever we heard the
anti-aircraft guns go off on Guadalcanal or
Tulagi, we could set in the entrance to the cave
and watch the light show. When the shells burst
in the sky, from a distance, it looked exactly
like the lights on the back of a pinball machine.

One evening, I had gone to sleep early and must
have been dreaming. The others were sitting outside the cave, watching an air raid in progress.
Suddenly, a plane came over Florida Island and
they heard the bomb dropping through the air.

They shouted, "Lookout" as they dashed into the cave. One of them bumped into my cot, just as the bomb exploded nearby.

I evidently incorporated the sounds and the bump into my dream. I heard the shout and knew a bomb was coming down. Then I felt the severe jolt at the same time as the bomb exploded. In my dream state, I actually believed that the bomb had hit our cave and killed me.

I felt a huge sense of relief wash over me. It was over, I was dead and it had been absolutely painless. I had hoped to survive the war, but I had experienced an amazingly easy death. Nothing else could touch me now. I was beyond fear of anything. I did not have to worry about returning as a mutilated cripple or a basket case. I suddenly thought about my mother and how she would grieve for me. However, I thought, we all have to go sometime. These thoughts went rapidly through my mind.

I began to wonder how I could be dead and still be aware of it. Then my cot was again accidentally bumped by someone and I woke up.

My dream had been so vivid and real to me that I was surprised to discover that I was actually still alive. The events had seemed so convincing that I felt a momentary disappointment that it had only been a dream. I knew, from that moment on, that I would never again fear death. I only worried about how it might happen. I was concerned about the possibility of being crippled or mutilated, however, death itself could no longer frighten me. My life became a lot easier after that night and I slept better than ever.

We used that cave for several weeks. Suddenly, one evening, everything changed. As I previously indicated, it was a long haul going up to the cave. At about the half way point, there was a large, flat rock. We would always pause at this spot and take a breather. On this particular

145

evening, we had reached the rock and I was
standing up, stretching my arms. I heard a loud
buzzing sound zing past my ear. I thought it was
a huge bumble bee. I heard it again and then we
all heard a bullet ricochet off a rock.
We were being shot at by a sniper.
 We dropped flat and slid backwards off the rock.
We could not see where the shots were coming from
and had no idea of what we had encountered. We
had our rifles, but the prudent thing was to
leave quickly and report the incident.
 We heard several more shots as we retreated
rapidly down the hill. We reported the shooting
as soon as we reached Calvertville.
 The following day, the Army sent a patrol to
Florida Island to search for enemy troops. They
did not find any but I heard that they had found
some evidence that someone had taken over our
cave, possibly Japanese soldiers. I never
returned to the cave after that. I even abandoned
my 'Studs Lonigan' book. It was several years
later before I located another copy and finished
reading the novel.
 The air raids continued and I was again losing
sleep. In early April, we underwent the largest
day light air raid I had ever seen in the
islands. Approximately 200 planes attacked the
Tulagi and Guadalcanal areas. One plane crashed
on Florida Island. It did not appear to be too
far from Calvertville. I went with a group to
investigate the crash site in the jungle. Native
guides led us, primarily so we could find our way
back. It took several hours to reach the wrecked
plane. The pilot had been flung out and was in a
sitting position at the base of a tree. He
appeared to be asleep, but he was definitely
dead. He was a stocky, powerfully built man. I
wondered if his family would ever know how he had
died.
 I looked the plane over and noticed that the

plane's tires were made in the U.S. I cut the
brand name from one tire as a souvenir. I was
glad to leave the crash scene and return to our
base.

One day, one of the Squadron officers asked me
when I would be eligible for advancement to
Boatswain Mate Second Class. I told him that I
was eligible now, but I had no way of studying or
preparing for any test while we were in the war
zone. He told me that I would not have to take a
test. They would advance me on May 1. He was as
good as his word. I was promoted to Boatswain
Mate Second Class a few days later.

At about this time, our squadron was told that
we were going to Auckland, New Zealand for two
weeks R&R (Rest & Rehabilitation). I was eagerly
looking forward to this trip and began trying to
find some type of dress uniform to wear. I asked
one of the Yeomen if he knew where I might locate
a uniform. He told me not to bother. I was not
going to go. I, and some of the other survivors,
who had joined the PT Boats in Tulagi, had been
transferred to Squadron Two. I was told that we
would go to New Zealand, with Ron Two, when Ron
Three returned.

I was bitterly disappointed, but I had learned
patience in the Navy. Ron Three loaded happily
aboard a PT Tender, I believe it was the
Jamestown. They sailed for New Zealand and
returned about six weeks later.

I was already packed and had managed to borrow a
dress blue uniform. It belonged to a Second Class
Motor Mechanic. It was a left arm rate, but I was
not particular at that point in time. The main
thing was to again be a member of civilization,
if only for a few weeks.

I asked the Yeoman when we would be leaving for
Auckland. It was like deja vu, he told me I was
not going to go. The others and I had been
transferred back to Ron Three. He said that we

147

were only in Ron Two on a temporary basis while Ron three was in New Zealand.

I was furious as I went to see the Commanding Officer of Ron Two. I controlled my temper as I explained the situation to him. He said that he had enough problems taking care of the people he had brought from the States. I told him that I had been in the South Pacific for a year before he and his squadron had left the States. He told me that I would have to talk to Ron Three, I was their problem, not his.

I recognized a run around when I was getting one. I was livid as I walked away from him. I met two other angry Boatswain Mates who had just found out that they were not going to New Zealand. I told them that I had struck out with the Ron Two C.O. I decided to go see Commander Calvert. He was in charge of all the Squadrons. We all went over to his quonset hut. Since I was senior, I decided to go in alone. I did not want it to look like a mutiny.

I went in and asked if I could talk to him. He was kind enough to listen to my entire tale. He said to me. "Tell your shipmates waiting outside to pack up. You are all three going to New Zealand."

I went out and gave them the good news. We quickly got ready to leave. About that time, the C.O. of Ron Two sent for us. We went to his office and he told us that he had changed his mind. He said he had decided to take us with Ron Two on R&R. Then he said that in return, he wanted us to change our rates to Quartermaster. In that way he could assign us to boat crews when we returned from our trip. He dismissed us and we went aboard the tender. Commander Calvert had ordered the C.O. to take us along. The C.O. was trying to take advantage of the situation by forcing us to change our rates.

I discovered that I had been selected as part of

148

a four man crew to ride aboard an empty PT
Boat hull. The engines and armament had been
stripped off. The tender was going to tow the
empty hull to New Caledonia. With all the weight
gone,the PT would bob like a cork.

The four of us got aboard and began our one week
trip to New Caledonia. We were continually
bobbing and bouncing at the end of the tow line.
We never stopped rolling and pitching as we took
turns steering the craft. We tried to steer in a
way that would reduce the pounding, but it was
not possible to do so.

The senior man aboard was a First Class
Quartermaster. I told him about the C.O. wanting
me to change my rate to his. The Quartermaster
rate was required to be expert in navigation,
signaling, codes and other areas that I only had
a rudimentary knowledge of. I did not think that
I had the necessary training to handle that job.
I asked his opinion and he agreed with me. I
would need to have some training or I would be
lost in that rate.

The constant bouncing and rolling was making us
queasy. When it came time to eat, the tender put
all of our food in an empty, five inch powder
can. They lowered it on a line and let it float
back to us. We retrieved it and opened the can.
The result was as if the food had gone through a
blender. It was one big gob of goo. We tried to
eat and that finished us off. For the first time,
I became sea-sick, we all did. When we were not
on watch, we were groaning in our bunks. A week
later we finally reached New Caledonia.

We were there for one day. I checked around and
found several Hornet men who had been assigned to
jobs on that island. I heard that Morelock, the
one who had been with me in the water when we
were bombed, was now Admiral Halsey's Coxswain.
He ran the Admiral's Barge. I was told that
another friend of mine, Ben Lee Hek, was

operating a tug boat in Noumea Harbor. I always liked Ben, we were similar in size and appearance. People sometimes thought we were related.

The visit was short, but I enjoyed it. About one week later we arrived at Auckland, New Zealand.

New Zealand was a beautiful, green, tree covered, charming land. They raised sheep and cattle. The people spoke with a British accent. Their cities were large and clean. They made you think of England. Everything seemed to be about ten years behind the times.

We were there for exactly two weeks. It was in July. Since we were on the other side of the Equator, the seasons were reversed from ours. It was the middle of their winter.

We first went to a rest camp called, "The Domain." It was noon and we had lunch before our liberty would commence. The food was plentiful and delicious, real milk and eggs. Nothing powdered. I believe that I gained about two pounds during that noon meal. Next we went into Auckland to begin our leave. Two of us rented rooms at a boarding house and started to explore the town.

The first thing we did was to have our pictures taken to send home. I wanted my folks to see that I was all right. Then I got weighed on a New Zealand penny scale. I inserted one of their large, copper pennies and received a card that said I weighed 8 stones and 6 pounds. I tried for days to find out how much I weighed in pounds. No one seemed to know how many pounds were in a stone. I would show my card to a new Zealander and ask them how much I weighed in pounds. They would look at the card and say, you weigh 6 pounds and 8 stones. It took awhile, but I eventually discovered that a stone contained 14 pounds. Therefore I actually weighed 118 pounds.

We had two glorious weeks of R&R. During that time, I discovered that New Zealand is the land of dentists. There is either something wrong with the water or they lack something in their diet. They have a great many young people with false teeth. There seems to be a Dentist Office in every block in Auckland.

One morning, my intermittent toothache started to bother me. Two of my buddies insisted that I see a dentist immediately. We went to the nearest one and he decided to pull the tooth. I had never had a tooth extraction before. He told me I was lucky because he had the latest thing, called Novacain. He told me I would not feel a thing. He gave me a shot to deaden the tooth and we waited. I did not notice any difference. He gave me a second shot. When I still did not feel any numbness, he said it was my imagination. He knew that I could not have any feeling in my jaw. He grabbed the tooth with his pliers and I felt every thing he did. It took my two buddies and his nurse to hold me down before he could finish yanking out the tooth.

Either the Novacain was defective or he did not administer it correctly. In either case, he pulled that tooth without deadening it.

During the months that we lived on Tulagi, we were exposed to malaria carrying mosquitoes. Interestingly, there are several varieties of these insects. Only the Anopheles mosquito carries the malaria parasite. You can tell this type when it lands on you.

Most mosquitoes bend their head down to sting you. The Anopheles straightens its back legs, then it jabs into you like a dart. These details may sound peculiar to you. However, if you spend eight or nine months in daily contact with mosquitoes, you learn a great deal about them.

Malaria has several forms. One, called Pernicious or Black Water Fever, kills your red blood cells. Your urine turns dark with these dead cells and thus, the name. It can kill you if

151

not treated promptly with quinine. The most common form was called, Benign Tertian. This is a very debilitating disease, it normally does not kill you, at least not right away. It does remain in your system and can re-occur at any time for up to seven years. Quinine, which comes from the bark of the Cinchona tree, was the only medicine that could control malaria. Unfortunately, the Japanese had captured the Netherlands East Indies which contained the world's supply of Cinchona trees. Because of this fact, the limited supply of quinine in the U.S. was strictly controlled. It was only given to those actually suffering from malaria.

Atabrine was a synthetic drug, designed to protect us from malaria. In the tropics, we took one pill each day. It caused the skin to turn yellow. If you took them religiously, it would prevent you from having malaria.

When we went to New Zealand, we quit taking the Atabrine. After all, there were no mosquitoes on the ocean. What I did not know was that I already had malaria. All the Atabrine did was to prevent the malaria symptoms from appearing.

By the time my two weeks R&R ended, I was feeling very ill. I had done a lot of unaccustomed partying and drinking and assumed that this was my problem. I lost my appetite and had severe headaches. By the time we returned to Tulagi, I was really suffering. An attack would start out with nausea and sudden chills. This would last up to an hour. Then an extremely high fever would develop and I would vomit. I would then sweat profusely until my temperature reduced to normal. The attacks would completely exhaust me. During an attack, it was impossible to do anything other than lay there and let it run its course. These sessions would occur about every third day. Without quinine, the attacks would increase in intensity.

I checked into our hospital and it was determined that I had Benign Tertian malaria. I was put on a course of Quinine and in a few weeks I was returned to duty.

The Ron Two C.O. sent for me. He wanted to know when I was going to convert to the Quartermaster rating. I explained to him that I was not knowledgeable enough in that rating to change over. I knew the basics but was not proficient in it, for example, celestial navigation, visual signaling and things of that nature. I told him I would volunteer to ride the boats, but only as a Boatswain Mate. He did not really listen to my rationale. All he heard was that I was not going to change my rate. He became very angry and dismissed me. The next day I was told that I was being sent to the Russell Islands. They were located North-West of Guadalcanal. I boarded a PT Boat. About two hours later, we arrived at the Russell Islands.

The Japanese had been on these islands but had abandoned them before we got there. I did not have a specific job to do so I tried to make myself useful on the Base Force. A few days after my arrival, I again came down with malaria.

I was sent to an Army Field Hospital. It consisted of a big tent. I went through the same routine of attacks until the quinine was able to control it. After about two weeks, I was feeling much better. However, I had a very difficult time in getting released from the hospital. Each morning the doctor would make his rounds. I would ask to be released. He would check my chart and invariably say, "Maybe tomorrow." As soon as he would leave, an Army Sergeant would come in and select several patients for working parties. He always picked me. Then I would spend the day doing some monotonous, heavy chore for the Army. We would clear fields of coconuts or tasks of that nature.

153

After about a week of this routine, I simply walked away from the hospital. I caught a ride on an Army truck and returned to the PT Base. The Navy medical corpsman, who had sent me to the Army hospital, wanted my medical records. I told him the Army said they would send them later. I never found out if he ever received my records or not.

One day, out of the blue, I received a letter from the girl in Chicago whom I had sent the musical jewelry box to. The one who had turned it into an ashtray. Since I had joined the Navy, I had never heard from her. She had not even acknowledged the birthday present I sent her. I could not imagine what the letter could possibly be about.

She wrote that she had recently heard about the sinking of the Hornet. Someone had also told her that I was now with the PT Boats. She said, "You must have had some exciting experiences. You probably are having lots of interesting things happening to you now. Why don't you write and tell me about them"? I sat down and answered her letter. I said that we had nothing to say to each other. If she wanted to help the war effort, she could do so by not writing to me anymore. Her letters tended to lower my morale. I never heard from her again.

Along those same lines, I heard a story about one of the squadron sailors who received a Dear John letter from his fiancee. She broke off the engagement because she was going to marry someone else, someone who was there. She told him not to be sad. He would find the right girl someday. The sailor was really broken up, but his buddies came to the rescue. They gathered up about a dozen pictures of various girls and mailed them to her along with her photo. They enclosed a letter from the sailor. It thanked her for her kind words and thoughts. The letter said that, unfortunately, he could not recall what she looked like. However, he assumed that she was among this group of girls. He asked her to pick out her photo and send the others back. I do not know if he got the pictures back or not, but I thought that was a great response to a Dear John letter.

The cook on Russell Island told me he needed a Mess Hall Master at Arms. I took the job to have something to do. It was simple work and kept me busy. During this time, we got word that Lieutenant Jack Kennedy's PT Boat had been run over by a Japanese destroyer while on night patrol. His entire crew was missing. A friend of mine, McMahon, a Scot who had taught me a Scottish drinking song was a member of his crew.

I had noticed Kennedy on two previous occasions. Once, his boat was in my dry dock and someone pointed him out to me. They told me that he was the son of Joe Kennedy, the former Ambassador to England. He was skinny, about six feet tall and looked like the other young officers that were in the squadrons.

One other time, I was on the pier at the Russell Island Base. A PT Boat came in much too fast and collided with the dock. It caused some minor damage. I noticed that the boat skipper was Jack Kennedy. I wondered if the Ambassador was aware of his son being missing.

One day the Ron Two C.O. came to Russell Island. The next day, a Yeoman told me that I was to return to Tulagi. They were getting ready to set up an 'advanced base' at Bougainville, a Japanese held island. They were going to tow a dry-dock there and I had been selected to ride aboard the dry-dock.

Being towed on a large, unwieldy target, through Japanese waters, was not my idea of a fun trip. However, I knew someone had to do it. It could have been my imagination, but I was getting a definite feeling that I was on somebody's list. I

155

packed up and caught a PT boat back to Tulagi Island.

Shortly after reaching Sesapi, I heard the news that Kennedy and his crew had been saved. All except one man who was killed during the initial collision. Kennedy was held in high esteem by the PT sailors after we heard how he held his crew together and managed their rescue. In my opinion, he had a lot of guts to do some of the things he did to save his crew. My Scot friend was one of the survivors. He got a kick out of my telling him that, since he had no insurance, the squadron insurance officer was using him as a horrible example during his lectures.

In those days, you had to buy insurance if you wanted it. It was not automatically provided to you. My friend was one of those who refused to buy insurance. He claimed it would have jinxed him. I had bought a five thousand dollar policy when I first joined the Navy. I later increased it to ten thousand which was the maximum amount you could purchase.

It was November 1943. I had left the States in April 1942, over twenty months ago. I had been in the islands with the PT boats for a year. I was preparing to go to Bougainville to help establish the next base. I had resigned myself to facing a new campaign. I only hoped I could survive it in one piece.

I had finished lunch and was talking to a couple of friends of mine. They were the cooks on the Base. One of them, Schaefer, asked me to go with him to the dentist at the new Army MASH (Mobile Army Surgical Hospital) Unit. He hated to go the dentist and needed moral support. I borrowed a jeep and we drove around the island to the MASH Unit. We located the dentist and Schaefer still hesitated about going in. He asked me to get my teeth checked first. I told him that my teeth

156

were fine. However, to satisfy him, I went in to get my teeth checked while he worked up his nerve.

The dentist checked me over and said, "That tooth has to come out, it has bothered you long enough". I was shocked. I said, "That tooth does not bother me, I just wanted a check up." He laughed and said, "Don't worry, I've got Novacain, you won't feel a thing."

Despite my objections, he gave me a shot of Novacain and pulled the tooth. To my great surprise, I did not feel anything. I told him of my New Zealand experience. He could not explain it. He assumed that either the drug was no good or that it was improperly administered.

Schaefer finally went in. His teeth checked out fine. All he needed was a minor cleaning. I complained to him all the way back to the base. By doing him a favor, I had lost a tooth.

One evening, after supper, I stopped by Schaefer's tent to pass the time. He said, "I hear you got your orders." I asked, "Do you mean to Bougainville? I told you before that I am taking the dry-dock there, whenever they tell me to leave."

Schaefer said, "Not Bougainville, to the States." Then he turned to the other Cook and said, "Can you imagine that? Here is a guy with orders back to the States and he does not even know it yet."

I thought he was pulling my leg. However, Schaefer insisted it was true. I went to the Base Office and checked with the Yeoman. He said that he had been looking for me. He told me that some replacements had come in and I was on the top of the list to be relieved. My orders to return to the States would be ready in the morning.

I was on cloud nine as I ran back to tell Schaefer that he was right. That was one of the happiest moments of my life. I went to my tent and packed. I doubt if I got any sleep that night. The next morning I picked up my orders and caught the mail boat to Guadalcanal. I not only was returning home, I could forget about riding that dry-dock to Bougainville.

16

BACK HOME

From Guadalcanal, I caught a ride on an oil
tanker and went to New Caledonia. I was there a
few days and then boarded the Matsonia. This was
originally a luxury liner belonging to the Matson
Steamship Company. The military had turned it
into a troop ship.

It was crowded, but it got us back to San
Francisco. It was really a thrill to again sail
beneath the Golden Gate Bridge. It had been
twenty-one months since the Hornet had passed
under it with Colonel Doolittle and his B-25
bombers. I could hardly believe that I had
actually survived the battles that I had
experienced. It was November 1943. I would be
home for Christmas.

We were sent to the Naval Receiving Station at
Treasure Island in San Francisco Bay. My orders
read to return to the States and report to the PT
Training Center at Melville, Rhode Island. I was
authorized to take thirty days leave en-route.
The Receiving Station had to process the paper
work. I also had to get an ID card made. I
definitely had to obtain at least one Dress
Uniform. I knew I would probably be there for a
few days even though I was anxious to head home.

I collected my back pay and went ashore with a
friend of mine from the PT boats. His name was
Aiello. I stopped at a Uniform Shop and ordered a
set of tailor made Dress Blues. Regulation uniforms were all right, but to really look sharp,
you needed a set of tailor mades.

That evening, dressed in our new uniforms and
campaign ribbons, we commenced celebrating. For
the first time I was wearing my Boatswain Mate
Second Class rating badge. After a steak dinner

we went to a cocktail lounge in San Francisco. It
was called the 'Car Club.' It was made like a
Cable Car. It had a bar down stairs and a piano
player and tables upstairs. Aiello and I were at
an upstairs table, drinking toasts to each other
and requesting songs to be played. I told Aiello
that if he requested Mr. Five by Five or Cow, Cow
Boogie I would shoot him.

The table directly next to ours was occupied by
two beautiful women and a tall well dressed man.
Aiello looked at them and said to me, "Hey,
that's Lyle Talbot." Lyle Talbot was a well known
movie actor. He appeared mostly in 'B' pictures,
but he had been around for years. I still see him
occasionally on TV shows.

In any case, I think Lyle heard Aiello's comment
to me. He looked over at us and smiled. Then he
invited us over to his table for a drink. We were
both thrilled to be meeting a celebrity and two
beautiful girls. We got up to move over to their
table. We found out later that he was appearing
in a stage play in town. As I started to sit
down, my left arm accidentally knocked a tall
drink into the lap of the girl I was going to sit
next to. Everybody jumped up as I stood there
feeling like a real ass. I did not know what to
do, so I apologized and left. Aiello reluctantly
followed me. For the rest of the night, all I
heard was how I had screwed up his big chance to
meet a movie star.

The next day, I picked up my leave papers, got
my train tickets and then found out that it would
take six more days before my ID card would be
ready. I grabbed my sea-bag and boarded the
train. I decided that if the Shore Patrol stopped
me, I had my leave papers. I could always say
that I had lost my ID card. It was true. I had
lost it on the Hornet.

The train trip to Chicago took about four days.
After I got there, I found out that all of my old

160

friends were in the service except the ones with police records. My parents had moved to Monroe, Wisconsin. My dad had quit the painting and decorating business and bought a house with two acres of land. Then he went to work for the County Road Department. I spent part of my leave in Chicago. I then went to Wisconsin to visit the folks for a few days. I came back to Chicago to finish up my leave.

Some of my neighborhood buddies were in Chicago, on leave, at the same time. I had a very enjoyable visit. It was a Christmas to remember. However, all good things must come to an end. I soon had to catch the train and head for the PT Training Center at Melville, Rhode Island.

I was assigned to the Master-at-Arms Force at Melville. It was a boring job. I had expected to finally receive PT training myself. I found out that things did not work that way. Since I had spent more than six months in an operating squadron, I was considered as being already trained.

Before long, I started pestering them to transfer me to a squadron that was getting ready to deploy. I thought I was set to receive a transfer when my malaria came back. I wound up in the hospital for a little over a week before they would release me.

Eventually, I was assigned to Squadron 37. I knew some of the boat crews and I asked one of my friends to recommend me to his skipper, to be part of his boat crew. I really thought that I had it all arranged. When I checked into the squadron, I discovered that I was once again in the Base Force.

We went to the Brooklyn Navy Yard in New York. After a few weeks, we were loaded, with our PT Boats, aboard a Merchant Marine Oil Tanker. We sailed for the Panama Canal. En-route, we stopped

at the Island of Aruba. She belongs to the
Netherlands. Germany was occupying the
Netherlands and Aruba was Pro-Nazi. They hoped
that Germany would win the war. The island had
oil refineries on it. It was rumored that German
submarines would secretly refuel there.

It was a strange town. They used Dutch Guilders
for their money. I remember that they had square
nickels.

Several of us were on liberty and stopped at a
local bar. It was early in the morning and we
were drinking rum and cokes. They had a juke box
and we managed to upset all the civilians in the
bar by continually playing the same record. It
was by Spike Jones and was called, "In Der
Fuhrer's Face." It was very derogatory to Hitler,
but it was funny to us.

The bartender complained but we ignored him. I
told him that it was his record, not ours. If he
did not like the song, he could take it off the
juke box.

Since we were not welcome there, we finally left
for a more sociable place.

After leaving Aruba, the ship arrived next at
Colon, the Atlantic entrance to the Panama Canal.
We were dropped off and rode a train across
Panama to the Pacific side. It was about 50 miles
and I enjoyed the chance to see the landscape. We
passed a prison near the center of the Panamanian
jungle. The main gate was open. I saw a line of
men, with several guards, filing out. From the
way they walked, they may have been a chain gang.
I hated to see all those wasted lives.

At Balboa, on the Pacific side, we took a motor
launch to Taboga. An island located about 12
miles off the coast of Panama. The PT squadrons
used this island for their final training before
deploying overseas. My squadron was slated to be
part of the campaign to capture the Philippines.

162

Things went fine for a few weeks until I suddenly had another attack of malaria. They rushed me to the hospital and covered me with a mosquito net. I told them I thought it was a little late for the mosquito net. They told me that I did not understand the situation. Currently, there was no malaria on Taboga. They had eradicated it. However, the Anopheles mosquitoes were still on the island. If any of them bit me, I could give malaria to the mosquitoes and start an epidemic.

I was transferred out of the squadron and into a Navy hospital in Panama. After several weeks, I was told that I was being sent to another Navy hospital in New Orleans, Louisiana. The Navy Doctor, who was treating me, told me that I was being sent back on an Army ship. He said that he had indicated on my chart that I needed additional medical treatment. He told me that in that way, I could live in the Sick Bay and would be considered a non-working passenger. I would be un-available for any work details.

I considered that very thoughtful of the Doctor. I remembered my experiences in an Army Hospital on the Russell Islands. I recalled how the Sergeant liked to put me on working parties.

I boarded the Army ship and was assigned to a bunk in the crowded sick bay. I had on pajamas and an Army bathrobe. I decided to go up on deck and enjoy the trip through the canal. To my surprise, there was an armed Sentry at the Sick Bay door. He refused to let me leave.

I waited until the Army Doctor arrived. I asked him why they had a guard at the door. He looked at me a little strangely. He got my record out and read it over. Then he called me over to the side, out of earshot of the other patients. He told me that I was the only malaria patient in the Sick Bay. All the others were Section

163

Eight's, Psycho patients. They had to be kept
under guard. I asked him to release me from Sick
Bay and let me be a regular passenger. He said
his hands were tied because the Navy Doctor had
specified that I needed additional treatment.
  Then he cautioned me not to let the other
patients know that I was different. He said that
they were very paranoid, suspicious and excit-
able. He told me to play it cool for the seven
day trip.
  The Navy Doctor's well meant gesture had
backfired. I was locked up with this group for
seven long days.
  Some of the patients were quiet and some were
loud. I tried to avoid conversations and did a
lot of reading. During the trip, several of the
patients came over to me. They seemed to have a
compulsion to tell me their stories. I soon
noticed that they all appeared to follow the same
pattern.
  In almost every instance, some minor event would
be the trigger that set them off. Then they would
blackout and not remember the details of what
they had done. When they came back to their
senses, there would be a victim lying there. He
would be either dead or badly wounded. The
patient would have a weapon of some description
in his hand, a knife, a gun, a hammer or a club.
Someone else would be accusing them of the
attack.
  They invariably wanted to know my story. I
truthfully told them that I was not sure why the
Navy had me locked up. I could not remember
anything that happened. When they pressed me for
details of what I had been accused of, I told
them I could not remember anything. They would
not be convinced, but eventually they would
wander away. The majority of the patients had
cracked up in combat. There were several violent

cases. They were kept locked in individual cells.

When we arrived at the New Orleans hospital, we were still under guard. I was lined up with the other patients from the ship. A Doctor called out my name and told me to report to a ward that was different from the psycho ward. Several of the ones who I had talked to on the ship became very suspicious of me. They wanted to know why I was not going with them. I told them that I had to get special treatment for malaria. That was the last time I saw them. I was glad to be away from this group and their guards. I imagine some of them thought that I was some sort of spy.

I was in New Orleans for several weeks. I had to wait until my case went before a medical board. It was December 1944. Our troops had landed in Normandy, France that June. After a rough start, they had been steadily pushing the Germans back. With the Russians also making progress against the Nazis, it looked as if the war in Europe might soon be over. Then we got the sudden news about the Battle of the Bulge. Hitler had launch- ed a surprise offensive and was tearing up the Allied Army. I wondered if Germany was still that strong. If it was, the war was far from over. My morale dropped.

Within a week or so, the Allies had stopped the German push and again had them retreating. Things were looking much brighter.

I finally was notified that I had been placed on Limited Duty for six months. That meant that I could not be sent out of the States during that time. They also informed me that I would be sent near my home of record, Chicago. I was trans- ferred to the Naval Air Station at Glenview, Illinois, about 60 miles North of Chicago. I was assigned to the Training Department as a Seaman- ship Instructor.

A large number of policemen had been brought into the Navy as Boatswain Mate Petty Officers.

They would primarily be used as Shore Patrol or Master-at-Arms. They knew absolutely nothing about the rate they were handed. My job was to give them some basic education in their new field.

Since I was training others, I took out the study courses for First Class Boatswain Mate. When the test was given, I passed it easily. I advanced to First Class on February 16, 1944. I had been in the Navy for three and a half years. It was unheard of for a 'Regular' Navy man to climb that fast. If a sailor made Third Class in his first four years, he was considered to be a ball of fire. Every First Class I had ever seen had at least three hash-marks. This indicated at least twelve years of service. I was a slick arm First Class, a "baby Boatswain Mate."

Admiral Mitscher had certainly been right when he told me that there would be many opportunities for advancement in the Navy. The way things were going, I felt that I might make Chief before my six year enlistment ended in 1947. I knew that I would have a good chance at it.

One day, a sailor came into the Training Office to order a study course. I had never seen him before. He kept looking at me. Then he said that he had met a Boatswain Mate in Noumea, New Caledonia that looked exactly like me. He mentioned that he ran a Tug Boat. He said that he had heard the sailor's name but he could not recall it. He asked me if I had a twin brother in the Navy. I said, "No, both of my brothers are in the Army. But you probably met Ben Lee Hek." He recognized the name and was astonished that I could possibly know whom he had been talking about.

I was contacted by a Lieutenant Cotter. He told me that German war prisoners were going to be working at the Air Base. This was the first time that they were going to be employed by the Navy Department. He already had 22 guards assigned, but he needed a Chief to run it. None of the Chiefs on the Base wanted to tackle the job. He decided to try it with a First Class Boatswain Mate, if I would agree. I grabbed his offer. I thought that it would be a good assignment and I was right.

The Army kept a large number of German prisoners at Fort Sheridan, Illinois, North of Chicago. There were 320 prisoners assigned to the Navy. The Army took over the Arlington Race Track, a few miles from the Air Station, and housed the 320 prisoners there. Every morning, Monday through Friday, the Army delivered the prisoners to me. I broke them up into 22 groups and my guards marched them away to their work stations.

We used the work details for cutting grass, pulling weeds, cleaning and things of that nature. The various Departments on the Base let Lt. Cotter know what work they needed done. Between us, we set the work assignments.

There were certain things we could not use them for, such as making servants out of them. If there was a gray area, like cleaning up the Officer's Club after a party, I could always find someone to take care of it. I always cooperated completely with Mr. Cotter. We worked well together as a team.

When the Army delivered the prisoners each morning, they turned them over to my waiting guards. When they were all assigned, I would give the order and they all marched away. The Germans would be in perfect step. Their arms would be swinging as they sang one of their German marching songs. They really looked impressive as they marched away.

Lt. Cotter was watching them one morning and he said, "I have to hand it to you, Ski, you really have them whipped into shape. By the way, what the hell were they singing?"

167

I said I had no idea what the song was. I told him, "If it helps them stay in step, who cares?"

He had to agree and I received credit for the German's marching ability. I imagined that the song was undoubtedly one that said the Germans would win the war.

The prisoners were allowed to use one mess hall for their noon meal. We provided mostly vegetables and a small portion of meat. The prisoners would do their own cooking. No matter what we gave them, they always made a stew out of it.

Being of German and Dutch extraction, along with my short, military haircut, I looked exactly like the prisoners. One day, during the noon meal I put on a prisoner's work jacket and leaned out of the Mess Hall window. A Navy enlisted girl happened to be walking by. I smiled and in my best German accent, I said, "Gutten morgan Fraulien." I expected her to blow up and tell me off. She gave be a big smile and said, "Good morning to you." I was surprised and disappointed. I never pulled a trick like that again.

We had one detail working in an area called the bone yard. Since the Air Base was a training station for new pilots, we had a lot of wrecked Stearman bi-planes. The prisoners were working there, taking the wrecked planes apart for salvage use. There was one older prisoner with a Kaiser Wilhelm mustache. I found out that he had also been an American prisoner during World War One. He could speak some English.

One day I told him, "If we have another war you should fight on our side. After all, everybody ought to be on the winning side at least once in their life." I don't think that he enjoyed my humor, but I thought it was funny.

Some of the younger Germans were ardent Nazis. They would give a bad time to any prisoner who they thought was cooperating, in any fashion,

168

with the Americans. They wanted to create problems for us. At night, in their compound at Arlington Racetrack, they would hold a kangaroo court. As punishment, they would beat the ones on trial. Whenever I could identify which of the prisoners were the ring leaders, I notified the Army and they transferred these individuals back to Fort Sheridan. As a result, the majority of the prisoners I wound up with were very little trouble.

Every evening the Army took back the Germans and I was free until the next day. I had every evening and every weekend off. I also had my own Jeep for use on the base. It did not take long for the Chiefs to discover that they had passed up a very nice job. Several of them visited Lt. Cotter and told him that he really should have a Chief in charge of the Prisoners. Cotter turned them all down. He said that things were running as smooth as a Swiss watch. He had absolutely no reason to change the organization.

The Army Master Sergeant, who delivered the prisoners and picked them up at night, always had a K9 guard dog with him. It was a Doberman Pinscher, a large, powerful, animal.

One morning he said he wanted to check on how we were working the prisoners. He and his dog got into my Jeep and I drove over to the gymnasium. I had a job scheduled to be done at that location. However, I was not sure if the work detail had arrived yet.

I hopped out and walked a few steps to the door and glanced in. The detail was not there and I started to get back into the Jeep. As soon as I touched the vehicle, the guard dog flew at me. I was off balance as I was getting in and he bowled me over. I was sprawled on my back. The dog had a paw on each shoulder and was snarling at my throat. I did not dare move. The Sergeant pulled him off me and I got up. I asked him why the dog had attacked me. He said that he was trained to not let anyone enter any vehicle that he was in. He was merely guarding the vehicle. The Sergeant claimed that it had not occurred to him that the dog did not know me. I had a suspicion that the Sergeant did it on purpose. After that, I could only get in my Jeep, if the dog was not already inside of it.

As we drove around the Base, the Sergeant was telling me how the Army differed from the Navy. He told me that he was actually senior to his Captain. I asked how that could be. He explained that the Army had temporarily appointed Corporals or Sergeants to the Officer ranks. When the war was over, they would revert to their enlisted status. I believe he said that his Captain had been a Corporal. After the war, the Master Sergeant would again be senior to him.

When Hitler died, I showed the morning paper to the prisoners. I told them, "Hitler Kaput!" They refused to believe it. They said it was all propaganda. I told them that with Hitler dead, the war in Europe would soon be over. I said they would be going home. They still said it was propaganda. Then I mentioned that if they were prisoners of the Russians, they would probably believe what they were told. They would not respond. They were deathly afraid of the Russians. They had a morbid fear of being sent to Russia instead of Germany when the war ended. They did not want to even mention the word Russia. If I had been in their shoes, I probably would have felt the same way.

An opportunity suddenly appeared for me to become an Aviation Cadet. They put out a Navy wide test. Once you took the examination, you could never take it again.. You either passed it or failed.

Several hundred Navy men took the exam, only six
passed. I was one of the six. I was really
excited. My childhood dream of becoming a pilot
was within my grasp. I went through the physical
exam and special vision tests with flying colors.
A huge, unexpected door had opened for me and I
was ready to leap through it. There was only one
problem I was still on limited duty for malaria
for six months. I had to be released from that
category to become an Aviation Cadet.

Fortunately, my six month period was up. I put
in an application, to the Medical Department, to
be released from limited duty. The head of the
Medical Department sent for me. He was a Navy
Captain. It turned out that he had been the
Senior Flight Surgeon on the Hornet when we were
sunk. He saw on my medical record that I was a
Hornet survivor and he wanted to talk to me. I
thought that I had it made.

I told him of my experiences in PT Boats after
the sinking and we talked for quite awhile. I
also told him that I was anxious to be an
Aviation Cadet. I had passed all the tests and
all I needed was his signature to release me from
limited duty. I also mentioned that the six month
period had expired.

He said, "Don't you remember all the pilots that
we lost on the Hornet? The average pilot in
combat can only expect to live for about ten
minutes. As a personal favor to you, I am going
to turn down your request."

I pleaded with him. I told him that I had
dreamed of this chance. I pointed out that the
war would probably be over before I became a
pilot. Nothing I said could make him change his
mind. He refused to clear me for cadet training.
He told me, "Years from now you will thank me for
this". He was wrong. I have never thanked him for
blocking my dream to become a Navy Pilot.

To make matters worse, he decided to really do

me a favor and release me from the Navy. He told
me that he had recently received an order that
allowed him to discharge anyone on limited duty.
He told me that I would be a civilian before the
majority of the servicemen were released. I would
have first crack at all the jobs.

I was totally stunned. I explained that I was
regular Navy. I had two more years to go on my
six year enlistment. I was First Class and
expected to make Chief and stay in the Navy. I
was a career man.

He would not listen to me. He insisted that he
was doing me a great favor. He not only closed
the door to becoming a pilot, he opened the door
to civilian life and shoved me through it.

I am sure that he meant well, but he sure
screwed up my life. As a result of having a
friend in high places, I was being forced out of
the Navy.

On 1 August 1945, I received an Honorable
Discharge, for medical reasons. I was eighteen
days short of having four years service. I did
not even earn my first hash-mark.

17

CIVILIAN LIFE

I had to start all over. I went up to Monroe,
Wisconsin to see the folks. While I was there, I
checked the job markets. Their primary product
was Swiss Cheese. I tried working for a cheese
maker. I really did not care for it too much. I
quit that job and returned to Chicago. I drove a
truck for awhile for the Manhattan Project. This
was the cover name for the project that developed
the Atomic Bomb. They had created the first
nuclear chain reaction at one of the University
of Chicago buildings. This was a few blocks from
where I had grown up.
 The truck driving job did not pay too much. I
quit and went to work as a bartender in a
neighborhood tavern. I had a great time helping
my buddies celebrate as they returned to civilian
life. We told each other our war stories and
enjoyed being together.
 I told them about the neighborhood jerk I had
met on New Caledonia after the Hornet was sunk.
They could not believe me when I told them that
he had said, "You didn't last long did you?"
 One evening, the bar was packed, as usual. One
of my friends said, "Look who just came in." I
looked up and saw the guy who had humiliated me
in front of my shipmates in New Caledonia. He was
with an older man. He had just returned home and
someone had told him I was tending bar. He had
purposely brought his Uncle to meet me. He was
smiling broadly as he came up to me. He said "I
want to introduce you to Richie. I know he saw
action because he was out there with me." He was

173

trying to imply that he had seen action also.

He leaned over the bar to shake hands with me. I refused to take his hand. I told his uncle, "I'll serve you a drink, but not that bastard that your with." Both he and his Uncle were flabbergasted. Naturally the Uncle did not want to drink alone and I steadfastly refused to even talk to his nephew. The Uncle wanted to know what the problem was and I advised him to ask his nephew. The entire bar was watching the episode. They were all aware of what had occurred in New Caledonia and they were enjoying the scene. The two finally left and things got back to normal.

Later that night, the Uncle came back alone. He asked me to tell him why I refused to serve his nephew. I explained how I first met him on liberty in Noumea. I told how he humiliated me in front of my shipmates when I met him accidentally after the sinking.

The Uncle finally understood my actions. He said that he did not blame me. He told me he had hoped his Nephew had changed during the war, but he could see he was the same as ever. Then he left the bar. I felt sorry for him and wondered if I had done the right thing or not.

Late that night, just before closing, the Nephew came in. He was half drunk and could not understand why I had treated him that way in front of his Uncle. I reminded him of how he had humiliated me on New Caledonia. I said that I could have really used a friend that day. I also told him that the sailors, who were with me, wanted to kick his butt.

He did not want to hear about his treatment of me, all he wanted to do was to moan about his troubles. He said his Uncle had never shown him any respect until today, when he returned from the war. He was almost crying as he said, "Now, because of you, he does not respect me at all." I

174

said to him, "You didn't last long did you?"

I do not know if he caught the poetic justice of my comment, but it was appropriate. I have never seen him since that day.

I got tired of tending bar after a year of mixing drinks. I went to work in Chicago at a company that manufactured battery operated fork lifts. I started as an Assembler and quickly moved up to become an Inspector. The work was routine but the pay was not great.

One Sunday night, a friend told me he had signed up for a construction job on Okinawa. This was a Japanese Island that had been the scene of the last big battle of World War Two. My friend, Jim Buckley, told me he was flying out on Tuesday. I got all the details from him concerning the job.

The next morning, I took off work and put in an application with the construction company. I was accepted and flew out with Jim on a DC3 that Tuesday. We landed in San Francisco and were taken to a barracks in Sausalito, just North of the Golden Gate Bridge. We waited there for several days while waiting for a ship to take us to Okinawa.

It was early April 1947. That first weekend, Jim mentioned that he was going shopping to buy his mother an Easter card. I thought that would be a good idea and I went with him. Then it suddenly dawned on me. I had left in such a hurry that I had not told any of my family that I was leaving.

I sat down and wrote letters to my parents, brothers and sisters to let them know I was on my way to Okinawa for a year.

We worked for the Guy F. Atkinson and J.A. Jones construction companies. They had combined on a Joint Venture. They had won a bid on a government contract to build Typhoon Proof Bases on Okinawa. I worked for the Warehouse Manager as a Material Expediter. Eventually I took over a job as a Dispatcher. I supervised about twenty native truck drivers.

The future of Okinawa had not yet been decided.
It was still under Army control and we lived
under Martial Law.

Our expenses were minimal. Room, board, laundry
and maid service came to $6.80 a week. I forget
exactly what our pay was, but it was very high
for those days. I kept a few dollars each week to
spend in the Army clubs. The rest of my money I
sent to my Mother to bank for me. The construction company had set up a gambling casino in a
quonset hut. I think they won most of their money
back each payday. I never heard of any one
winning in the casino, but I heard about a lot of
men who lost their paycheck there. I never had
any urge to risk my wages. I sent the money home.

The company held back 25% of each check until we
had accumulated enough money to pay our own
transportation home. That was in case we quit and
did not finish the one year contract. After the
year was up, the company paid for the trip home
and refunded the money they had retained.

I had no trouble in finishing my year. I enjoyed
the experience. I learned to speak some Japanese
since that was the local language. On weekends, I
would go sightseeing or on fishing trips. There
was always something to do and I had a good time.

When my year was up, I was interviewed, on
Okinawa, by another company that had a contract
in China. The Chinese Nationalists, under Chiang
Kai-shek, were in a life and death struggle with
the Chinese Communists. The Nationalists had been
buying surplus Army equipment through the company
that interviewed me. The surplus equipment was
repaired and then shipped to China. By the time
it got there, it usually needed repairs again. It
was decided to ship the equipment, as is, and
repair it only after it arrived in China. They
were in the process of setting up a repair
facility in China.

Since I had finished my contract with Atkins and

176

Jones, I was made available to the China company. I was offered a job with them at a salary that was about four times what I had been earning in Okinawa. It sounded great until I got down to the details.

I would be working directly for the Chinese Nationalist Government. They would pay me, every three months, in gold. It would be up to me to figure out how to protect the gold and get it safely out of China. In addition, since China was in the middle of a civil war, there was another problem. I was informed, by a State Department representative at the interview, that I would be completely on my own. The U.S. Government could not give me any protection.

It was April 1948. I had already saved several thousand dollars and decided that the China offer was too risky. The door to a fabulous salary was wide open but I turned it down. If they could have paid me in a way that ensured my money would go to a U.S. bank, I would have accepted the job.

I returned to Chicago and decided to try going to college. I thought that I might like to become a lawyer. I registered at Wilson Junior College and was soon hitting the books. I worked in a gas station at night while I attended for two semesters. I had an A average but I eventually lost interest in continuing on. I dropped out of school and continued working at the gas station. About that time, the Gasoline Truck Drivers, in Chicago, went out on strike and all the gas stations closed.

With time on my hands, I took a trip to Monroe, Wisconsin to see my folks and my brother Paul. He was living with them and working in Monroe as a carpenter. Paul was a highly skilled carpenter and actually became a cabinet maker. I saw some of the furniture that he made. It was excellent work.

During the visit, I found a job as a combination, truck driver and ground-man for the Wisconsin Power and Light Company. A ground-man assists the linemen who work on the poles. The work was interesting and outside. I enjoyed the job. However, the pay was not that great. It was near the end of 1949. I thought maybe I had made a mistake in turning down the China job.

At about that time, the Communists won the Chinese Civil War and Chiang Kai-shek fled to Taiwan (Formosa). The movie theater news reels were full of scenes showing the Chinese Communist winners beheading the losers who had not been able to escape to Taiwan. I knew then that I had made the right decision. I would have been working for the losing side. I would have been lucky to have escaped with my life.

18

THE KOREAN WAR

By the start of 1950, I had gotten myself
situated as an Apprentice Lineman. I still drove
the line truck but I would be getting a chance to
advance. Things progressed nicely for me until
June of 1950. In that month, Communist North
Korea invaded South Korea. The United States and
the United Nations sided with South Korea.

America had demobilized after World War Two
ended. She had to start drafting quickly to come
up with the necessary troops to send to Korea.

Monroe, the town I was living in, had a
population of about 5,000. They were primarily
Swiss people. They are very clannish and consider
anyone, who has not lived there for over two
generations, as outsiders.

One day, the Draft Board sent for me. They
wanted to know why I had never registered for the
draft. I explained that I had already been in the
Navy when World War Two started. When I got out,
four years later, the war was over. There had
been no reason to register.

They said, that was no excuse. I was told that
they would get back to me in a few days. I could
read the hand writing on the wall. I was 27,
healthy, a stranger and not Swiss. I no doubt
would be drafted into the Army, as a Private, in
place of one of their own home town boys.

There were no Navy Reserve organizations in
Monroe. I called the Navy Department and
explained my situation. They told me not to
worry. They would air-mail me an application into
the Inactive Navy Reserve. They would enlist me
for four years as a Boatswain Mate First Class,
the same rating I held when I was discharged. I

179

filled out the papers when I received them and air-mailed them back to the Navy.

A short time later, the Draft Board sent for me. I notified them that I had joined the Navy In-active Reserve and was no longer subject to their authority. I had out maneuvered them.

A few days later, I received an official notice from the Navy. They had placed me on Active Duty and ordered me to report to the Great Lakes Naval Station. I found out later that the Army Reserves are called up by Units. The Navy Reserve can order up individuals.

I took a military leave of absence from my job and caught the bus to Great Lakes. They issued me a set of uniforms and a full sea-bag. I was given a physical exam. The Doctor wanted to know if I had any complaints. I explained about being given a medical discharge for malaria in 1945. He said, "No problem, we can give you a waiver on that." He wrote something in my health record and I was back on Active Duty.

I was slightly chagrined to discover that the Navy had done away with right arm rates. Everyone now wore their rates on the left arm. At least I was able to sew on one hash-mark. I would no longer be a slick arm First Class.

A Yeoman interviewed me. He was happy to learn that I had previous sea duty. He told me that I would be going back to sea. They were short of sea going Boatswain Mates. I asked him, "Do you mean to tell me that if I had not had sea duty in the last war, I would not go to sea in this war"? He said, "That's right. We don't have time to train anyone."

I was sent to San Diego to help re-commission a destroyer, the USS Walke (DD-723). The ship had been placed in mothballs at the end of WW2. There were about 17 Officers, 16 Chiefs and 310 other enlisted in the crew. As a BM-1, I was the senior white hat

on board. The only ones over me were the Chiefs
and Officers. It helps, if you can reduce the
number of people who can officially order you
around.

I was in charge of the Second Division. The
Gunners Mates and Torpedo-men were in this
Division, as well as the forty Seamen and
Boatswain Mates that I supervised. My battle
station was Mount Captain of Mount 52, a twin,
enclosed, 5 inch 38 caliber gun. The same type of
weapon that I had been assigned to on the Hornet.

The Commanding Officer was Commander Marshall
Thompson, a real fine gentleman. The Executive
Officer gave me the definite impression, from our
first meeting, that he disliked me. I didn't know
if it was me, or if he was the same with the rest
of the crew. He may have hated his job. My
Division Officer, Lt. Bob Mullen was a really
great guy. The last one in the direct line above
me was Klepach, the Chief Boatswain Mate. He was
very easy to get along with. In general, I was
happy to be aboard the Walke. I hoped that Lt.
Mullen would be a buffer between the Exec and
myself.

We re-commissioned the ship on 5 October 1950,
in San Diego. We went on sea trials and conducted
training and drills until we were ready for sea
duty. We sailed to the Mare Island Naval Shipyard
at Vallejo, California and finished up some minor
repairs. We were tied up to a pier and scheduled
to load ammunition in a few days.

One evening I went ashore. As I walked down the
pier, I happened to glance back at the Walke.
The ship looked strange to me. I looked at it
more closely. The ship was definitely not riding
level. It seemed to be much lower at the stern. I
walked back to the ship and asked the Officer of
the Deck if the Engineers had flooded the after
part of the ship. He said, "No." I told him then

he had a problem because he was sinking.

He went out on the pier with me and immediately
saw that the ship was down by the stern. We
started checking and found that one of the, Aft,
ammunition magazines was completely flooded. The
sprinklers had gone off for some reason and
filled the space with sea water. We secured the
sprinklers and began pumping out the magazine. We
had to remove all the insulation from the bulkheads. Then we had to dry the compartment and re-
insulate it before we could load ammunition. We
spent the entire weekend completing that task. I
had to forget about my liberty, but we finished
the work in time to load ammunition on schedule.

On 2 January 1951, we sailed under the Golden
Gate Bridge and headed West. We were ready for
war. We stopped at Pearl Harbor, Hawaii for a
week of training in hunting for submarines.

I noticed that Honolulu had more hotels and
restaurants than I had seen in 1942. It was
becoming more and more crowded. It was still
beautiful though. The water was a brilliant blue
and the weather was always mild. Where ever you
went you could smell the fragrances of the exotic
flowers. I have always had bitter-sweet memories
of Hawaii, ever since my first trip ashore there
to bury a shipmate of mine.

We soon headed out again with two other
destroyers. We stopped off at Midway Island. It
brought back memories to me of the Battle of
Midway. This was the first time that I actually
saw, or stepped ashore on, the island. Our visit
there was brief and we headed for Japan.

We sailed right into a typhoon. The waves were
mountainous and crashed furiously onto our decks.
We could feel the bow go under the heavy seas and
bury itself, then, it would shake and struggle to
surface again. I think the crew held its breath
each time, wondering if it would come up or not.

We could barely see the mast tops of the other destroyers.

Our Motor Whaleboat was heavily damaged and the Main Deck outer bulkhead to our Post Office was caved in. The water would rush through the Post Office, through the inside passageway and into the Officers Staterooms. Some water would manage to enter the hatches to the Engineering spaces. It was imperative that we shore up the Post Office if possible.

We shoved mattresses into the space and tried to block the inside door to the Post Office.. The waves quickly ripped out the mattresses and smashed open the thin aluminum door that we were trying to shore up. We would have to place a cargo net over the outside bulkhead of the Post Office to keep the mattresses from being washed away.

BM3 Elmer Mellsen and I put on life jackets and life lines and went onto the Main Deck. We worked quickly to secure the cargo net in place. Our life lines were being tended by men on the Boat Deck, the next deck up. We were hit by several waves as we worked, each time it was as if a solid wall had struck us. We would be knocked sprawling. The only thing that saved us from being washed over the side was the lifelines. If either of us had gone over in that typhoon, nothing could have saved us. It would have been a death sentence. I felt very relieved when we had finished the job and were again safely inside the ship. This time, when we stuffed the Post Office with mattresses, they stayed in place.

The typhoon continued for days as we sailed toward Japan. When we finally arrived, we had to go into the Japanese Naval Shipyard at Yokosuka. We had to repair the storm damage before we could go to Korea.

It was my first trip to Japan. It was a fascinating experience for me. I was able to speak some Japanese due to my year on Okinawa. I soon became acquainted with one of the Japanese shipyard workers. He was the Foreman of the Sheet Metal workers.

One day he invited three of us to join him for dinner at his home. It was still the typhoon season and it poured rain the night we went to his house. It was a typical Japanese home. It was small, with sliding doors, but it had a warm, snug feeling to it. Of course, we had to remove our shoes when we entered. The rooms were very Spartan but attractive. They had tatami mats on the floors. We all sat on the floor around a low table. We had entered a completely different culture.

There was a small charcoal stove in the center of the table. It had a large frying pan on it. There was a small fire glowing under it. There were various dishes set in place and small sake cups before each of us. He poured the hot sake into the cups and we toasted each other. Then his wife and daughter began bringing different, prepared, ingredients to the table. When they had set their dish on the table, they would not turn and leave. They would bow very low and back out, still facing the table. He announced that he was going to prepare Sukiyaki. I asked him, "Aren't the women going to eat with us?" He looked at me as if I had lost my mind. He laughed and said something in Japanese that I did not understand. However, I caught his drift. In that time and place, the Japanese women were treated as servants.

We each had a raw egg, in a cup, next to our plate. We were served some delicious braised vegetables as he began cooking strips of beef in the frying pan. The routine was that he would

indicate when the meat was ready. We would use
our chopsticks to pick up a strip of beef, dip it
in the raw egg and then eat it. It did not look
appetizing at first, but the combination of beef,
egg, vegetables and hot sake was very delicious.
It was the first time I had eaten sukiyaki and I
have enjoyed it many times since then. I never
again had it with raw egg, that variation must
have been a family recipe.

After dinner, we sat around the table, talking
about the differences between the American and
Japanese ways of life. I smoked in those days and
I asked him for one of his cigarettes. I wanted
to compare it to our tobacco. He did not have any
left. He summoned his wife into the room and I
realized that he was going to send her to the
store for cigarettes. We could hear the storm
raging outside and I told him to forget it. He
assured me that it was no problem and he sent her
out into the drenching rain. She came back about
fifteen minutes later. The cigarettes were dry,
but she was completely soaked. I felt guilty
since I had been the cause of her trip into the
storm. I smoked a couple of the cigarettes. They
reminded me of the cheaper brands of American
cigarettes.

When we were ready to leave, he again sent his
wife out into the storm to find a taxi cab. He
was a great host, but I felt sorry for his wife.

We eventually finished our repairs and sailed to
Korea. We became part of Task Force 77, the U.S.
Aircraft Carrier Force. Our job was to screen
the carriers from submarines, planes or anything
else that tried to attack them. The day finally
came when we were detached from the Task Force
and ordered to report to the United Nations
Fleet. They gave us a bombardment assignment. We
sailed to the coast of Korea to shell the enemy
forces.

We were at General Quarters when the bombardment started. It was night and it was snowing heavily. My battle station required me to have my upper torso sticking outside the top of the gun turret. As we continued the shelling, the snow storm turned into a full blizzard. The gun mounts were under Director control. The Director is a unit that sits high above the mounts and uses radar to aim the guns. Since I was totally blind in the snow, I requested permission to close the hatch and go inside the turret. The Director agreed with my request and I went inside the mount.

A few minutes later, we secured from General Quarters. We set the normal Condition Three watch. My section had the first watch and we continued to man our gun mount. When the Director had secured from General Quarters, he had our turret slewed around against the Port side stops. The barrels were almost parallel to the Bridge and slightly below it.

When the Condition Three section manned the Director, they told us to load and close our firing key. Since I was inside the turret, I did not realize that the mount was jammed up against the Port stops and was not following the Director as it trained around. When the Director fired our mount, the concussion from our twin muzzles, a few feet from the wing of the Bridge, knocked down most of the Bridge personnel. It also severely damaged the Bridge windshield.

The cease firing order was given and we discovered what had happened. After this fiasco, I never again fired the mount without having my head sticking outside of it, regardless of the weather. Technically, I was not at fault, but I was involved in the incident and I definitely felt responsible for it.

We had to traverse a mine field to enter or

leave Wonsan Harbor. After we were safely inside, we would anchor and start bombarding, night and day. Every five minutes we would fire two five inch shells into the coast road. Through this action, we denied use of the road and bridges to the North Koreans and made them pack their equipment and supplies over the snow covered mountains.

The enemy would set up one or more shore batteries that were zeroed in on our ship. When they were ready, they would open up on us. General Quarters would sound and we would duel with them as their shells splashed around us. If we could not silence the shore guns, we would hoist anchor and retreat through the mine field. We would remain out of range until help arrived. It would usually be a cruiser with heavier, longer ranging guns.

She would send us back in as bait to draw fire. As soon as the enemy revealed their position, the cruiser would begin firing at them. I always hated this phase of the operation. It was bad enough going through a mine field. You also knew that you were in the sights of an enemy gun. Once the shore guns opened up on us again, the cruiser usually made short work of them. They could knock out the gun positions fairly rapidly.

I recall on one occasion that we were sent to the Northern border of North Korea. We were within about 50 miles of Vladivostok, Russia. We began at this extreme location and sailed South by ourselves, down the East coast of North Korea. We were to destroy any targets of opportunity such as factories, villages, boats or power stations.

I was manning the turret one day when two Koreans on horse back trotted out of a grove of trees. My mount trained around and fired at them.

I often wondered what went through their minds when they saw a ship swing her guns around and fire at them. The last I saw of them, they were high tailing it back into the trees.

We would normally rendezvous with supply ships to replenish fuel, stores and ammunition. From time to time, we would return to Japan for a rest. We would either go to Yokosuka on the East coast or to the nearer port of Sasebo on Japan's Southern tip.

I recall one time we were headed for Japan and I happened to be on the Bridge with Captain Thompson. He said that he hated to take a ship into Sasebo. I asked him why and he said that there were more prostitutes there, per capita, than any other port in the world. I said, "That's not all bad, at least it keeps the boys in off the streets." He gave me a disgusted look, but he laughed. I knew he had taken it as a good natured joke. He and Lt. Mullen were getting used to my brand of humor. I never did try it out on the Exec though. He still appeared to heartily dislike me.

They had a lot of rickshaws in Japan. They were towed by a bicycle instead of a trotting man as they still were in China. They soon developed a motorized bike to pull the rickshaws. That is exactly how the Honda Motor Company got its start.

In 1950, prices in Japan were very reasonable. The Yen was maintained at 360 to an American dollar. A night on the town was inexpensive. We always enjoyed ourselves there. I made Japanese acquaintances in Sasebo and Yokosuka so that wherever we went, I had friends to visit.

One of them gave me a narrow strip of paper covered with Japanese writing. It was about three inches long and one inch wide. It was encased in

a clear plastic. I was told to wear it around my
neck. It was a Japanese prayer card and supposed-
ly would keep me safe from harm. I do not know if
it was from their Shinto or Buddhist religion.

 I thought back to my mental promise on the
Hornet, to never ask for help again. Though I
never knew if I had gotten help or not that day,
I had kept my promise. I never again asked for
anyone or anything to help me. Now, nine years
later, out of the blue, I was offered the
protection of a Japanese God. I thought to
myself, it can't hurt, I have not requested it,
and I hung the prayer card around my neck with my
dog tags.

My shipmates soon spotted the prayer card and
began kidding me about my Japanese dog tags.
Since I had my name stenciled on my shirt, in
Japanese, they figured I had really gone Asiatic.

 I remember an incident that occurred and caused
me to give an impromptu, philosophical talk
regarding my own patriotic beliefs. We periodically received new men aboard. They would
normally join us when we were in Japan. One
afternoon, in the berthing compartment, a group
of men were talking. One of them, a new seaman,
asked me how I felt about being involved in a war
when most of the people in America were un-
concerned about events happening in Korea. I am
not sure, but I believe that he was a Reserve who
Had been activated to Active Duty. Since I was
the senior white hat on board, other sailors
would at least listen to my opinions.

 I had never thought out my feelings, but I
responded that I felt that we were fortunate to
be Americans. We lived in a free society that our
ancestors had provided for us, with their blood.
However, it was always possible to have it taken
away from us. We had just finished WW2 to keep
our country free. Now our government had decided

that we had to draw the line again to prevent a larger war from occurring.I said that some Americans are born at the right time and manage to have a peaceful existence. Others, such as us, live at a time when our country is threatened and we are called upon to defend it, not only for ourselves but for future generations. We happened to be in the Navy, as Regulars or Reserves, at a moment when the Navy needed us. If we did not step forward, who would do it? I said that if the Korean War could be handled without mobilizing the entire U.S. then we were doing our job of keeping the Korean War from spreading into a larger one.

After my little speech, one of the new men told me that he had tried to explain the same thing to his wife before he left. However, he had not been able to find the right words to express himself. He was going to try and incorporate my thoughts into his next letter to her. I had not heard any negative reactions to my words. I just hoped that I had not sounded like a pompous ass.

We headed back to Task Force 77. We soon were in our normal position of screening the carriers. The days seemed to blend into each other as we carried out our routine duties.

One day, Lt. Klein, the Combat Information Center Officer came to see me. He said that he had been assigned to schedule a Happy Hour for the coming Sunday afternoon. He had assembled several acts and wanted me to work up a skit of some type to present.

I had never attempted anything of this nature before. Being a happy-go-lucky individual, I joked and kidded around as a matter of course. I could always see the humorous side of events. However, I had never tried to be a stand up comedian before. I don't know why Lt. Klein thought I could handle it and my first impulse

was to turn him down. Then I thought about it for
a moment and agreed to do it.

I had about four days to prepare a script. It
was a real challenge to come up with something.
It seemed logical to center the bit around our
own circumstances. Whenever Bob Hope put on a USO
show, his biggest laughs came when he kidded the
troops.

Once I decided on a theme, the writing came easy
to me. I soon had enough material for two shows.
I checked with Mr,Klein to see how long I would
be on and trimmed my script accordingly. He told
me I would be the last act.

As I imagined myself presenting the skit, I
realized that I needed a straight man to really
make it work. I asked BM3 Elmer Mellsen to go on
with me and he quickly agreed. We rehearsed
briefly and soon had it down pat.

Sunday afternoon rolled around and the various
acts appeared. There were singers, musicians and
harmonica players, mostly harmonica players. I
began to have second thoughts about my skit, but
it was too late. I was being announced as the
next act. Since no one had a clue what I was
going to do, I borrowed a harmonica to take on
the stage with me.

I approached the mike and I could hear the
audience groan as I pretended to get ready to
play the harmonica. Suddenly, Elmer dashed onto
the stage and interrupted me. He said, excitedly,
"Ski, Ski, the men, they are revolting!" I turned
to Elmer and said, calmly, "Yes, aren't they."

This line brought the house down. It was a show
stopper. I even saw the Exec laughing. We were
home free as we went through the rest of our act.
All the sketches worked. For the final "bit," at
the close of our act, two more sailors joined us
on stage.

I told the audience that the four of us had been

caught in a rain storm one day. We took refuge in a convenient doorway for a few minutes, until the rain stopped. It happened to be a Geisha house. While we waited, we happened to overhear a lovely Japanese song titled, "China Nights".

Then the four of us sang the entire song in Japanese. Of course, the implication being, if we were in a Geisha house for only a few minutes, how could we possibly learn an entire song, in Japanese.

Just as we finished our song, the word was passed to relieve the watch. The happy hour was over. The applause was genuine and appreciated. I was relieved that everything had worked out so well. I even had enough material for another show in case we had another happy hour. Elmer told Mr. Klein that we were going to get an agent to represent us as we basked in the afterglow of a fun day.

The following morning, I was lying on my bunk in our compartment. I was fully dressed, except for my shoes. It was a few minutes before Eight and I was waiting for the word to be passed to Turn to. A friend of mine, Gunners Mate First Class, Jackson, stopped by my bunk. He said, "Let's go up on deck." I glanced at my watch and said, "No, I'll just have to come right back down and chase every one out when turn to sounds". That decision of mine, undoubtedly saved both Jackson and my lives. If I had gone with him, he would have waited while I put on my shoes. That would have delayed him for about 10 seconds. As it was, since I said no, Jackson immediately went into the next compartment forward and up the ladder. He just reached the top of the ladder when the compartment, that he had just walked through, was rocked by a tremendous explosion. It killed many men. If I had put on my shoes and gone with him, we would have both been in the middle of the compartment when the explosion occurred.

My Division lived in the last berthing compartment Aft. My bunk, a middle one of a string of three, was against the Starboard (right) side of the ship. It was at the forward end of the compartment and butted against the bulkhead that separated us from the next berthing compartment. In our normal steaming condition, the only door open to the next forward space was the one next to my bunk. When in the open position, it swung against my bunk, shielding me from the waist up. I slept with my head facing forward.

When Jackson left, I slipped on my shoes and lay back down. Just as my head hit the pillow, I heard and felt the tremendous explosion. I felt sharp stings in both legs as I ricocheted off the bulkhead and the door. I rattled around like a pea in a can. I could smell burnt powder. Since my bunk was next to the ammunition ready room for Mount 53, the after five inch gun, I thought at the first instant that something had blown up in the ready room.

I jumped out of my bunk to find myself in waist deep water that was rapidly rising. I could see that there was no possibility of going forward. I went aft to the ladder that exited from my compartment. The ladder was packed with men trying to escape. We normally steamed with the main deck hatch closed and only a small scuttle open to the deck. Only one man could leave at a time. If the large hatch were opened we could all get out quickly. I worked my way over to the ladder and called out, "Don't panic and
 we will all get out. Pass the word to un-dog the hatch." By this time I was treading water. Whatever had struck us had hit on the Port (left) side, of the next compartment forward. It had ripped a huge, 20 by 25 foot hole in our side.

The Walke had been doing 20 knots when we were hit. It was still moving through the water and the sea was pouring into our compartments. My head was getting close to the overhead in the compartment and I could taste fuel oil in the saltwater. It reminded me instantly of the Hornet. I was glad I had my shoes on this time.

I called out again for the hatch to be undogged. Then I looked around for an alternate way out.

There were two doors leading aft from my compartment, one on the Starboard side, led into the Ship-fitter's Shop. That was a dead end. There was no way out of that space. The other door, almost amidships, led to the Steering Engine room. That door swung into the Steering room and I would not have to fight the water pressure to open it. It had an escape ladder and scuttle. The problem was that if I opened the door to that space, I doubted if I could close the door against the on-rushing water. By escaping, I would flood the steering engine compartment and disable our steering. I was on the horns of a dilemma as I continued to tread water. I had a chance to escape drowning, but it meant that I would risk disabling the ship. I decided to wait until the last possible moment before deciding. A few moments later, someone opened the main deck hatch to my compartment and we were all able to rush up on deck.

General Quarters was sounding and we rushed to our battle stations. As soon as I got there I manned my phones. The word was passed to stand by for a Jet plane attack. Evidently our carriers had launched anti-sub planes and Russian Mig aircraft were interfering with them, or, someone thought they were.

I asked the Director what had hit us. He said it

was either a torpedo or a mine. Prior to the
explosion, we had a submarine contact. We were
doing about 20 knots, on a straight course. We
were screening the carriers when we were hit on
the Port side aft, about 60 feet from the stern.

By this time, we were dead in the water. I asked
permission to secure from my battle station and
return to my compartment. I felt sure that there
may be some men still trapped there. I received
permission and raced back to my berthing space.
Several men joined me as we went through the
spaces to seek out any survivors and to extricate
the dead. When it was over, there were 26 killed
and 40 wounded. I was included in the wounded due
to cuts on my hands and legs. However, it is hard
to consider yourself as wounded when you see
others lying there who have lost their lives.

The bodies were being laid out on the Fantail.
Once more it reminded me of the Hornet as I saw
the bottoms of their feet. Again it struck me as
a most unusual sight. You normally do not see the
bottoms of anyone's feet.

Our Damage Control parties shored up the
weakened bulkheads to the best of their ability.
With a sea going Tug for an escort and power on
our Starboard shaft only, we slowly returned to
Sasebo for temporary repairs. We were closely
questioned by Navy investigators and placed under
censorship. They were trying to find out what had
really hit us.

Shortly before we arrived in Sasebo, the
Russians announced that they had given six
submarines to the Chinese Navy, several months
ago. This was obviously meant to cloud the issue
if we claimed that we had been torpedoed. The
Navy advised us that we were the victims of an
enemy explosion of un-determined source. It was
generally accepted that we had hit a mine.
However, it could also have been a torpedo.

My first night ashore, I visited the family of the one who had given me the Prayer Card. They had read in their paper about the Walke being hit. However, they had assumed that the Prayer Card would keep me safe. Maybe it did. You never can tell about these things. The next day on the ship, I noticed several other sailors were wearing prayer cards.

We were in dry-dock for quite a few weeks undergoing emergency repairs. A temporary patch was placed over the huge hole in our side. The ruptured deck was strengthened by welding heavy rails on top of it. It gave the appearance of railroad tracks on our
deck. Our Port screw was removed and we became a single screw ship.

Our Division Officers were required to censor their own Division's mail. I wrote a letter to my Mother. I started it off, "Dear Mom," then I filled the page with all the Japanese writing that I could find. I used old laundry tickets and anything that held the old style Japanese characters. At the end of the page, I signed it, "with love Richard." I turned it in to Mr. Mullen, unsealed, and waited for his reaction.

The next morning, he smiled at me. He said, "You think you're smart, but I mailed it to your Mother." I don't know if he did or not. I never heard anything about it from my Mother.

We received a Navy notice that Boatswain Mates were urgently needed to man several Frigates that were being, home ported, in Sasebo. They were much smaller than a destroyer or a destroyer escort. I was single and enjoyed being in Japan. I immediately put in a request to be transferred to one of the Frigates. I never received an answer. I assumed that either Mr. Mullen or the Captain had killed my request. I complained but it did no good.

Before too much longer, we headed back to the States. We were escorted by another destroyer, the USS Stickell. We arrived in San Diego and tied up at the foot of Broadway Street. A few days later we headed for the San Francisco Naval Shipyard at Hunters Point.

I met Katherine Roberts who worked at the shipyard. We started going together. She had two children from a previous marriage, Ronald 13 and Dolores, 11. Around the middle of November 1951, we got married in Reno, Nevada.

An All Navy message came out about that time and authorized Inactive Reserves to be released to Inactive Duty if they had been on Active Duty for at least a year. I went to the ship's office to ask the Yeoman about the message. He said that all I had to do was to request my release and they would have to let me go. It was strictly up to me.

As we were talking, the Exec walked in to the office. He made a sarcastic remark about my being there. That made up my mind, I told the Yeoman, "Make out the request and I will sign it." The Exec wanted to know what was happening and the Yeoman explained it to him.

The Exec said, "I'll be glad when all these Reserves are back out of the Navy." I guess that was one of the reasons he didn't like me, because I was a Reserve. In any case, I had the last word this time and he could not do a thing about it. Mr. Mullen tried to talk me into staying for one more cruise to Japan. I really liked him, but I refused to sail with that same Exec again. I took the discharge.

19

CIVILIAN LIFE AGAIN

I was released to Inactive Duty in December
1951. I was now married and living in low income
housing in San Francisco. I went to work for the
Pacific Gas and Electric Company. They hired me
as a Ground-man. The pay was low and advancement
was slow. I decided to try the Hunters Point
Shipyard. I was hired into Shop 72 as an Apprentice Machinery Rigger.

In this job, I worked inside of the ship's
engineering spaces with chain falls. We had to
move heavy pieces of machinery around. I also
worked with the large dock cranes to move loads
on and off of the ships. The hardest part for me
was to climb to the top of the masts and work on
the Radar Antennas. It would not have been so bad
if we did not look down. However, we had to look
down to signal to the crane operator.

I also had to look up while working aloft on the
masts. I had to ensure that the boom of the crane
did not cause any damage by striking the ship's
mast or antennas. I almost got knocked off the
mast of an aircraft carrier on one occasion,
while guiding the crane operator. The ship was in
dry-dock. Shop 64 had to stage the upper part of
the mast. There was a small platform about 150
feet up the mast. The staging was going to be
built up from the platform. I had to land several
12 inch by 12 inch timbers on the platform. They
were each 20 feet long. Once the timbers were in
place. Shop 64 would use the them as a base to
build the staging on. When they were finished, I
would have to lay wooden planks on the staging
for the workers to walk on.

I climbed up to the platform and crawled through a manhole next to the mast. I started to guide the crane into position by using hand signals. As I looked up, to watch the distance between the crane boom and the mast, I almost lost my balance. The sky was full of small, white, fast moving clouds. It created a dizzying illusion. The platform did not have a rail around it and I had to hold onto the mast with one hand to steady myself. In that position, the crane operator could not see me.

I had them send me up the large, heavy, box of clamps that were needed to build the staging. I landed the box on the platform. Then I sat on it to steady myself as I looked up to guide the boom of the crane. The crane had two timbers hanging from the hook as it rolled down the tracks toward me.

As I concentrated on making sure the boom did not strike the mast, the crane operator had hoisted the timbers up to my height. I did not notice this as I maneuvered him closer. The timbers began to swing but I did not see them as I watched the boom and mast nearing each other. Fortunately, at that moment, a Shop 64 man stuck his head up through the scuttle of the platform and saw the danger. He hollered "Look-out". I looked down and saw the ends of the timbers heading straight towards me. I just had time to raise my legs up and out of the way, when the two beams smashed into the heavy box of clamps. The force of the blow shoved the box and me about a foot along the platform. If it had not been for that Shop 64 man, I would have been knocked off the box and fallen to my death. He wiped the sweat from his brow and said, "Don't ever do that to me again". I thanked him for saving my butt. Then I landed the rest of the material.

After I got back down off the mast, I realized
how close I had come to disaster. A little delayed shock set in. I told the Foreman that he
would have to get someone else to put the planks
in position on the staging. The hard part was
already done.

My son Richard was born on 18 March 1953. We
managed to buy a new home at a place called Pedro
Point. It was about 20 miles South of San
Francisco on Highway 1. It is now a town named
Pacifica. It was a three bedroom, one bath house
for just under $10,000. I used the World War Two,
GI Bill, to help buy it. The VA guaranteed the
loan.

On 10 October 1954, my second son William was
born. I now had the responsibility of supporting
a wife and four children. For the first time, I
started thinking seriously about my future.

I had a permanent Civil Service job as a
Machinery Rigger, as long as the shipyard stayed
open. After thirty years combined military and
Civil Service, I could retire at the age of
fifty-five. It looked as if this was going to be
my only possible option.

I worked hard at the yard and had a good
reputation. I received several Letters of
Commendation from various shops that I worked
with. I soon became a Journeyman Rigger.

The Department of Defense built a six story,
windowless, building at Hunters Point. It was
known as the Rad Lab. They performed nuclear
experiments there. I helped them relocate their
various, scattered facilities, into the Rad Lab.
As I worked around these various laboratories, I
realized that I had the capability to have become
a scientist or an engineer. However, I lacked the
actual education. I did not see how I could
possibly gain it at this late date, especially
with my family responsibilities. I definitely

felt that I had missed the boat.

In December 1955, everything changed. I read a Navy Message that stated that from that time on, broken service would count for retirement purposes. The previous policy was that you had to serve twenty years, continuously. Any break of over thirty days required you to start your twenty years over. Now, with the new directive, I already had six years in. I only had to do another fourteen to retire. I was thirty-three years old. I would have to work twenty-two more years in Civil Service to retire. It was no contest. I went to see the Navy Recruiter.

The maximum age to enlist was 31, I was 33. However, the Navy deducted my 6 years Active Service from my age. This made me 27 for enlistment purposes. The only hitch was that they cut me back to BM3, Third Class. This was a drop of two grades. They told me that they had plenty of Boatswain Mates and really did not need me.

They did offer to make me a First Class Steelworker in the CBs, the Navy's Construction Battalion. However, it would be in the Reserves. I told them no. I wanted Regular Navy only. As a Reserve, you could always be forced out of the Navy during an economy wave. You might never be able to complete your retirement. Besides, as a BM3 with over four years in, I was eligible for all the family benefits.

I went home and talked it over with Katherine. I would take a military leave of absence from my Civil Service job. In case the Navy did not work out, I would have the Civil Service as an ace in the hole. If I could make Chief in four years, or get close enough to it, I would stay in the Navy until retirement. To provide a nest egg, we would sell the house and move into Navy housing.

In January 1956 I re-enlisted in the Navy as a BM3, the same rate I first reached in October

1942, fourteen years earlier. I thought about the Flight Surgeon who not only kept me from being an Aviation Cadet, but had forced me out of the Navy for my own good. I hoped I would not meet any more well meaning blunderers like him. From now on I would not let anyone arbitrarily shove me around. In the past, it had been just me, now, I had a family to consider

20

THE ELECTRONICS TECHNICIAN

I received orders to the Treasure Island Naval
Station near San Francisco. I was outfitted with
uniforms and a new sea-bag. I was back in the
Navy. I received orders to report aboard the USS
Onslow (AVP-48), a small Seaplane Tender. It was
tied up at Alameda Naval Air Station. The same
place that the Hornet had picked up Jimmy Doolittle and his sixteen bombers in 1942.

I applied for Navy housing at Alameda and reported aboard the Onslow. It was like a small
yacht. It had a crew of about one hundred. The
Navy had four of these tenders. They were being
used as Station Ships at Hong Kong, China. The
Station Ships provided Shore Patrol, Embassy
Communications and Embassy storage facilities.
They also briefed incoming military personnel and
their dependents on the current rules and
regulations to observe while in Hong Kong.

The four AVPs would take turns. Each tour at
Hong Kong was for a six month period. Shortly
after reporting on board, the Onslow set sail for
China. Once more I sailed under the Golden Gate
Bridge.

I had sold the house and settled the family in
Navy housing before I sailed. I did not have any
thing worrying me at the moment. I took out the
Correspondence Course for Boatswain Mate Second
Class and began studying. I suddenly realized
that I had never actually taken the test for the
BM2 rate before. It had been handed to me in 1943
when I was in the PT Boat squadrons. With that
thought in mind, I really buckled down to study
as hard as I could for the coming examination.

After I had been back in the Navy for six months, I applied for the BM2 test. My Division Officer, a Warrant Officer, said I would have to be back in for a year before I could take the test. I went to the ship's office and checked with the ship's Yeoman. The instructions were a little vague concerning my specific case.

I finally convinced my Division Officer that since the instructions were not clear, the Bureau of Personnel would reject my application if I was not qualified to take the test. On that basis, he agreed to forward my application.

I was allowed to take the test. When I had completed it, I was sure I had answered every question correctly. However, the Boatswain Mate rate was considered as frozen. It was deemed unlikely that there would be many openings in that rating. The Navy just had too many BM2s.

I used to play chess with a First Class Electronics Technician. He was a Filipino. I invariably beat him. I asked him one day how he had become an ET. He said that he had converted from his previous rating of First Class Stewards Mate. I discovered that the Navy had a program that encouraged men in frozen rates to convert to critical ratings.

I went to the ship's office and talked to the Yeoman about the conversion program. He told me that I would first have to determine if I was qualified to convert. He would have to check the results of my aptitude tests. These were a battery of tests administered in boot camp. These tests did not measure knowledge so much as they did the ability to learn. We checked my record and discovered that I had scored high enough to go to the Academy. The problem was that I was too old.

The other possibilities were to convert to Guided Missile-man or Electronics Technician. After reviewing all the options, I selected

Electronics Technician. I applied for the one
year conversion course.

The ship's Executive Officer, a pleasant man,
had to approve my request. He called me into his
office and tried to talk me out of converting. He
told me that he thought I was an excellent
Boatswain Mate. He said, "We can't have a Navy
full of ETs. We need good Boatswain Mates too."

I held firm. I recognized a well intentioned
blunderer when I met one. I told him that I
appreciated his kind words, and I liked my job,
but I was determined to convert my rate. If
necessary, I would have to request to see the
Commanding Officer.

He said that would not be necessary. If I was
that determined, he would sign the request.

By the time the Onslow returned to Alameda from
China, my request had been approved. I received
orders to report to ET Conversion School at
Treasure Island.

I transferred there and moved the family into
Navy housing at Berkeley, California. I would be
a BM3 until I successfully graduated from the
conversion course. Then I would become an ET3.

A few weeks after starting the school, I was
notified that I had been promoted to BM2. I had
one of my lost ratings back and the pay raise was
most welcome. I had also accomplished it in a
frozen rate.

The year went fast and I really enjoyed my
studies. I was soaking up the Electronics
knowledge like a sponge. At the end of the first
six weeks, we had a comprehensive exam. It was
designed to determine how much of the electron
theory we were able to retain. I had a perfect
score. This was a very difficult accomplishment.
We continued studying theory and then covered the
different equipment that we would encounter in
the Navy. We studied, Radar, Sonar, Loran and

205

Communications gear. I was one of their top students.

One year after I had taken the BM2 test, I was eligible to take the First Class test. I applied for the ET1 test. A Warrant Officer who was in charge of the training phase that I was currently in, called me into his office. He told me that since I was a Boatswain Mate, I had to take the BM1 test, not the ET1 test. He asked me to change my request. I had met another well intentioned blunderer.

I was prepared for this eventuality. In my wallet, I had a copy of the Navy Notice that authorized me to convert my rate. In the fine print, it clearly stated that a student, while still in conversion school, could apply for an advancement test in his current specialty or the specialty he was converting to. It was up to the student.

I showed it to the Officer who had never before read the Conversion Notice that closely. I told him I would have to request a meeting with the Exec or the Commanding Officer if I was denied an opportunity to take the ET1 test.

He quickly assured me that he would forward my request to the Bureau. He tried to convince me that he only intended to have me go up for BM1, for my own good. He thought I would have a much better chance if I went up for BM1.

To let him save face, I told him that he was probably right. However the BM1 rate was frozen. I told him I probably would not pass the ET1 test but I would know what the ET test was like for my future attempts.

Despite what I had told the Officer, I had every intention of passing the ET1 exam. I had almost completed my year in school and I was at the top of my class. If I did not know the Electronics field at that time, I never would know it.

I took the ET1 test and passed it with flying

colors. I knew that I had an almost perfect score. All I had to do was wait for the results. It always took about a month before the Navy published the names of the advancements.

A few weeks later, I was graduated near the top of my class. I was officially converted from Boatswain Mate to my new rating, Electronics Technician Second Class.

I received orders to report aboard the USS Pollux (AKS-4). It was tied up in the Triple-A Shipyard in San Francisco, a civilian shipyard.

The Pollux was a Navy Supply Ship. It was being modified to also be an Electronic Repair Ship. The shipyard installed several electronic repair shops. They also installed a large number of radar, communication and crypto equipments on board. These equipments were actually set up to operate. They represented a pool of emergency exchange equipment for the Pacific Fleet. If a warship had an electronic equipment that could not be repaired, they could exchange with us. We would repair it and have it ready for the next exchange. We were the ace in the hole for electronic equipment repairs in the Pacific Fleet.

We had a sister ship, the USS Castor (AKS-1). She was also similarly rigged for electronic repair or exchange. We were both scheduled to be home-ported in Japan. With that designation, our families were authorized to accompany us to Japan.

A week or so after reporting aboard the Pollux, I was notified that I had made First Class ET. It was December 1, 1957. I had regained my First Class rating in less than two years after my re-enlistment. I was really rolling. The pay raise was doubly appreciated, it was just in time for Christmas and my daughter Kathy had recently been born. She arrived on 19 October 1957.

When the shipyard work was completed, we sailed to the Naval Supply Center at Oakland, California to load our Supply Ship. A few days later, our new Commanding Officer came aboard. He was Captain Wells. He turned out to be one of the most fascinating individuals I have ever met. He was the Navy's answer to General Patton.

The day after Captain Wells came aboard, we were scheduled to move the ship to another pier. The ship's Quartermaster said that he had heard that I used to be a Boatswain Mate. He mentioned that he was short handed because of having one man on emergency leave. He wanted to know if I could help him out during the move and shoot bearings for him. I agreed to do it. He said he only needed me for this one occasion. I told him it was no problem.

When the word was passed, "Go to your stations, all the Special Sea and Anchor Detail," I headed for the Bridge. I was assigned to a Pelorus on the Port wing of the Bridge. The Pelorus is a cylindrical stand, about four feet high, with a gyro repeater compass installed in the top of it. Above the gyro repeater was an Azimuth or bearing circle used for taking bearings. I was connected by earphones to the ship's Navigator. I was instructed regarding which landmarks I was to take bearings on. When I was given the word, "Mark," I would shoot the bearing of the object and read it off to the Navigator. It was more interesting than standing at Quarters, which was my normal 'Sea Detail' station on the Pollux.

The move went smoothly. The Quartermaster thanked me for my assistance and I chatted briefly with the ship's Exec. He was a real nice guy. He told me that he had known Captain Wells previously. "One thing about him," said the Exec, "he never carries a grudge."

Everything was going fine until the next time the ship got underway for sea. They passed the word, "Go to your stations, all the Special Sea and Anchor Detail." I fell in with my Division on

the Main Deck at Parade Rest. This was my assigned Sea Detail Station.

Suddenly the word was passed, "Nowatzki, ET1,
report to the Bridge on the double." I ran up to
the Bridge and Captain Wells began chewing me
out. He wanted to know why I had to have a
special invitation before I would man my Sea
Detail Station. I politely explained to him that
my station was with my Division. The other day,
when I manned the Pelorus, was a one-time event
to replace a missing man.

I noticed that the Navigator and the
Quartermaster were keeping completely silent.
They did not volunteer any information.

Wells glared at me and said, "Who is the Captain
of this ship?" I said, "You are sir." He pointed
at the Pelorus, saying, "From now on, that is
your Sea Detail Station." I saluted and said,
"Aye, aye sir."

It was no big deal. I would just as soon be on
the Bridge while entering or leaving port. It was
much more interesting than standing on the Main
Deck with my Division. However, the way he had
handled it got under my skin a little.

Neither of us realized it at the time, and I'm
not sure that he even realized it later, but his
assigning me to the Pelorus would one day help
keep his career from being endangered.

I soon found out that the ship's officers
treated the Captain with kid gloves. He could fly
off the handle very easily. This could be
disastrous for any officer's future. At certain
scheduled times each year, all officers receive
Fitness Reports from their Commanding Officers.
These become part of their permanent record and
are the basis for promotion within the Officer
Corps. Bad Fitness Reports can prevent an officer
from being promoted. If he is passed over twice,
he can be forced to resign. It is easy to see why

an Officer would be extremely reluctant to get on the wrong side of their Commanding Officer.

One time in San Diego, we were having a field day in preparation for an inspection of our spaces. We were in the process of scrubbing the decks in my spaces. Captain Wells walked into one of my shops with a visitor. He chewed me out because the shops were in a mess. I explained that we were in the middle of cleaning them for inspection. I said that they had to look messy during the cleaning process. He refused to buy that and chewed me out again before he left.

I complained to my Division Officer, Warrant Officer Van Horn. Incidentally, my mother's maiden name was Van Horn. He just shrugged his shoulders and smiled at me. I told him, "I don't see why Captain Wells is so difficult. When, with just the slightest bit of effort, he could be impossible!" Van Horn cautioned me, "Don't ever let the Captain hear you making jokes about him. He does not appear to have a sense of humor."

The next time I had a run in with the Captain was a real wild one. We had just entered port and were tying up to a dock. We had sent line handling parties on to the pier and we were doubling up the lines. There were three lines forward.

Number one line went out the bow of the ship and could not be seen from my station on the bridge. Only lines two and three could be seen from where I stood. My phones were connected to the line handling parties on the pier. The Captain glanced over the side and noticed that line number two was slack. He told me,'Get the slack out of line number one.' I saw his mistake and tried to advise him that he meant line number two. He blew up and demanded that I repeat his words exactly.

Every time I told the line handling party to take the slack out of number one, they went to line one, no one was touching line number two and

the Captain was getting more frustrated by the
minute. It was actually getting comical except
for the fact that Wells was so angry. Then he
caught me trying to whisper over the phones that
we really meant line number two.

He furiously grabbed me by both shoulders and
dragged me over to the side of the ship. The cord
to my phones would not reach that far and they
momentarily hurt my ears as they pulled off my
head.

He pointed over the side and hollered at me,
"Look damn it, line one and line two." He was in
a rage, but I was now angry also. I looked him
straight in the eye and said, "All right, if that
is line one and line two, where the hell is line
three?" He looked down at the dock and realized
that he had to be wrong. There were only two
lines in view. He angrily shoved me back to the
Pelorus and stomped away without another word.

I was feeling pretty good as I told the line
parties to take the slack out of number two. I
had finally won an argument with the Captain. The
Exec came by and said, "You sure like to live
dangerously." I reminded him about his comment
that the Captain never carries a grudge. I said,
"He doesn't have to remember a grudge, he has a
new one against you each time you meet him."

The Exec cautioned me with almost the same words
that Mr. Van Horn had used, "Don't ever let the
Captain hear you making jokes about him." I was
beginning to get the message. I would have to
watch my brand of humor.

In spite of the run-ins I was having with him, I
really liked Captain Wells. He always had a point
in whatever he did. He was a very interesting guy
and demanded excellence. He did not always get
it, but he always demanded it.

The Pollux had several cargo holds. Whenever we
replenished other ships, while underway, a line

throwing gun would be used to connect the first
line between the ships which were sailing
alongside of each other.

As soon as the line was made fast, a Pollux
Signal-man would release a 50 foot banner which
would trail back from the Pollux yardarm, It was
inscribed with the words, "WELL'S CARGO".

Captain Wade C. Wells was not one to hide his
light under a bushel basket

Each cargo hold had their own team of men
working the high lines and booms. Captain Wells
had issued different colored "T" shirts for the
personnel assigned to each separate area. If one
hold was not presently engaged in work, they were
required to stand in formation, at Parade Rest.
It was a very imposing scene and reflected a high
state of discipline aboard the Pollux.

Pollux sailors, that were not engaged in the
transfer of stores, were not allowed to be sight
seeing on deck. From the customer ships, all they
could see was teams of men working or standing in
formation. No one lounged about as they did on
the customer ships. Ships that were steaming
alongside, receiving stores, were suitably
impressed and slightly fascinated by our
professionalism. The Pollux was certainly
different since Captain Wells had come aboard.

We had our families living in Yokohama in
military housing. The Japanese Yen was still 360
to an American dollar and prices were very
reasonable. I had my car, a 1951 Chevrolet, in
Japan. It took awhile to get used to driving on
the wrong side of the road. Everyone in the
family was there except my step-son Ronald. He
was now working and living on his own in
California. We had a maid and the living was
easy. We could drive to Tokyo and have lunch.
Then we could see a live show at the Kabuki
Theater and have dinner afterwards, all for about
twenty-five dollars.

The Pollux and Castor took turns making supply runs and replenishing the fleet. A competitive spirit existed between the two ships. We claimed we did all the work while they rested. They claimed that it was the other way around. In actuality, I believe the work was shared fairly equally.

On a supply run, we would sail to Subic Bay and Manila in the Philippines. Then we would swing by, Kaohsiung, Taiwan, (formerly Formosa). We would re-supply ships at sea and in port. We exchanged large quantities of electronic equipment and became expert at repairing equipment that other techs had given up on.

To keep Technicians from leaving the Navy for higher paying civilian jobs, the Navy came up with a deal called Proficiency Pay for Electronic Technicians.

You were given a special test in your rate. If you passed, you got the higher pay scale. I took the test and soon was receiving Pro Pay. This brought my salary close to Chief's pay.

Besides repairing exchanged equipment, I occasionally was sent to nearby ships to help them solve their equipment problems. I became our traveling expert. Despite my protests, I went aboard one ship to help them fix their Electronic Countermeasures gear. I had never seen this type of equipment before. The Exec told me that the Captain had ordered me to go help them with their problem.

When I arrived on the other ship, the ship's ET was upset because they had not sent someone who was familiar with his equipment. I informed him that none of us on the Pollux were familiar with his gear. I asked him what the problem was. He said that the equipment was designed to detect the emission of electronic signals and indicate the direction they were coming from. He had been checking out his equipment and found that it detected an electronic signal but, indicated that it was coming from all directions.

He demonstrated the problem. As he rotated the gear through 360 degrees it continued to detect an electronic signal. I noticed that the frequency of the signal was the same as one of the Navy's air search radars. I stepped out on deck and looked up. The ship's own air search radar was on and the antenna was rotating. I pointed it out to a very red-faced ET. He was detecting his own ship's radar that was setting directly above his equipment. He admitted that he should have determined that his own ship was not transmitting before he turned on his detection gear.

We turned off the ship's radar and his problem was solved. I chalked up another victory to plain old common sense.

When I returned to the Pollux, the Exec asked me if I had fixed their problem. I explained that it was simply an operators error. There was no malfunction with the equipment.

On one other occasion in the Philippines at Subic Bay, we were anchored out and were scheduled to sail that night. Captain Wells told me to go aboard a destroyer that was tied up to the pier. He wanted me to fix their Attack Plotter. I told him that I did not know anything about that equipment. I told him that Fire Control Technicians were the only ones who were qualified to work on that gear. I should have known better than to argue with the Captain. He sent me anyway.

I took a boat into Subic and went aboard the ship. I met with the ship's Gunnery Officer and he took me to the Plotting Room. The Attack Plotter is a device about three feet high and four feet square. It is packed full of interlocking gears and shafts. It has thick, multiple wired cables running all through it. It is used to figure out solutions to Fire Control problems so that the ship's Gun Director will hit what it is shooting at. It takes into account the course and speed of its own ship. It considers the course and speed of the target ship. It considers the height of the ship's guns above the water line. It takes into account the temperature, the wind velocity, the roll of the ship and any other factor that could possibly affect the aim of a weapon fired from the ship. I had heard about them but I had never seen an 'Attack Plotter' before.

There were two Fire Control Technicians sitting in the compartment which was located at the lowest point of the ship. I asked them what the problem was.

They told me that it would not pick up any flags. I asked them what they meant by that phrase. They said it was a signaling system used between the Director and the Plotting room to designate targets. They explained that the AC power was interrupted somewhere between where it entered the Attack Plotter and where the flags, , in the Plotter, were located.

I spent a short time trying to imagine how I could possible isolate anything in that monstrous Swiss watch. I asked them for the manual on that equipment. They informed me that they did not have a manual. I asked the lead tech how long he had been on the ship. He said he had been there about a year. I asked him how they worked on the gear without a book. They told me that whenever something happened, they wrote down how they fixed it. This current problem had never happened before so they were stuck.

I looked again at the Plotter, but it would be impossible to trace any wire through that maze of

215

gears. I had an idea though. I located a wire in the Plotter that had an AC voltage on it. I placed a temporary jumper from that wire to the wire connected to the flags. The Gunnery Officer was in the Director and I asked him, over the phones, to try the flag circuit. To his delight and mine, they worked fine.

The two techs were upset, they wanted me to find and repair the actual broken wire. I told them that my ship was sailing and I was going with it. I advised them to get a book so that they could repair their equipment properly. I notified the Gunnery Officer that the fix was temporary, but he was satisfied, the Plotter was working. I also advised him to make sure his techs located a manual for the gear. The techs were not happy but I had fixed their problem.

When I returned to the ship, Captain Wells asked me what happened. I told him that I had jury rigged the equipment to get it to work. He looked at me and said, "Does it work?" I said, "Yes sir." He said, "Don't argue with me the next time I tell you to go somewhere. Just do as I tell you." All I could say was, "Aye, aye sir."

As I walked away, I began to suspect that the Captain had more faith in my ability than I did myself.

On one of our supply runs, we pulled into Buckner Bay, Okinawa. The same island I had spent a year on with the Atkinson and Jones Construction Company. I was on the bridge taking bearings as we sailed toward our anchorage. I had been in this same Bay when I sailed on the Onslow and I was very familiar with it. There was a small Isle in the harbor and it looked to me as if we were on the wrong side of it, if so, we were in danger of running aground.

Everyone was busy and I tried to flag the Navigator. I could not attract his attention. I took off my phones and went over to the chart. I saw immediately that we were definitely headed on the wrong side of the small Isle. I walked over to Captain Wells and said, "We are on the wrong side of that Isle, we could run aground."

He did not look at me but my words spurred him into action. He dashed over to the chart and took one look. He looked up at the Isle and reversed his engines. It took some maneuvering but he finally brought the ship around to the correct heading.

Then he chewed out his Navigator and Exec. He never mentioned the incident to me, but he must have appreciated my action. Any Captain who allows his ship to run aground has just destroyed his career. Also his Exec and Navigator usually are destroyed along with him. The day he assigned me to the Pelorus had paid off for Captain Wells. I was glad to have been of service.

During the latter part of 1958, I read a Navy announcement that offered an opportunity to Chiefs and First Class to apply for advancement to Warrant Officer and LDO (Limited Duty Officer) status. The LDO would be as an Ensign. It was the same exam for either advancement. You merely indicated which you were applying for. According to the details of the announcement, I was too old for LDO but I was still within the age limit for Warrant. I applied for the Warrant program.

The Exec and Captain Wells approved my application. One day I was called into the Officer's Wardroom. I was told that I was to be interviewed as part of my application for Warrant. I sat in the center of the Wardroom and was surrounded on all sides by the ship's officers. They began asking me a wide variety of questions. Besides answering the myriad of questions tossed at me, I would have to twist and turn to face each questioner while responding. I found out later that I had been interviewed under adverse con-

217

ditions as required by the Warrant/LDO exam.

About a week later I took an eight hour exam. I was given a four hour test in the morning. This test was to determine my overall knowledge. In the afternoon, I was given a separate four hour exam. This one was to determine how well I would compare to college graduates. This test, together with my interview, completed my examination for advancement to Warrant Officer. My fate was now in the lap of the Gods.

As I waited for the weeks to pass before the Warrant Officer results were published, I began to think about how it would affect me if I did make Warrant. Whenever an enlisted man reached the end of his enlistment, he was offered a bonus to ship over (re-enlist). In my case, I had never had the opportunity to ship over. If I made Warrant, it would be too late to ship over. I would miss out on any possible bonus.

I went down to the ship's office and discussed it with the Yeoman. He told me that I could ship over, up to one year early. I could receive my bonus but I would not receive travel pay to my home of record. To get the travel pay, I had to ship over when my enlistment expired.

On 6 January 1959, one year before my 4 year enlistment would expire, I re-enlisted for six years. This gave me the maximum bonus possible. I received 6 months pay, one month for each year of re-enlistment. I had been back in for three years and had just collected a handsome nest egg.

About three months later, the Warrant and LDO lists came out. I was not listed. I had struck out. For the first time in my life I had failed to be promoted as a result of an examination. I was philosophical about it. At least I had failed while reaching high. I could still take the Chief's test when I became eligible for it. In the meantime, I was doing well in the Navy and enjoyed my career as an Electronic Technician.

The Pollux was at sea, en-route from the Philippines to Japan when we received a message from the Bureau of Naval Personnel to transfer one ET1 to the Castor, our arch rival..

There were two ET1s on the Pollux. A fellow named Mason, a real nice guy, and myself. Mason took care of the ship's operating equipment. I ran the repair shops and the exchange equipment. I went up to the Bridge and asked Mason if he had heard which of us was to be transferred. He said no, he had no idea who would be sent. I told him that the Exec told me that he was being transferred. Before he realized that I was pulling his leg, he blurted out, "What! He told me that you were going!" My little ruse had succeeded. I now knew which way the wind was blowing.

Mason was embarrassed but I told him to forget it. I had assumed that the ship would prefer to keep their own operating personnel and transfer someone from the Repair Department.

Due to the years of rivalry between the Pollux and Castor, I really did not look forward to reporting to the Castor for duty. Besides that, I was very happy aboard the Pollux and enjoyed my tour with Captain Wells.

However, orders were orders.

21

THE WARRANT OFFICER

When we arrived back in Yokosuka, I discovered that the Castor was in Sasebo, Japan. I packed my sea-bag and said good-bye to my shipmates. One thing you learn in the Navy is to never let your shipmates pack your sea-bag for you. They have a nasty habit of putting heavy weights in the bottom of your bag, items such as large shackles. When you arrive at your destination, you discover why the bag was so damn heavy.

I caught a train for an interesting two day ride across Japan. It was a great opportunity to view the country side. They had a dining car and I thoroughly enjoyed the trip.

I eventually reached Sasebo and located the Castor. I reported aboard for duty and was welcomed aboard by the Exec. He seemed to be a friendly sort of an Officer and I was feeling a little better about my transfer. If they were all like him, I would get along fine. I still had the feeling that I had been delivered to our competition.

The ET1 that I was scheduled to relieve, was very anxious to meet me. He was eager to be transferred, but they had refused to let him go until another ET1 came aboard.

He took me on a tour of his spaces and happily pointed out all the various equipments that they were unable to repair or get parts for. He was really looking forward to leaving all these problems behind when he was finally transferred.

I could see that I was going to be very busy, trying to get all that equipment ready for exchange. In a way, I looked forward to the challenge. I really enjoyed repairing the equipment and solving problems that had stumped other technicians.

I went back to my berthing compartment to finish unpacking. The ship's Yeoman came up to me with a big smile. He said, "Let me be the first to congratulate you, Sir." Then he shook my hand. I did not know what he was talking about. He told me that I had made Warrant Officer. I told him he was wrong. I had seen the list and was not on it. He told me that he had a letter from the Bureau to advance me. I accompanied him to his office and read the letter.

He was right. I had been selected from an un-published alternate list. According to the letter, only the original selection list is published. If for some reason, a selectee does not accept the appointment or does not pass the physical, a replacement is picked from the top of the un-published alternate list. All I had to do was pass a physical and say yes. Then I would be a Warrant Officer. I noticed a paragraph in the letter that specifically prohibited me from shipping over after the date of the letter. They were too late. I had already collected my bonus.

I got a copy of the letter and immediately went to the sick bay for my medical exam. As soon as I passed it, I went back to the Yeoman and arranged to get sworn in as a Warrant Officer. He said the Exec had mentioned that it would be nice if they could do it during the next week's Personnel Inspection. I asked the Yeoman, when my Warrant pay would actually start. He said, not until you are sworn in. I asked him, who makes the decision. He told me it was up to me. I said, "OK, we will do it tomorrow."

I located the ET1 that I had been scheduled to relieve and asked him to take a walk with me. As we re-traced the same route he had taken me on earlier, I pointed out all the equipment that they had been unable to repair or get parts for. He looked at me like I gone bananas. Finally he asked me, "Why are we doing this?" I told him, "I hate to be the one to tell you this, but I have just been promoted to Warrant Officer. I get sworn in tomorrow and you are stuck until they can locate another relief for you."

To put it mildly, he was extremely upset, especially since I was so obviously happy. I don't recall him ever speaking to me again after that day.

I was sworn in on 1 September 1959 as a Warrant Electronics Technician. I moved up to the Officer's Quarters. I was really thrilled at the way things had turned out. As soon as we got to the Philippines, I went ashore and bought several khaki uniforms and insignia for my new rank.

The way the Navy ranks go, the Chief Petty officers are senior to the First Class Petty Officers. Then next in line are the Warrant Officers (W1). Then there are three levels of Chief Warrant Officer (CWO-2, 3 &4). Next in line they have, Ensign, Lieutenant Junior Grade, Lieutenant, Lieutenant Commander, Commander, Captain and Rear Admiral. There are several categories of Admirals.

When I had re-enlisted for four years, in January 1956, I had hoped to either reach Chief or be in striking distance before my enlistment expired. Now, in three years and nine months, I had by-passed the Chiefs category and was senior to all of them.

To work my way through the Warrant and Chief Warrant categories would be a long process. It would take me fifteen years to reach CWO-4, but I was happy to have reached the level I was at. I was truly a happy man.

There was one small cloud on my horizon. My

appointment said that I was a Temporary Officer. There was always the possibility that I could be reverted to Petty Officer First Class if the Navy ever had to cut back. I remembered the Army Master Sergeant telling me during WW2 how the Officers would be cut back in the Army to their former enlisted rating.

However, I always read the fine print. The authorization for my promotion had discussed the case of a First Class going to Warrant. It had stated that in that instance, if the First Class so requests, when he would have been eligible to take the test for Chief, he can be administratively advanced to Chief. I made a copy of that authorization. On the day when I would have been eligible to apply for the Chief's test, I stopped at the ship's office, showed the authorization, and had the Yeoman advance me to Permanent Chief ET in my Enlisted Record which always stayed with my Officer's record as long as I remained a Temporary Officer. Now if I got cut back I would at least be a Chief.

Shortly after we returned to Japan, I received orders transferring me to the USS Talledega (APA-208). An APA is an Attack Transport, the type of ship that is used for amphibious landings of troops. The Talledega was home-ported in Longbeach, California.

I packed up the family and we boarded a passenger liner to sail back to California. We all enjoyed the cruise home on the luxurious passenger ship. It was a pleasure to again return under the Golden Gate Bridge.

We traveled to Longbeach and located a Duplex to rent. I reported aboard the Talledega and assumed my new duties as the ship's Electronics Officer. I had a small crew of ETs working for me and we kept the ship's equipment in top condition. I can honestly say that I enjoyed every facet of my new station in life. The pay was good, the work interesting and I had pleasant shipmates. I had my own, spacious stateroom. I ate well and traveled around the Pacific to places like Hawaii, Japan and Hong Kong. Who could ask for anything more?

As an Attack Transport, we were part of a squadron of other amphibious type ships. On one occasion, we were scheduled to sail from Longbeach to San Diego. One of the ships in our squadron, the USS Mathews (AKA-96), a Supply Ship, had been having problems with her air search radar. My Commanding Officer, Captain Spencer, asked me if I had any suggestions to help them out. I offered to ride the Mathews to San Diego and check out their equipment during the trip. It was all arranged and I sailed aboard the Mathews.

They had two ETs aboard but they did not have much experience. I worked with them and we corrected their radar troubles along with a few minor problems. Then I showed them how to keep their equipment tuned up. The entire process did not take long and we had a lot of time left over.

I decided to check out the rest of their gear. They had one 'radar repeater' on the Bridge that was very dim. The radar repeater is the unit that displays the radar scene. The ET told me that he had isolated the problem to a large "J" shaped, sealed unit. This sealed unit had several output points that tied into various parts of the circuitry. All the outputs were fine except one. This one point was supposed to provide an output of three volts DC (Direct Current). It had a zero output. I asked him why they did not replace the unit. He said it was too expensive. They cost $1,300 and his Department did not have that much money left in their budget.

As he talked, I got to thinking about the three volts DC. A flashlight has two, one and one-half volt cells. They are in series. That means that they add up to three volts DC. I had him find a flashlight. I removed the bulb and wired the rest of it into the circuit. I turned on the flashlight and the brightness came up like magic.

The ET said, "You can't repair equipment that way." I told him that I had just proven that the sealed unit was indeed the problem. I also had provided a usable piece of equipment. All he had to do was to turn on the flashlight whenever he used the radar repeater. In the meantime, when they could afford it, they could replace the sealed unit.

The Captain of the Mathews was appreciative of my efforts and ingenuity and sent a nice letter to me, via my Commanding Officer. He sent an info copy to our Squadron Commander, a Rear Admiral. As a result, my Captain received some points from the Admiral for our novel, intra-squadron cooperation. It was sure to improve the marks on my Captain's next Fitness Report.

In November 1960, I received a letter from the Navy Department offering to promote me to Ensign if I so desired. They said they would back-date it to correspond to my appointment to Warrant Officer. As an Ensign, I would be senior to all the Chief Warrant Officers. I would by-pass the entire category just as I had done to the Chiefs. In addition, Ensigns were advanced to Lieutenant, Junior Grade after eighteen months. By back-dating my appointment, I would be advanced to LT(JG), six months before I would even reach the zone for promotion to CWO-2.

Despite the well meant advice from the CWOs, to turn it down, I told the Bureau that I would accept the appointment. On 17 January 1960 I became an Ensign. I was in the LDO (Limited Duty Officer) category as an Electronics Specialist.

As an LDO, I could never advance beyond Commander.

At the time I received the offer for Ensign, and before I was advanced, the Talledega was anchored in the Outer Breakwater of Longbeach. As the Electronics Officer on my ship, I would see the reports concerning the Electronics Readiness of our entire squadron.

I noticed that the USS Navarro (APA-215) had their air search radar marked as un-satisfactory. There was an additional comment that indicated that the equipment had been in-operative for 24 months.

I was curious and asked our Operations Officer about the Navarro. He told me that the ship had been unable to get their radar to work for over two years. They even had factory experts come out to the ship. They had taken the antenna off and re-conditioned it at the factory, nothing had helped. The Navarro was currently in the Longbeach Shipyard to have the radar removed. They were going to scrap it and install a new radar set.

The next day, I had the Quarter Deck Watch. It was a Friday night and we were still anchored in the Outer Breakwater. I saw the Captain's Gig approach the gangway and Captain Spencer came aboard. He told me that he had just had dinner with Captain Manown, the Commanding Officer of the Navarro. They had decided that they wanted me to take a look at the Navarro's radar set. He said he had promised Captain Manown that I would be over in the morning. I told the Captain that it would probably be a waste of time. I repeated the list of repair efforts that our Operations Officer had related to me. However, he insisted that I go take a look at it and I arranged to have a boat take me to the Navarro, early the next morning, a Saturday.

As our boat approached the Navarro that morning, I noticed the air search radar antenna was rotating. I went aboard and knocked on Captain Manown's cabin door. When I entered, I explained who I was and why I was there. The Captain thanked me for coming, but told me that I could forget about it. He said he had thought it over and decided that it would be a waste of time. He said also that they were getting ready to hold Personnel Inspection in a few minutes and it would be a bad time for me to inspect the radar. Then he said, "On Monday, the shipyard is going to start removing the radar set. It is too late to do anything to it."

After my long boat ride to get there, plus my own natural curiosity, I wanted to inspect a radar that had been inoperative for two years. I told him that I could not possibly go back and tell Captain Spencer that I had not even looked at it. Captain Manown said "OK, if you insist, you can probably catch the Electronics Officer in the Wardroom. He can assign someone to open the Radar Room for you."

I was surprised to hear that he had an Electronics Officer on board. I assumed that he had merely designated some Line Officer to fill that position. When I got to the Wardroom and met him, I was surprised again. He was a Chief Electronics Warrant Officer. I was still a Warrant Officer and this fellow was very senior to me.

I explained my mission to him and he told me that it was a complete waste of time. He repeated all the things that the Operations Officer had told me. When he finished, I told him that my Captain and his Captain had both ordered me to look at it. I had no choice but to go ahead with it.

The CWO said, "OK, it is a waste of time, but I will send for the ET2 who handles the radar. He can take you around. He will be glad to get out of Inspection anyway."

We had a cup of coffee while waiting for the ET. When he arrived, we went up to the Bridge. I wanted to see what the problem really was.

The radar had been turned on and, as I had observed from the boat, the antenna was rotating. I looked at the radar repeater on the Bridge. All that appeared was a small white spot, exactly in the center of the screen, where the rotating sweep originated. It was about one inch in diameter. I should have seen the entire screen filled with a video display. The ET told me that all they ever could see was that small spot in the center. It was the same on all the radar repeaters.

There were several radar operators lounging around the Bridge. They were waiting for the word to be passed to start the Personnel Inspection. They began a good-natured banter with me. They said I was another in a long line of experts who would soon give up. They wondered where they found guys like me. One of the operators mentioned that he had been on the Navarro for over a year and had not seen a plane on the radar yet.

The ET and I went down several decks to the Radar Transmitter Room. He unlocked it for me and we went inside. I shut the radar set off. I told him that I wanted to turn it on and tune it up myself. In that way, I could observe how it reacted during the tuning process. Sometimes you can find clues to various problems by using that method. I told him not to give me any suggestions unless I asked him a question. I had previously discovered that if a tech cannot fix a certain piece of equipment, it is useless to ask his

228

opinion. All he can do is send you up the same
blind alley that he got lost in. I wanted to have
a completely fresh approach to the problem.

To appreciate what happened next. You have to
understand the basic principle of how radar
works.

It is essentially the same as hearing an echo in
the mountains. Someone hollers out and the sound
of their voice travels outward. The sound has a
frequency and travels at the speed of sound. If
it hits a flat surface it will rebound back to
the sender who hears his own words echoed back.

Radar is basically a powerful radio transmitter
and sensitive radio receiver. The transmitter
sends out a strong, short, radio pulse, through
the wave guide and out the antenna, at the speed
of light. Then it waits for a pre-determined
length of time before it sends out another pulse.
During the delay between pulses, if the
transmitted pulse hits a solid object, it will
send an echo back to the antenna, through the
waveguide and into the radio receiver. A video
screen is connected to the receiver to visually
display the echoes that have returned.

The heart of the transmitter is a large
magnetron. The magnetron is a special metal
cavity that is surrounded by a magnet. When ever
it is triggered, it will radiate a tremendous
burst of energy that travels up the 'wave guide'
and out the antenna. This is the transmitted
pulse.

A large, negative, trigger pulse is applied to
the magnetron to start the process. Each time the
magnetron fires, the frequency of the pulse can
vary over a short range of frequencies. To ensure
that the receiver is tuned exactly to the correct
frequency, each transmitted pulse is sampled. The
sample is used to tune the receiver to that exact
frequency before any echoes can return from that

specific pulse. The samples are obtained by way
of a small crystal that is inserted in the
waveguide. The crystal can be tuned to ensure
that the sample is not too large. The transmitted
pulse is powerful and a strong sample could
damage the radar receiver circuits.

When echoes are received, it is possible that a
nearby target will return a powerful echo. This
could damage the receiver. To prevent that from
happening, another crystal is inserted in the
waveguide. This crystal is the entrance to the
receiver. It ensures that the returning echoes
are not too large.

Now, as I turned on the radar equipment, I
observed the various circuits as they energized.
My first act was to adjust the Transmitter and
Receiver Crystals to a safe level before I
proceeded. There was a multi-purpose meter installed with a switch. I could not adjust the
indicated current to either of the crystals. I
asked the ET if he had ever noticed this problem
before.

He said that the meter was in backwards. Then,
he flipped the switch to Transmitter and adjusted
the Receiver current. Then he flipped the switch
to Receiver and adjusted the Transmitter current.

I asked him why they had never corrected this
problem. He explained that the Electronics
Officer had told him not to bother with these
little problems until they had fixed the main
problem.

I kept thinking about this condition. I shut the
radar off and opened up the front of the set. I
traced the wiring to the two crystals. The
crystals are about the size of pencil erasers and
are made to be replaced if they burn out. As I
looked at the two parallel wires coming from the
waveguide, I suddenly realized why the radar did
not work.

The wires leading from the crystals were reversed.

Evidently, two years prior, some ET had replaced both crystals and accidentally reversed the wires. They merely screwed on to the crystal holders. It was a matter of seconds to reverse the leads and close up the radar set. This time the crystals adjusted properly and I quickly tuned up the radar. I noticed an oscilloscope mounted on the radar indicated returning echoes.

We locked the radar room and went back to the bridge. We had been gone about ten minutes. I was anxious to see the radar display.

The radar operators were all crowded around the repeater where a beautiful radar scene filled the entire screen. "What the hell did you do to it?" they exclaimed to me. I said, "That's the way we real experts do our work." I stuck around for a few minutes, basking in their amazed reactions.

The ET kept looking at me with his mouth open. He was completely dumbfounded. Now that I had fixed the radar, it was amazingly obvious what the problem had been, all along. For two years, they had been looking at the sample of the transmitted pulse. That is why it was only a small, white, spot in the exact center of the screen.

The returning echoes were mistakenly routed to the Receiver to tune it. They were never displayed on the screen. No one, including the factory experts had ever sat down and tried to analyze why they were seeing only a small white spot.

I asked the ET how long he had been aboard. He told me, two years. I wondered if he could have been the one who mixed up the crystal leads. I asked him how long the Electronics Officer had been aboard and he told me eighteen months.

I cheerfully went back to Captain Manown's cabin

to report my magnificent accomplishment. His Stewards Mate told me that he had left for Personnel Inspection. I was disappointed not to see him. I wanted to watch his reaction when I gave him the news.

I went back to the Wardroom to have a cup of coffee. I was surprised to see that the CWO was still there. Evidently he was going to miss Inspection also. He looked up at me with a smile and said, "Boy, you gave up fast didn't you?" I had been gone only about fifteen minutes.

I relished the moment as I said to him, "Why don't you get us both a cup of coffee while I tell you a story?"

He looked at me strangely as he got the coffee. When he sat down, I told him, "I fixed your radar." He stared at me. I said again, "I fixed your radar, I found the problem and I fixed it."

He was totally flabbergasted. He did not believe me. He sounded angry as he said, "You just came aboard. How the 'hell' could you possibly find the trouble and fix it in fifteen minutes?"

I calmed him down and explained what I had found and how I corrected it. It was as if light bulbs were turning on in his head. I explained what the white spot meant. It was the main clue.

I suggested that he cancel the scheduled removal of the radar. I told him that the equipment he had was performing beautifully. The factory experts had reconditioned all the other circuits and they were performing flawlessly. Unfortunately, they had not discovered the basic problem.

He looked at me with amazement. I saw the same expression that I had seen on the ET's face. He was a study in mixed emotions. He was glad that the equipment was repaired, but he had been aboard for eighteen months. A stranger came aboard and fixed it in a few minutes.

He gave me a bewildered, respectful look and asked, "Are you some kind of repair expert or specialist?" I told him, "No, I'm just an Electronic Technician, but I get lucky sometimes."

I really felt good as a Navarro boat took me back to the Talledega. I had definitely earned my pay on that day.

It was about noon when I arrived. I went into the Wardroom for lunch. Captain Spencer sent for me and I went to his cabin. He was a little upset as he said, "I thought you agreed to go to the Navarro today and check out their radar equipment?"

I told him, "I already went. A Navarro boat just brought me back." Then I explained to him that I had found the problem and fixed it. The radar set was operating and in first class condition.

At first, Captain Spencer could not believe what I was telling him. He listened in growing amazement and delight as I told him the story in as much detail as I could. When I finished, he said, "Boy, you are one in a million." I had proven his faith in me. I had made both of our days. My reputation was soaring.

A few days after the radar episode, I was advanced to Ensign. It was 17 January 1961. The effective date of rank was 1 September 1959. This was the same date that I had made Warrant Officer. With this date of rank, I would automatically be advanced to Lieutenant, Junior Grade in three more months.

There was a Warrant Carpenter on board, a CWO who was a stickler for Navy protocol. When entering a vehicle, such as a boat or a car, the junior officer enters first. When leaving, the senior officer exits first.

As a Warrant Officer, I was the junior Officer

aboard the Talledega. Whenever we were going ashore, I used to try and enter the boat after this particular CWO because I knew it bothered him. He would find me standing behind him and angrily insist that I enter the boat first. When the boat neared the landing, I would pretend that I was going to get in front of him. He always made sure that I was the last one to leave.

After I became an Ensign, I was senior to the entire CWO category. A short time later, this particular CWO and I were going to ride in the same boat. I gave him a big smile and pointed to him to enter the boat ahead of me. I could see his ears turn red and I knew he was burning up inside.

When we got to the landing, I made sure that I left in front of him. His face was beet red. Revenge may be wrong, but it sure is sweet.

Within a few weeks, we were scheduled to sail to Seattle, Washington. I received orders to report to the San Francisco Naval Shipyard at Hunters Point. The same shipyard that I had worked in for four years as a Machinery Rigger. It would be like going home.

I moved the family to San Francisco. Then I returned to Longbeach and sailed with the Talledega to Seattle. When I arrived there, I caught a bus back to San Francisco and started my new job.

22

THE SHIPYARD YEARS

I rented a house in the town of Colma, near San Francisco. It was a very nice location but there were no young children in the neighborhood that were near Kathy's age. She had no one to play with. For that main reason, we signed up for the Foster Parent program. We soon became foster parents of a young girl named Genie. She was slightly younger than Kathy, who was around four at the time.

The Foster Parent group warned us not to get too attached to Genie. They said that foster children rarely remain with one family for any length of time. They were completely wrong. We wound up raising Genie to adulthood.

Our daughter Dolores had met and married a young American sailor while we were in Japan. His name was Eric Martin. With Ronald on his own and Dolores married, we had our three children and Genie at home. I think the entire family enjoyed living in the Colma area.

On the job, I met many shipyard employees that I had worked with during my four years as a Machinery Rigger. The Commanding Officer of the Shipyard, Captain Curtze, who soon made Rear Admiral, told me to make sure I remembered whose side I was now on. In other words, I was now part of management and not a civilian worker.

I assumed that he was not too thrilled to have an ex-Rigger as one of his officers. I could not help that. It was his problem. I knew that I could do as good a job, if not better, than his other officers. I looked forward to the opportunities.

I was assigned to the Production Department as a Ship Superintendent. I was the liaison Officer between the shipyard shops and the ship being repaired. I had a civilian assistant to help me. Depending on the workload, it was not unusual to supervise several ships, at the same time.

The Planning Department actually issued the Work Orders that controlled the repairs to be done. They would issue these jobs after consultations with the ship and the ship's Type Commander. The Type Commander had the funds. The ship had the work they wanted done and the Shipyard had to satisfy everybody.

I recall one of my civilian Assistants, who was nick-named Dutch. We went aboard a ship, one time, that had just arrived in the Yard. We were in the Wardroom talking to the ship's Officers. They had just come from the Mare Island Shipyard.

The Engineering Officer complained that Mare Island had the nerve to charge the ship $40, just to write up a Work Order. He was obviously looking for a sympathetic response. Dutch slammed his fist on the table and hollered, "Are those bastards cutting our prices again?"

Everyone looked at him in astonishment before they realized that he was kidding them. Now there was a guy with my brand of humor. There must be something in the Dutch genes that enjoys teasing people.

It sometimes became hectic trying to resolve disputes between the customer ship and the shipyard shop that was doing the work. However, by listening to my civilian assistant, I soon developed a knack for it. The Planning Department would give me a special Work Order for each ship. This would allow me to authorize small amounts of work to cover gray areas between the ship and the shop. There were always small, aggravating, items that were overlooked by the ship or the Planner when the Work Orders were written. This special Work Order had a maximum limit to it so that the Planning Department could keep me under control.

Evidently, I developed a good reputation as a liaison Officer. One day a friend of mine, a Navy Commander, asked me if I would like to transfer into the Planning Department and work with him. I forget his last name, but his first name was John. I liked him and I was flattered to be asked. However, I was happy where I was at.

Now, just like many other things, there was a natural rivalry between the Planning and Production Departments. Instead of telling him a simple, No, I said, "Transfer to Planning, why I would rather have a Sister in a whore house than a Brother in the Planning Department." That is an old joke, but, evidently, John had never heard it before.

He eventually retired from the Navy as a Captain. About twenty years after this episode, I happened to meet John at the Officers Club at Moffett Field in Sunnyvale, California. We were both retired and accidentally met at the entrance to the Dining area.

In a loud voice, clearly heard by the numerous people present, John hollered out, "Ski, did you ever get your Sister out of that whore house?" Old John had waited twenty years to get back at me. Now, that is what I call humor.

On 1 March 1961, I was promoted to Lieutenant, Junior Grade. If I had turned down Ensign, I would have still been a Warrant Officer. I would not even be in the selection zone for CWO-2 yet. I obviously had made the right career decision.

The two year tour of duty at the shipyard was going by very fast. I worked on a variety of ships and had a good reputation with the shops

and the customer ships. One day I was having
lunch at the Officer's Club with the Commanding
Officer of one of the destroyers that I had
overhauled. His repair work had gone very well
and we had become friends during his three month
yard stay.

During lunch, he suddenly asked me, "Doesn't the
Admiral like you?" I told him that we were not
friends, but, I always assumed that he was
satisfied with my work. I said, "Why do you ask?"

He told me that he had been at a meeting with
the Admiral and other Commanding Officers of the
ships being repaired. Just before the meeting
broke up, the Admiral asked for any comments. He
said that he stood up and told the Admiral that
he thought that Lt. (JG) Nowatzki was a particularly fine Ship Superintendent. He said the
Admiral merely looked at him with a sour face and
said, "They all are."

My friend said that he, and several other
Commanding Officers, got the distinct impression
that the Admiral did not care for me at all. He
said that he hesitated to tell me about the
incident, but he liked me and decided to warn me
to watch my step around the Admiral.

I thanked him for his candor and filed the
information away for possible future use. It is
always nice to be aware of any lists that you may
be on. I got along fine with Commander Fellows,
my immediate boss. I decided not to lose any
sleep over this knowledge. If the Admiral
actually did not like me, there was nothing I
could do about it. However, I was on my guard
around him from that time on.

The Navy was accomplishing drastic overhauls to
modernize their aging destroyers. These overhauls
were called FRAMs. This stood for the Fleet
Rehabilitation and Modernization program.

They removed everything above the Main Deck and replaced it. They installed new deck houses, new armament, new missiles and new masts. They expected to get at least twenty years out of each rebuilt ship. These FRAM jobs were all the same and were being accomplished at several of the Nation's shipyards. For the first time, the Navy would have a yard stick to measure one shipyard's capability against another shipyard, if they wanted to.

I was assigned to handle the FRAM on the USS Hamner (DD-718). It arrived in the yard about one week before the overhaul was to start. I had the crew move off and started doing a lot of preliminary work. The deckhouses were all cut loose with cutting torches and I had a great deal of equipment removed. On the day the overhaul was to start I would have a tremendous jump on the work. I would be way ahead of schedule.

The day before the overhaul was to start, John, my friend in Planning, called to tell me that the Bureau of Ships was thinking about deleting the Hamner from the FRAM program. My heart sank. It would cost a small fortune, and several weeks, to repair all the preliminary work that I had done to the ship. None of the work had been authorized by anyone but me. I was in a very precarious spot. Especially for someone who could be on the Admiral's list.

I explained the situation to John and asked him to use any influence he had to get the Bureau to keep the Hamner in the program. John called the Bureau and was able to keep the Hamner on the FRAM list. However, he made me squirm all weekend before he let me know what had happened.

At the end of the eleven month overhaul, I held the record, from any shipyard, for expending the least amount of man-days on a FRAM. I also had the least amount of problems to resolve during the sea trials after a FRAM. My early start had paid off in the end. However, it did give me several gray hairs at the beginning. Thanks to John, I came out smelling like a rose.

One evening at home, after the FRAM was completed, the Exec of the Hamner called me. He said, "Well, we finally got the fire out." I instantly visualized that beautiful ship in flames. I shouted, "What fire?"He said, "Didn't you hear about it? We had a pier fire next to us and moved the ship to another pier. They just now got the fire under control." I was relieved to learn that the Hamner was safe.

When the Shipyard pier caught on fire, shipyard fire engines, San Francisco fire engines and Fire Boats responded. Pier fires are almost impossible to extinguish. They start burning from under-neath. You just cannot get to the fire source.

They eventually cordoned off the pier and let it burn itself out. Two of the San Francisco fire engines collided with each other while responding. Another fire engine got trapped on the burning pier. It was a very expensive evening.

A few months later, on a Sunday, I happened to be the Shipyard Duty Officer. My friend John, the Commander, was the Command Duty Officer. We were sitting in the Shipyard Duty Office when the phone rang. I answered it. It was the Admiral. I asked him if he wanted to speak to the Command Duty Officer and he said no. He said he would give me the message and I could pass it on. John was reading the Sunday papers and he looked over at me, curiously. I did not tell him who was on the phone.

The Admiral told me that he had received orders to the Bureau in Washington, D.C. He only had a couple of weekends left before he had to leave. In the meantime, he had his own personal boat in a civilian boat yard in Marin. Just North of the Golden Gate Bridge. He gave me the phone number and said that he wanted to finish some work on his boat. He only wanted to be contacted in case of an emergency. He re-iterated the same instructions several times. I told him that I understood and I would only call him if it really was an emergency. In the meantime, John had put down the paper and was trying to find out who I was talking to.

The Admiral repeated his instructions again. I said, "I understand Admiral. I will only contact you if we have a real emergency. For example, if we should have a pier fire."

The Admiral stopped talking for a few seconds. Then he said, "Nowatzki, you are as funny as a kick in the balls." Then he hung up.

John was getting frantic. He asked me if that was really the Admiral. When I told him all the details of the call, he shook his head. He said, "You sure like to live dangerously." Those were the same words that the Exec on the Pollux had said to me when Captain Wells and I had gotten into an argument over the mooring lines.

I felt that I had managed to even the score a little, between the Admiral and myself. However, I knew it was probably going to cost me on my Fitness Report.

23

HAWAII

Near the end of 1961 I was transferred to the USS Markab (AR-23), a Repair Ship. She was home-ported in Alameda, California. I rented a house in Alameda. Later on, we bought a house in San Leandro.

I was assigned to the Repair Department as the Electronics Repair Officer. I did not know it at the time, but this would turn out to be my last sea duty station in the Navy. I sailed on the Markab for two years and enjoyed it thoroughly. It had a pleasant group of officers and the work was interesting. We operated just like a floating shipyard.

I had qualified as Officer of the Deck Underway and stood my watches on the Bridge. I was advanced to full Lieutenant on 1 September 1963. Evidently my Fitness Reports were still satis-factory, in spite of my occasional wise remarks to my senior officers.

One morning, at sea, I was in my cabin shaving. I was getting ready for breakfast. Being the Electronics Officer, I had a short-wave radio installed in my room. I was listening to some music when a news flash interrupted the program. North Vietnam PT Boats had attacked a US Navy destroyer in the Gulf of Tonkin. President Johnson had called an emergency meeting of his cabinet. It might mean war between the U.S. and Vietnam.

I went into the Wardroom for breakfast. I was relating the news flash to my fellow officers when our Navigator, Lt. Bauer came in. He listened to me for a moment and then, with a look of horror on his face, he said excitedly, "The Exec doesn't want that information released yet. That is classified information. How the hell did you find out about it?"

Under the circumstances, I had to laugh at him. I told him that I had just heard it on the news broadcast on my radio. I told Bauer, "I don't think the radio station cares what the Exec wants."

Then I found out that, during the night, an encrypted message had been received by the ship. They had some difficulty decoding it and had just finished it. The Exec told Bauer not to reveal the contents of the message until he had briefed the Captain. Bauer had come directly into the Wardroom and heard me giving out all the details that were contained in the message. He thought that I was passing out classified information.

Bauer notified the Exec that it was too late to keep the information secret and I had an amusing memory of life in the Navy.

One day I came into the Wardroom for lunch. There was a large group of Ensigns arguing. They appeared to be upset. I asked them what the problem was. They told me that a new Navy Notice had just come out. They would now have to wait twenty-four months, instead of eighteen months, before they could be advanced to LT(JG).

I could not resist the opportunity. I told them, "I know exactly how you guys feel. Why I was an Ensign for almost three months myself."

I found out later that they checked with the ship's Yeoman to see if I was pulling their legs or not.

In 1964, the Markab had just returned from a six month trip to Westpac. Katherine and I were not getting along too well and we were having a trial separation. I was living on the ship.

One night, I had severe stomach cramps. I went to see the Ship's Doctor. He immediately transferred me to the Oaknoll Naval Hospital at Oakland, California.

The Hospital Doctor told me that I had Diverticulitis. This is caused when your lower Bowel gets small pouches in it. These are called, Diverticuli. They are similar to a soft spot, that bulges out, on a tire's inner tube. These Diverticuli can become inflamed, causing Diverticulitis. It normally requires surgery to correct the problem.

They told me that I was very young to have this condition. I was forty-one. It would normally be expected to occur to an older man. I told them about being bombed in the water in 1942, twenty-two years earlier. I could still recall that moment vividly. I imagine that the Diverticuli were formed at that time. Fortunately they had never caused me any problem before.

When any infection attacks your body, your system gears up to defend itself. They told me that my white blood cell count was much too high. Before they could operate, they would have to feed me antibiotics to reduce my fever. When that was done, they would do the operation. They kept me in bed and fed me intravenously for eight days while dosing me with antibiotics.

During this time, some married friends of mine, from my Chicago youth, came to see me in the hospital. They were Melvin and Barbara Larson. He was my best friend, who had upset the Nun at Saint Thomas because he was a Lutheran. They were living in Los Altos, California. It was fun to see them and Barbara brought me a book to read about Hawaii. It was by James Michener. I was

feeling in great spirits and was completely un-
concerned about my forthcoming operation. Barbara
asked me what the operation was for an
d I explained it to her. She got very excited and
said, "My God, don't let them put a bag on your
side." I asked her what she was talking about and
she described a colostomy to me. It is a system
designed so your body can dispose of waste matter
when your Bowels can no longer operate. She said
a friend of hers had this done and it was awful.
Barbara managed to scare the Hell out of me.
 When they finally left, I was very distraught.
When my Doctor made his evening rounds, I asked
him about the colostomy. I assumed that Barbara
had upset me needlessly and I wanted to hear his
reassurance that I did not have to fear this
outcome.
 I told him I wanted to make sure that he did not
plan on doing that to me. He became angry and
told me that those decisions would have to be
made, during the operation. He said that I could
not expect him to guarantee that any particular
procedure would not be done. He said that he
would not do it unless he had to.
 I was really depressed after that. I wished that
Barbara had kept her advice to herself. Now,
instead of waiting patiently for the operation, I
lived in dread of the moment it would happen. I
thought to myself that my normal life would be
over if I had to have this procedure done.
 One evening, my Doctor told me that the fever
was sufficiently reduced and they would take some
X-rays of my Bowel in the morning. This would be
in preparation for the operation. I had the X-
rays and that day my Doctor gave me some
miraculous news. The antibiotics had cleared up
the Diverticulitis. I still had the Diverticuli,
they would always be there, but they were no
longer inflamed. An operation would not be

necessary. I was on cloud nine. I relaxed for the
first time since Barbara had visited me. I
vowed to myself, that if I ever visited anyone in
a hospital, if I could not say anything to cheer
them up, I would keep my mouth shut.

That evening, a different Doctor made the
rounds. He asked me when I was scheduled for my
operation. I happily told him that it was canceled. He said that if it was him, he would insist
on the operation. He told me that it was like
having a time bomb in your colon. I ignored his
advice. I still have the Diverticuli.

I returned to the Markab and found out that I
had received orders to report to the Naval
Shipyard at Pearl Harbor, Hawaii. I would be
there for three years. It was quite a coincidence
that I had just read all about Hawaii in
Michener's book.

I had a few weeks before I had to report in and
I took a quick trip back to Chicago to visit my
family and friends. It had been about twelve
years since I had last visited Chicago and it was
fun to note all the changes. I met friends that I
had almost forgotten about. I was in a bar one
afternoon and a guy came in that I used to know.

He came over and said, "Hey Nowatzki, you old
Polack, what's new?" I told him that I had
changed my name. I said that my name, Richard
Nowatzki was just too long. So, I shortened it.
He was really surprised and said, "What's your
name now?"

I told him, "Al Nowatzki." He stared at me for a
full minute and then said, "Just like a dumb
Polack." Then he started laughing and from then
on he called me Al.

I returned to the Markab and prepared to
transfer to Hawaii. Since I was going to be there
for three years, I contacted Katherine and
suggested that we get back together so the kids

could enjoy the tour in Hawaii.

I went alone to Hawaii and located housing while she arranged to rent out the San Leandro house. We moved to the Island of Oahu and lived in Navy housing. Katherine and I did not get along too well, but the kids loved Hawaii. Richard and Billy were soon riding surf boards like natives. Genie and Kathy were busy taking hula lessons.

I was once again assigned to the Production Department as a Ship Superintendent. My civilian assistant was Peter Teves. I became close friends with Peter and his charming wife Eleanor. We are still friends to this date and exchange cards each Christmas. I look them up during my 'infrequent' visits to Hawaii.

I remember asking Peter once if he had any children. He said that he had three daughters. He said that they were all married, all had children, all were divorced and had all moved back home. He did not sound too happy about it.

After one year, I was transferred to the Planning Department. I was the Planning Officer for Auxiliary Ships and Destroyer Escorts. There was also a Planning Officer for all other combat ships and a separate Planning Officer for Submarines. The three of us reported to a Commander who was responsible for our work.

At the beginning of an overhaul, I would meet with the ship's Officers and their Type Commander. We would review all the work requests that the ship had prepared. The Type Commander would assign the work to either the Shipyard or to the ship's force. It all depended on how much work had to be done and how much money the Type Commander had.

I had a civilian Assistant. I believe his name was Perez. He was a fine individual and invaluable to me in the Planning job. As each work request was reviewed, my Assistant and I would place a cost estimate on it. If the job was assigned to the Shipyard, we would enter the amount on our adding machine. As the meeting progressed, the Type Commander would ask for a sub-total. If we were getting too close to the total money he had available, he would assign more and more work to the ships force.

A normal overhaul takes about three months. The work usually grows as new problems are uncovered during the repair process. For example, a water pump is removed for repairs. When it is sent to the shop, we discover that the foundation is corroded and has to be replaced. Numerous things such as this can cause most overhauls to increase in cost.

A Type Commander has many ships to maintain. He has a limited amount of money to spread over all the ships. He has a big problem if he has to wait for a three month overhaul to end before he knows how much the authorized work will really cost him. It typically takes a month after the overhaul before all the miscellaneous charges are finally received. To avoid this problem, half way through the overhaul, the Planning Officer must offer the Type Commander a Fixed Price to accomplish all the authorized work. In other words, after six weeks, I would have to predict the cost of the overhaul that still had six weeks to run.

The Type Commander could reject my Fixed Price offer. However, he would then have to wait until all the work was completed and all the charges were accumulated. He had assistants who were free to check all my books and figures. He would normally accept the Fixed Price.

To prepare the Fixed Price offer, I would receive estimates, from the Planning Department and the Production Departments, to complete all the work that had been authorized as of the Fixed Price date. Each estimate was prepared, independently. They never agreed with each other.

I asked my Assistant about the previous success rate of the Fixed Price offers. He told me that they never were successful. It was an extremely time consuming process. The Fixed Prices and the Actual Costs varied all over the place. Sometimes they were way low and the Shipyard had to make up the difference. Sometimes they were much too high and the Type Commander would be very upset. The basic concept was to come out even. We were not to make money or lose it.

I pulled the files on the last two years of overhauls that were assigned to my desk. I made up a master chart of the Fixed Price offers, the actual costs, the Planning Department estimates and the Production Department estimates. Personal computers were not available in those days and I generated my charts and data by hand.

I could see what my Assistant meant. My desk never had even come close to the actual cost of an overhaul. As I analyzed the figures, I made an interesting observation. Sometimes the Production Department estimate was closer to the actual cost and sometimes the Planning Department estimate was closer. Regardless of which Department had been closer, if the highest figure submitted was used, and 10% added to it, the Fixed Price would have been extremely close to the actual cost in almost 95% of the overhauls.

From that time on, we used this system. When we received the estimates from Planning and Pro-duction, we simply selected whichever estimate was highest. We added 10% to it and that was our Fixed Price offer. We had an amazing success rate with this arrangement. Besides that, it was a simple procedure and took practically no time to accomplish.

After a few months, my boss, the Commander, asked me how I was able to come so close on my Fixed Price offers. He thought that the first ones I did were just pure luck. However, since then, I was consistently close to the actual costs. I explained my system to him.

He frowned and told me that I could not Fix Price overhauls that way. It was not scientific.

I pointed out to him that my system worked. I showed him my charts that proved that my desk had never correctly fixed priced an overhaul before. If they had used my method in the past, they would have had an excellent success rate. Despite his objections, I still used my system. I continued to be extremely close to the actual costs. I got along good with the Commander, it was just that we looked at things differently.

We were overhauling a Destroyer Escort, the USS Vance. My boss asked me to work up the Fixed Price and show it to him before I gave it to the Type Commander. I gave it to him and he said it was much too high. I refused to change the figures and he said that he would fix price the ship himself.

I made sure that the file showed my figures and I put a memo in the file that the Commander would handle the Fixed Price on the Vance. My memo clearly stated that my Assistant and I were not to be involved or responsible in any way regarding the Fixed Price for the Vance.

He may have used a scientific method, but he managed to Fix Price the Vance extremely low. We lost a bundle of money. The Shipyard had to make up the difference. I told my Perez to make sure that my memo stayed in the Vance file so we could not be blamed for this fiasco at some future date.

A few days later, my Commander handed me a hot potato. Before I had taken over the Planning job, the Shipyard had overhauled a Mike Boat for the Air Force. A Mike Boat is a huge landing craft that is capable of transporting a large Army tank and landing it on the beach.

The Shipyard had overhauled this boat, loaded it aboard a Merchant Marine ship and sent it to the Air Force at Christmas Island in the Pacific. The Air Force planned to use it during some Atomic Bomb tests.

I forget the exact figures, but my predecessor had given the Air Force an estimate of about $20,000 to do the work on the Mike Boat. It actually cost about $50,000 before it was finished. The Navy had asked the Air Force for the additional $30,000.

The Air Force not only refused to pay the increase, they stated that the Mike Boat was in such a deplorable condition when they received it, they wanted a refund of the original $20,000.

I investigated the entire episode. I discovered that the Mike Boat had indeed been completely overhauled and was in first class condition when it was loaded aboard the Merchant Ship. By interviewing some passengers on the ship, I found out that the ship had made one or more stops before reaching Christmas Island. The ship had used the Mike Boat, without authorization, to load and unload cargo at these intermediate stops. When they finally delivered the Boat to the Air Force, it evidently was in very bad condition. I now knew what had happened. However, I did not know how to resolve the situation.

I needed to create a file that included all the pertinent documents concerning the Mike Boat repair. I obtained a copy of the $20,000 Fund Transfer form that actually transferred the money

from the Air Force to the Navy. I had never seen
this form before and I reviewed it closely. I
read all the fine print.

It was set up for a three month overhaul of the
Mike Boat. The Air Force had transferred the
$20,000, but, I noticed immediately that they had
inadvertently written the figure in the wrong
block. Instead of inserting the amount in the
Final Cost block, they had placed it in the Cost
per Month block. They had actually transferred us
$60,000, $20,000 a month for three months, more
than enough to pay the $50,000 actual cost. I had
the problem solved.

I prepared a letter to the Air Force and
explained exactly what had happened to the Mike
Boat. I enclosed a copy of the Fund Transfer
document and told them that the Navy had retained
$50,000 and was returning the $10,000 balance. I
gave them the name of the Merchant ship and her
Captain. I suggested that they direct any damage
claims that they had, to the ship and her owners.
I had the entire package prepared for my boss's
signature and waited for him to give me a well
done.

To my surprise, the Commander called me into
his office and berated me. He said I was a
"Shyster Lawyer." He told me that I would have to
find a more gentlemanly way to solve this
problem.

I explained that there was no other way to solve
it. We either returned the $20,000 to the Air
Force as they demanded and have our Shipyard
absorb the repairs to the Mike Boat, or we did it
my way.

He refused to listen to me. I filed the package
away and did not do any more work on it.

A few days later, the Commander and his wife

took a vacation to Hong Kong. During his absence, the Shipyard Planning Officer, Captain Johnson came to see me. He wanted to know how I could have possibly lost so much money on the Vance overhaul.

I took the file out. I showed him my figures and my memo. I told him he would have to ask the Commander about the Fixed Price that we used. The Captain said that he had wondered what had happened since all my other Fixed Price offers were right on the money.

Then he changed the subject. He told me that the problem regarding the Mike Boat was becoming very much heated up. If we could not solve it between the Pearl Harbor Shipyard and the Air Force at Hickam Field, it was in danger of being escalated to much higher levels in the Air Force and the Navy Departments in Washington. He said that would be bad news for everyone concerned. He told me that I had to work on this problem on a priority basis.

I pulled out the Mike Boat file and my prepared package. I explained exactly what I had found out and I showed him the way I had solved it. He was astounded that the Commander had not sent the package to the Air Force. He asked me why he had not sent it

I told him that the Commander said I was a Shyster Lawyer and had to find another solution. I told the Captain that there was no other solution.

Captain Johnson took the package and signed off on my letter to the Air Force. He said he would mail it to the Air Force. He thanked me for doing a good job. He said, "You may be a shyster, but by God you are our shyster."

When my boss returned from Hong Kong, he never mentioned either episode to me and I never

mentioned them to him. We were still friends but
we thought along different lines.

24

VIETNAM

The Vietnam War was going hot and heavy. The newspapers and television programs were filled with controversy about the American involvement in the war. Many career military men were openly criticizing the fact that they could be ordered to go there.

In my personal opinion, a professional service- man should not be creating problems for the government that he serves. If he is a career military man, he should go where he is needed. If he cannot, in good conscience, obey his orders, then he should either resign, if an officer, or not re-enlist, if he is an enlisted man.

To place myself squarely on the record, in November 1966, I wrote a letter to the Navy Bureau of Personnel and volunteered for an early assignment to Vietnam. I received a letter back that stated, "Your interest and willingness to serve in a forward area is noted with pleasure." My name was placed in a ready pool of volunteers.

My Hawaiian tour ended in 1967. I was trans- ferred to the 12th Naval District in San Fran- cisco. The people who had rented our house had moved out and we moved back into our San Leandro home.

I was actually assigned to the San Francisco Naval Communication Station. The Headquarters were at Stockton, California, on Rough and Ready Island. It got this name because President Theo- dore Roosevelt, nick-named, Old Rough and Ready, had once visited a wealthy family who had a large estate on the island. The family had donated the island to the Navy with the stipulation that they would maintain and use the main house. This house became the Commanding Officer's quarters and was considered to be a desirable tour of duty for any officer.

Besides the Stockton Headquarters, the rest of the Station was spread around the Bay Area. The main message center was at Treasure Island. I ran a message center located in the Federal Office Building on Market Street in San Francisco. We had a High Frequency Receiving Site at Skaggs Island, North of San Pablo Bay. We had a Transmitter Site at the Mare Island Shipyard. We also had another Transmitter Site at Dixon, California. We were all electronically connected to each other via Micro-Wave Communications. This is line-of-sight equipment and our main relay antenna was installed atop Mount Diablo.

A few months after reporting for duty, I was assigned as Officer in Charge of the Skaggs Island receiver Site. We moved to Navy housing on Skaggs Island and sold our San Leandro house. About a year later, we moved to a much larger Navy house, located at the Mare Island Naval Shipyard. It was located about ten miles from Skaggs Island.

At the Receiver Site, we operated High Frequency Radio Receivers for the Navy. It was an interesting job and I was my own boss. Near the end of 1968 I was promoted to Lieutenant Commander. I had one more grade that I could advance to before I would reach my legal limit.

Once each month, the various O-in-Cs (Officers in Charge), would meet with the Commanding Officer, Captain Lyons. We would journey to Stockton and meet at his Headquarters on Rough and Ready Island. We would have a business meeting in the morning and then have lunch together at the Officer's Club. It was a long, boring, drive. One month, I arranged to ride with the O-in-C of the Treasure Island Message Center.

He was driving on this particular day as we headed for Stockton. He was also a Lieutenant Commander. However, I can't recall his name. In any case, he asked me if I had ever been in Chicago. I told him that I grew up there. Then he asked me if I knew where 55th Street and Lake Park was. I really looked at him this time. I told him that I used to tend bar at that location, after WW2. Then he asked me if I had ever heard of a bar called the Old Bear. It was like the Twilight Zone. This guy was talking as if he knew all about me.

I told him that the Old Bear was next door to the bar that I had worked in. Then he really blew my mind when he asked me if I knew a guy named Sam Blair. I had grown up with Sam. He was the friend who had asked Johnny Sotos and me, in Johnny's garage, which one of us would die first. Then a few months later, Johnny died in that same garage.

I could not figure out how this stranger could know so many intimate details of my life. I asked him how he could possibly know Sam and not know me.

He said, "Sam married my Sister, Eloise." I thought for a minute and then I said that I had met Eloise. I remembered Sam telling me that she did not have any brothers or sisters.

Then my companion told me that he and Eloise had been placed in an orphanage, at an early age. They were both adopted by different families. He had searched for, and located her, after they were adults. He traveled to Chicago and met Eloise and her husband Sam. They had dinner and Sam had taken him to the Old Bear afterwards.

He had just been making conversation during the drive and it was a pure coincidence that I was acquainted with Sam and Eloise.

I was relieved to learn that there was a simple explanation to this weird event. I must admit, he really had me going there for a while. It was mind boggling that two relative strangers could possibly have so much in common.

That day at the luncheon, I sat next to the Executive Officer. After the meal, the Officer in charge of the Club, passed out a questionnaire. He wanted to know what we thought of the meal and the arrangements. I answered all the questions logically, until I came to one that asked, "Were the waiters unobtrusive?" I wrote down, "I never noticed."

The Exec happened to see my answer to this question and he busted out laughing. He said, "You are either real smart or real dumb. I have not yet figured out which one it is."

I have always enjoyed slipping witty comments into ordinary conversations, rather than actually telling jokes. Of course, I could tell jokes if the occasion called for it, but I only told clean jokes. I never cared for off-color stories.

As an example of witty comments, I recall one occasion when I was aboard a ship that was in dry-dock. We had been undergoing several days of sand-blasting to remove the barnacles from our hull. The sand penetrated into everything and made life generally miserable.

I was in the Wardroom and one of the Officers commented that he hated to go through a shipyard overhaul. I spoke up and said, "I don't mind the repair work so much, if it were not for this blasted sand." My humor went right over their heads.

Evidently, no one had caught the play on words.

Suddenly, after several moments, one of the officers laughed. He said, "That was very funny." Then he said, "I wonder how many more of Ski's comments have sailed past us like that without anyone catching them?"

I recall another time when an Insurance Man phoned me at home. This type of sales person is very tenacious. They are usually extremely hard to politely escape from. As soon as he identified himself, I broke into his prepared speech. I told him that, "I never talk to Insurance agents."

This was like waving a red flag at a bull. I could visualize him gearing up to give me at least a fifteen minute lecture on why I definitely needed to talk to an Insurance man. He said to me, "Why would you say that you never talk to Insurance agents?" I told him, "It is against my policy." Then I hung up.

Now, to me, that was a really funny play on words. It had not been a pre-arranged answer. My comment was completely ad-lib.

Of course, I was not above borrowing funny lines from other sources. I lifted one from something I had once read about the Marx Brothers. I was aboard the USS Walke, the Destroyer that I had sailed on in Korea. We were tied up between two Buoys in the harbor. One Forward and one Aft. This method of tying up a ship was known as a Mediterranean Moor.

At our location, we had to have our garbage removed by a Garbage Barge. When we needed the Barge, we would hoist a special signal flag. The Fantail Sentry would notify the Quarter Deck when the Barge was approaching. The word would then be passed, "All compartment cleaners, lay Aft to the Fantail to handle garbage."

On this particular day, I happened to be in charge of the Quarter Deck Watch. We had hoisted the Garbage Barge signal. Suddenly the Fantail Sentry came up to the Quarter Deck and saluted me.

259

He said, "Sir, the Garbage Barge is approaching." I saluted him back and said, "Tell him that we don't want any." He saluted, turned around and started back towards the Fantail. I watched him as he walked away. He stopped for a moment and then turned around and came back to me. He saluted again and said, "Sir, they want to 'pick up' our garbage." I saluted him back and said, "Oh, OK, we can do it that way." He was shaking his head as he went back to the Fantail.

My favorite memory along those lines was when I was stationed on board the Markab. There was a Chief Warrant Officer on the ship who had a passion for playing pinochle. This is an interesting card game that four people normally play as partners. All the cards are dealt out and each player counts up how many points he has in his hand. There is one catch to the point counting process. Regardless of how many points you have in your hand, you have to have the King and Queen of the same suit, called a marriage, before you can name the suit that will be trumps.

If you do not have the King and Queen, you have to throw in your cards and deal over. On this particular occasion. We were getting ready to deal and the CWO I mentioned was called to the Bridge. He said "Go ahead and deal the cards, I will be right back." I was playing as his partner.

While he was gone, we fixed up his hand. I gave him all the Aces in the deck, and most of the kings, but I did not give him a single queen. If we played the hand, he would take every trick, however, his partner would have to name the trump suit.

When he returned from the Bridge and picked up his cards, we watched his eyes widen. He had the hand of a lifetime. He tried to maintain a poker face as he indicated with his extremely high bid that he had a powerful hand. The other team had passed and it was up to me to bid. I looked at him for a few minutes and let him squirm. His hand was so strong that it made no difference what suit I named as trump, he would still take all the tricks. Finally he could not stand it any longer. He said to me, in a strained voice, "Will you please say, something." I said, "I could name it, but, I am going to let you name the suit, I pass."

I thought he was going to have a stroke. He could hardly control himself as he shouted out, "Goddamn it, I can't name it!" He slammed his cards onto the table and glared at me.

He was in such a rage that I think he could easily have strangled me. We were all rolling around with laughter and we finally told him that it was a phony deal. We had deliberately fooled him. Even after he understood that we had tricked him, he was still upset that I could have possibly dropped the bid on him under such circumstances.

I had to reassure him that I would never do that to him during a legitimate game. I don't think that he ever fully trusted me in pinochle after that game.

In 1969, I received orders to Vietnam. I was assigned to the Defense Communications Agency, Southeast Asia Mainland (DCA-SAM). I was to report to an Army Colonel in Saigon and then go on to Korat, Thailand. It was an unaccompanied tour. The family could not go. I investigated the orders as well as I could and discovered that I would be relieving a Navy Officer in Bangkok, Thailand. I would be attached to a Military Advisory Group. Since I would be in Bangkok and not Korat, I could bring the family with me. We all packed up and flew to Bangkok. This was the first war that I was to be in without being shot at.

The DCA-SAM was a combination of Army, Navy, Marine, Air Force and Civil Service personnel. I worked directly under an Air Force Lieutenant Colonel. I had an Air Force Captain, a GS-14 Civil Service Assistant and several Army Sergeants in my group.

One day, I heard several Sergeants talking. One of them mentioned my name. Someone asked, "Who is Nowatzki?" The first one said, "He is that Navy 'Major' who sits at the front desk." They were not familiar with the Navy Officer designation of Lieutenant Commander. However, I did wear the gold oak leaves that an Air Force Major would wear.

I got a kick out of the mixed up rank that they had assigned to me. From then on, during my tour in Bangkok, I was known as the "Navy Major."

I enjoyed my job in Thailand. However, I began to feel tired and rundown. I assumed I was just getting old, besides, the high heat and humidity in Bangkok were very tiring to live with. I went on a short vacation to Singapore and immediately felt better there. The weather was cooler in Singapore. Upon my return to Bangkok, I again felt tired.

About this time, I received a message from the Navy Bureau. They reminded me that I had not submitted my annual physical exam. Time was getting short. Every Navy officer had to get a physical within 30 days of his birthday. July 28 was my deadline and it was fast approaching. I had completely forgotten this requirement.

I checked around and found that I could have the exam done by the American Embassy doctor. The problem was that I had to drive across Bangkok to get there. The traffic in that town is almost impossible to believe. It has been described as a slowly moving parking lot. Vehicles come from all directions and at all speeds, regardless of the normal traffic flow. It took me most of the afternoon, but I finally got to the Doctor's office.

A Chinese Nurse took some blood samples and then I finally met the Doctor. I believe that he was a German fellow. After the exam, I was putting on my Khaki shirt. He looked at me and said that I appeared to be too pale. He told me to get an additional blood test before I left. I asked him if I had passed the physical and he said that he would not know until he had seen the lab results from my blood tests.

The next day the Nurse called me and said the Doctor wanted to see me again. I really did not want to drive across town again but she insisted that the Doctor had to see me. She said I might be anemic.

When I arrived at the Doctor's office, he told me that I had lost about half my blood. My hemoglobin count was about half what it should have been. He said that this caused my pale condition. His tests indicated that I was losing blood somewhere. He sent me to a civilian doctor for an upper GI (Gastro-Intestinal) Barium Test. It turned out negative. He next sent me for a lower GI test, a Barium Enema. When I brought the films back this time, he showed them to me.

They displayed my intestines, up to a certain point. Then the film became blank. Several inches farther on, the intestines again came into view. He pointed to the blank spot and said that I had a growth in my ascending colon, on my right side. He said it was undoubtedly dripping blood into my bowel movements and that is why I never knew that

263

I was bleeding. Then he asked me if I had any
idea of what caused the growth. I asked him,
"Cancer?" He said, "It always is." He told me
that I had to have an immediate operation.

I was sent to an Army Field Hospital. They had a
Philippine Army Major who was their Surgeon. He
looked at the film and agreed that I needed an
operation right away. I assured him that I had
complete confidence in him, but I doubted that I
would heal very rapidly in the high heat and
humidity of Bangkok. I told him that I was going
to see if I could possibly return to the States
for the operation.

He said that he did not blame me. If the Navy
turned down my request, he would be glad to
operate on me.

Due to the time differential, I had to wait
until later that day to call the Bureau. I
decided to go home and returned to our apartment
house. I entered the slow moving elevator to go
to the third floor. When the door closed, with a
loud clang, it seemed as if a coffin door had
closed on me. My thoughts suddenly overwhelmed
me. I realized that I had a life threatening
disease and there was probably no escape this
time. I needed to calm myself quickly. I told
myself that they had found it early, by accident.
I had a fighting chance. By the time I reached my
floor, I had myself under control. I never
worried about the outcome of the operation again.

25

THE END OF THE NAVY YEARS

I called the Navy Bureau in Washington, D.C. and explained my situation. They immediately issued me orders to report to the Naval Communications Command at D.C. They authorized me to take a Pan Am flight back to San Francisco. They told me to check into the Oaknoll Hospital at Oakland, California. If Oaknoll agreed, I could continue on and they would operate at Bethesda, Maryland. If Oaknoll decided that the delay was too risky, they would operate on me there.

I had lost so much blood that I was given a transfusion before I was allowed to fly back. When I got to the office to say good-bye, after the transfusion, everyone remarked on how much better I looked. I was no longer pale and peaked.

The Pan Am flight returned via Hong Kong. We were there for one night. When we arrived in California, I put the family in a nearby motel and checked into the Oaknoll Hospital. They immediately ran another Barium Enema test. They then told me that they would operate the next day.

That night, my Doctor explained the operation to me. I had always heard stories about people who had advanced Cancer. The Doctors would open them up, see that they were too far gone and sew them up again without operating. They just let them die.

I asked my Doctor if my Appendix was near where he would be operating. He said it was, "Right near the firing line." I asked him if he would remove it while he was inside me. He agreed that

it would be a good idea and marked it on my
chart. I figured that if I was too far gone with
Cancer to operate on, they would not bother with
my Appendix. If they removed it, I would know
that I had been worth saving.

As we were talking, a Navy Dentist, who had
sailed on the Markab with me, came into my room.
He said that he was stationed at the hospital and
had seen my name on the list of patients. He had
dropped by to say hello. I explained to him about
my operation. He mentioned to me that if I needed
any dental work, he could take care of me while I
was in the hospital.

I pointed at the Surgeon who was still in the
room. I told the Dentist, "Doc, if I survive his
operation, I will call you. If this guy kills me
tomorrow, I will at least have the satisfaction
of knowing that I went to my grave without having
my teeth fixed first." They both laughed at my
comments. Then my Surgeon said, with a smile,
"You sure have a 'rotten' attitude."

It was 20 August 1970 when I was into the
operating room. They gave me a shot to relax me
and began dripping a solution into my veins. I
was told to count backwards from 100. I got to
about 97 and that is all I can remember.

The next thing I can recall was a Nurse, who was
trying to wake me up. It was five hours later and
I was in Intensive Care. The Doctor was there. I
asked him if he had removed my Appendix. He said
he had and everything had gone very well. I felt
much better because I now knew that I had been
worth saving.

I had a long vertical wound down the center of
my stomach and a lot of stitches in it. I felt as
if I had been kicked in the stomach. However, the
operation was over with. All I had to do now was
recover from the surgery.

Approximately one week after my surgery, my
Doctor came to see me. He told me that the
Pathologists report was finally finished. It
revealed that I had a malignant Cancer removed
from my Ascending Colon. He described it as,
Duke's C-1. He said that he needed to discuss
some pertinent things with me.

He told me that twelve Lymph Nodes had surrounded the Cancer site and were removed with the
Cancer. They had removed approximately two feet
of my intestines and then joined the ends
together. They had not detected any Cancer cells
in the Lymph Nodes. He told me that this result
did not mean that Cancer cells had not migrated
from the original tumor. However, he did say that
it was a very encouraging sign. I would not need
any Radiation or Chemotherapy treatments However
I would have to have a Proctologist Examination
every three months for a few years.

He went on to explain that the Ascending Colon,
the one on the right side, is known as the silent
side. He said that everything moving through that
area is in liquid form. The liquid would not tend
to irritate a growth on that side, until it
became too large to ignore. By that time, it is
normally much too late to save the patient.

On the left side, most of the moisture has been
removed from the waste matter, by the intestines,
before it gets there. A growth in that area will
normally be irritated by this solid material and
reveal itself early enough to give a better
chance of survival to the patient.

Then he asked me the $64,000 question. How did I
know that I had a growth in my right side, so
early in the process? He said that he had removed
many of them and had 'never' before caught one at
that location before it had become much more
difficult to deal with.

I told him the entire story of my physical exam

267

at Bangkok. I started with the letter from the
Bureau that reminded me to get my physical. Then
I told him how the Embassy Doctor said that I
looked a little too pale to him. Then, on that
basis, he checked my Hemoglobin count. It started the entire chain of events.

My Doctor was very impressed. He said that the
Doctor in Bangkok had made a magnificent call,
and had undoubtedly saved my life.

I later composed a one page letter (suitable for
framing) to the Embassy Doctor. In it, I personally thanked him for saving my life. At least he
would know that I realized what he had done for
me.

I was happy that I would not have to undergo any
radiation treatments, but the Proctologist Exam
every three months was nothing to look forward
to. In 1964, before they would release me from
Oaknoll after my bout with Diverticulitis, I had
to undergo such an examination. It did not help
my frame of mind when one of the other patients
referred to the exam as, visiting the Silver
Stallion.

On that occasion, I reported to the Lab. The
Proctologist was not yet there. I questioned a
Medical Corpsman about the procedure. He showed
me a small table with a side platform attached to
it. It also had two handles. He explained that I
would kneel on the platform, bend across the
table and grasp the handles. They would then,
rotate the table, to stand me on my head. While
in that position, the Proctologist would be able
to insert his instruments into me and explore my
lower colon, anus and rectum. They even could do
minor operations through this process.

I was really dreading this procedure, but I
knew I had to go through with it if I wanted to
be released from the Hospital. I asked the Corpsman where the instruments were that he would use

on me. He pointed to a nearby table. I saw several large, shiny, stainless steel tubes. They appeared to be over two inches in diameter in about ten inches long. I asked, "Are they in those containers?" He laughed at me and said, "Those are not containers, those are the instruments."

The exam itself was just as uncomfortable and humiliating, as I assumed it would be. The Proctologist was very considerate but my intestine refused to cooperate. He urged me to relax and I really tried to cooperate. However, the intestine is very muscular and has a mind of its own. He finally was able to insert enough of the instrument to examine me and released me from the hospital.

Now, I would be faced with a Proctologist Exam every three months for a long time. I would just have to learn to accept it. At least I was alive and I knew that the exam was really a minor inconvenience when compared to chemotherapy or radiation treatment.

A few weeks later, I had recovered from the operation. I drove the family across country to Bethesda, Maryland and rented a house. The couple that rented the house to us chatted with us for awhile. Katherine mentioned that I had just had a colon operation. The woman said that her husband had the same operation about a year ago. I asked him how his check-ups had been since the operation. Before he could answer, his wife said, "He wont go near the Doctor since the operation."

I reported in to the Naval Communication Command Headquarters in Washington, D.C. I was assigned as the Director of Material Requirements for Naval Communication Activities Ashore. It was a staff job, a little boring, but I managed to make it interesting.

I had a very capable civilian Assistant, Bill
Stephenson. He was fun to work with. Whenever I
had to send any type of letter or message, I
would first draft it out myself, on a typewriter.
I would tell Bill that I wanted it typed up
exactly as I had drafted it. Bill would always
look at it and say, "I'll put it in English and
get it ready for your signature."
  There were about twenty personnel, military and
civilian, in my department. I had one group of
about five people working for me. It was headed
by a Lieutenant in the Supply Corps. I interviewed him to find out what his basic mission
was. He told me that he kept track of the actual
communication equipment that was assigned to each
Communication Shore Station. The information was
needed so that we could make sure that each
station had the necessary Test Equipment to
maintain their equipment. I asked him how he
accomplished this task. He told me that they sent
inventory sheets to each station every year. I
asked him what the 'accuracy' rate was,
concerning his inventory data. He said that it
ran about 70%.
  With my practical experience as an ET and later
on as an Electronics Officer, I knew that this
exact same data was obtained annually by the
Electronic Supply Office (ESO), located at Great
Lakes, Illinois. All ships and stations were
required to annually submit a form, known as the
4110, that listed all their installed electronic
equipment. Annual ship inspections always checked
to see if this form was up to date and submitted
on time. This document had to be completely
accurate. The spare parts to repair the equipment
were provided by ESO. If the 4110 was wrong, you
had the wrong spare parts.
  I also knew, based on practical experience, that

periodic data requests, from shore staffs, did
not generate the same sense of urgency that the
ESO 4110 required. They were frequently shoved
aside to allow work with a higher priority to be
accomplished.

I suggested that the Supply Officer visit the
ESO at Great Lakes and see if they could provide
us with a copy of their annual data. We only
needed the information that was submitted by our
shore stations.

He was gone less than a week. When he returned,
he told me that I had been right. The ESO was
collecting the same data and they had an accuracy
rate of 97%. He had concluded an agreement with
them to provide us with the information each year
on magnetic tape. It would cost the Naval
Communication Command, $350 a year.

I notified my Captain that I no longer required
the services of the Supply Lieutenant or his five
man team. I declared them surplus. They were
immediately absorbed by other Departments whom I
considered, Empire Builders. For some reason,
some military staffs believe that the larger
their group, the more valuable they are.

I believe that the most valuable staff has an
authentic and clearly defined mission. It also
accomplishes its mission with the fewest
personnel necessary and in the most efficient
manner. I hate to see a huge staff, spinning
everyone's wheels without accomplishing anything
worthwhile.

By eliminating my Supply group, I saved manpower
from being wasted and eliminated unnecessary
paper work at the shore stations. I also improved
the information coming into my department because
it was now 97% accurate versus 70%.

One day, in 1970, I attended a conference
between my command and the Naval Electronic
Engineering Command. They had a big problem.
There was a British Island in the middle of the

271

Indian Ocean called, Diego Garcia. The Navy
wanted to build a Communication Station on this
island. They had removed the entire local
population and relocated them to a new homeland.
The Navy needed this station to ensure reliable,
world wide communications. As part of this
project, the Naval Electronics Command had
designed a $250,000 micro-wave system and had
already issued the contract to have it
manufactured.

To order a Micro-wave system, you first had to
determine the frequency you were authorized to
use, then you placed the order and waited at
least six to eight months for delivery. The Diego
Garcia equipment was ready to be delivered.

At the same time as this was happening, the U.S.
was having problems with the Ethiopian Government.

We had a Communication Station in that area that
also used a micro-wave system. Unfortunately, the
Ethiopian Government had signed a contract with a
Japanese Company that was to install some
communication equipment near our existing micro-
wave. We knew nothing about this development
until the Ethiopian Government told us that we
had to change the frequency of our equipment
because it interfered with the Japanese
equipment. To respond in time to meet the
deadline, the Diego Garcia micro-wave was being
diverted to Ethiopia.

One problem was solved but it left two big ones
in its wake. Where would we get the $250,000 for
the replacement micro-wave for Diego Garcia?
Also, where would we get the necessary six to
eight months time it would take to manufacture
the new equipment? The scheduled completion date
for Diego Garcia was imminent.

During the meeting, I asked the Electronic
Engineering Command to describe exactly how this
micro-wave was to be used on the island. I

discovered that it was designed to cover a link of several miles. I had a good solution. I told them that in my experience, we used micro-wave for security and ease of installation over rough or impassable terrain. Since they had already moved everyone off of the island except Navy personnel, they did not have to worry about security. The terrain was not impassable. All they had to do was string the necessary telephone lines and cancel the micro-wave installation. They would save $250,000 and could install the lines immediately. They could meet their deadline. I said, "In my opinion, we have no problem."

They all looked at each other with pleased expressions. It had never occurred to the engineers to change their equipment design. They agreed to my concept and the meeting broke up.

A few weeks later, I found out that the Electronic Engineering Command had claimed the deletion of the Diego Garcia micro-wave as a cost saving idea for their Command. They had completely swiped my idea and gave me absolutely no credit for it. Not even a thank you. I figured that at least the tax payer will get a break regardless of who gets the credit for the idea. I decided that if I had any more bright ideas I would not toss them onto the table. I would document them first.

We bought an older home in Bethesda in 1971. It had been built in 1938. It was a three story, brick house. It was a nice home and a great location. We could walk to downtown Bethesda. We invested quite a bit into it and really fixed it up. We enjoyed living there and I faithfully had my Proctologists exams every three months. I was convinced that if I had any problems, my only chance of survival was to give the Doctors all the time I possibly could. It would do me no good to   delay things.

One day, Katherine told me that she met our ex-landlady at the store. She asked her how her husband was doing. The landlady said that he never would go to see the Doctor for any check-ups. Then, he began to get severe stomach pains. He finally went to see the Doctor. They examined him and told him that he had waited too long. There was nothing they could do for him. He went home and committed suicide by shooting himself in the head. I was more determined than ever to continue my check-ups religiously.

Before we left the rental house, I injured my back. I had been hanging storm windows. I was standing on top of a ladder and the wind caught the window. I managed to hang onto it and not let it drop. It was a bad decision, I should have let it drop.

As I twisted to catch the window, I felt something pop in my lower back. Within a few days, I could not walk and I ended up in Bethesda hospital with a ruptured disk. I was there for two weeks until I could again walk. I still have the ruptured disk but I have learned how to live with it.

The last thing that I was involved in, at the Communication Command, was the reorganization of my Division. I was the Chairman of the Reorganization Committee. We completely revamped the group. We wrote new position descriptions and detailed the personnel to fill the slots.

When we had completed the task, it resulted in a considerable monetary saving for the Navy. It also increased the overall efficiency of the Department.

I had reached the promotion zone for Commander. I also was due for a change of duty. I called my Detailer to find out where I was slated to go next. He told me that they were going to keep me at my present position for another three years. This was not welcome news. Katherine was anxious to return to California. Her mother was getting older and she wanted to be near her. I told the Detailer that I would accept any ship or station on the West Coast. He told me that the main reason I was not being transferred was that the Navy Department was short of funds for transfers. I told him that I would pay for my own transfer. He told me that I could not do that. It was against Naval regulations.

I said that if I retired, the Navy would have to pay my transportation costs to California. He said that he did not care, the funds for that came from a different pocket.

I next called the Bureau of Naval Personnel and asked them how long I would have to stay in the Navy if I was selected for Commander and accepted the position. They told me that I had to give them at least two years more.

I thought my situation over, very carefully. I wanted to make Commander, but there was not that much difference in the pay. It was strictly an ego thing for me. By law, I could not advance beyond that level. If I stayed in the Navy, I was stuck in Washington for at least three more years. I would still be doing staff work. If I made Commander, I might as well finish my working days in the Navy and stay as long as I could. That could be another eight or so years. I would be almost 60 when I retired if I went that route.

On the other hand, I was fifty years old. If I ever was going to get started on a new civilian career, time was rapidly running out. I could retire as a Lieutenant Commander and begin again.

I still had an adventuresome streak in me and I opted to retire.

26

THE TRAFFIC BUSINESS

On 1 July 1973, I retired from the Navy. I sold
the Bethesda house at a nice profit and we headed
for California. We had two new cars, a Buick
Electra and a Ford Maverick as we drove West, off
on a new adventure.
We bought a new house in Campbell, California.
They were still in the process of building it. We
moved into a motel until it was finished. One
fine day, about two weeks after I had retired, I
headed out for a job interview. I had previously
arranged to meet the Personnel Manager of a
civilian shipyard. I was looking forward to the
chance to work there.
I crossed the San Mateo Bridge just at noon. I
was headed West and I had passed a truck and
trailer on the bridge. The truck had been
traveling at 65 MPH. This was before the 55 MPH
limit was imposed in California.
There was a traffic light at the Hayward end of
the bridge. I pulled up into the heavy noon
traffic to wait for the light. Paul Harvey was
just starting to announce the news on my radio. I
glanced into my rear view mirror and was
horrified to see the truck and trailer, that I
had passed, barreling down on me. He was still
doing 65 MPH.
I was hypnotized by the sight. I suddenly had a
wild thought that I may have blacked out and all
the other cars had driven off. It took an extreme
mental effort, but, I tore my eyes away from the

mirror and looked out of my windshield. The
traffic was still setting there, waiting for the
light to change, oblivious of the danger hurtling
towards us.

Before I could again look into the mirror, the
tractor and trailer slammed into me at full
speed. My Ford Maverick was catapulted into a
pick-up truck parked in front of me. The pick-up
truck flew off the road into a ditch. A load of
iron bars, loaded in the body of the pick-up,
flew over my car and into the windshield of the
truck that hit me.

At the moment of impact, I felt two sharp stabs
in my shoulders and a sharp bang on the back of
my skull. I did not have my seat belt on and that
may have saved my life.

When the noise of the collisions and all the
movement stopped, I was physically jammed into a
small space under my car's dashboard. I did not
know if I was in one piece or not. I could have
lost one or more limbs and not been aware of it
at that moment. My back or neck could be broken.
I was alive and awake but I was reluctant to move
anything. My car was bent almost double. The cab
of the truck was setting above my back seat.

A man's face appeared at the window opening on
the driver's side. My head was covered with
blood. "Are you alive?" he asked. At that
instant, we both heard the gas tank ignite with a
muffled boom. I hollered, "Yes I'm alive but
don't let me burn up in here!" I saw panic on the
man's face and he disappeared. He was gone. He
was saving his own skin.

If I was to escape, I would have to do it
myself. I never knew for sure, but I suspect that
the face I saw, in my window, was the driver of
the truck that hit me.

Fire provides a tremendous motivation,

especially if you are in danger of being burned
alive. I decided that I would get out whether I
had all my arms and legs or not. I struggled
violently and soon freed myself from the dash
area. I was trying to reach my window when some
brave bystander managed to force open the
passenger door. He called to me and I crawled out
that side. I heard fire extinguishers being
turned on. Fire engines had arrived and they
quickly extinguished the blaze.

Medics pulled up in an Ambulance. They could not
believe that I had escaped from the Maverick
alive. They said that when they drove up, they
expected to take me out with a spoon. They
insisted that I continue to lie down. I told them
that I was a retired Navy man and they took me to
Oaknoll Hospital.

I was treated for puncture wounds to my head and
back and released. I never did get to that job
interview. I thought to myself, civilian life is
more dangerous than the military.

The Police report said that the truck driver
claimed his brakes failed. The police checked his
brakes and did not find anything wrong with them.
I think that he fell asleep.

His insurance company contacted me, but I had
engaged an attorney. I referred the matter to
him. It took several years but the case was
eventually settled out of court. I was happy to
have come out of it in one piece.

When I was all healed up, I answered a help
wanted ad. The Singer Company wanted applicants
for an Applications Engineer job in Traffic. They
had a plant located in Santa Clara. In the
communications business, messages are called
"traffic." I knew that the Singer Sewing Machine
Company also owned an Electronic Test Equipment
Company. I assumed that they had also gone into

the Communications Equipment business.

The interview was just about over before I discovered that the company manufactured automobile traffic equipment. They had a Division that built intersection lights and controllers.

I wound up with the job. Then I had to teach myself how to do it. A real engineer, with a degree, will not take a job as an applications engineer. They want to design their own products. An applications engineer takes a product that is already designed and adapts it to fit a customer's requirement.

I first had to become familiar with the Singer Traffic products. Then I had to learn all the buzz words in the Traffic industry. Eventually, through, on-the-job training, I learned how to make the Singer equipment fit our customers needs. Sometimes I had to design special electronic logic modules to accomplish various required tasks that the Singer products did not do. I would look up previous job prints in the files to see how other applications engineers had handled similar problems. I taught myself by using this method. It was definitely a job designed for a self starter.

Once I knew that I had the job under control, I had time to think about other things. Katherine wanted to buy a small business. We finally purchased a small beer bar in San Jose. In the meantime, I had started attending evening classes at Foothill College in Los Altos. I carried 12 Units, that is a full course at night. I was majoring in Business.

Between working at Singer, tending bar and going to College, I had my hands full. In the meantime, things were deteriorating between Katherine and myself. One day she said that she wanted a divorce. It was 1974. Richard was 21, Billy was 19 and Kathy was almost 17. I agreed and moved

out of the house. We used the same lawyer and a
year later the divorce was final. In the meantime
we had sold the bar.

I continued working at Singer and going to
college. An opening came up in the Estimating
Department and I transferred to it. This job
required me to read the customer specifications
that were written by the various States, Counties
and Cities across America. I really had to read
the fine print on these documents because the
winner of the contract had to perform everything
that the contract spelled out. Each contract had
a job completion date and contained liquidated
damages for each day's delay in meeting the
completion date.

It was a challenging job to prepare accurate bid
offers on these contracts. You had to cover
everything that was required and still ensure
that you did not go overboard. We had many
competitors and the low bid submitted would win
the contract. To obtain work for the Company, we
had to win contracts that would allow us to make
a reasonable profit. It was very interesting
work.

Singer eventually sold the Traffic Division to a
company called Safetran. They were in the
Railroad Crossing Gate business. Besides buying
us, Safetran also bought one of our competitors
who was located in Colorado Springs, Colorado.
Safetran tried to blend the two companies
together, but a natural rivalry always existed
between the two facilities.

I had moved up to become the Estimating Manager.
Eventually, I became the Production Manager of
the Safetran Santa Clara Plant.

In the meantime, in 1975, I had met an
attractive and delightful lady at a Christmas
dance. Her name was Aida Watts. She was divorced
and had five children. They were practically all

raised. Two were married and three still were at
home. Aida was originally from Guatemala.

We went together for a number of months and
eventually became engaged. We were married
eighteen months later on 9 July 1977. We bought a
new house in Sunnyvale and settled down. We have
been very happy together. It took awhile to
adjust to each other but we managed to work
things out. We took a trip to Guatemala and I met
the rest of her interesting family.

In 1978, I became the Plant Manager of the
Safetran Plant. I ran this operation for eighteen
months until they decided to eventually combine
both factories at Colorado Springs. While things
were still in the planning stages, Aida and I
took a trip to Colorado Springs to see if we
wanted to relocate there. We decided that, when
the Santa Clara plant closed, we would prefer to
stay in California.

It was 1979 and things were going very well for
us. Aida's older Sister, Marina, was visiting
with us from Guatemala. Then, with dramatic
suddenness, tragedy struck.

David, Aida's 29 year old Son, was critically
injured in a traffic accident. He was returning
home from his aircraft mechanic job. He was
driving his Lotus car. It evidently went out of
control on Highway 84, at Livermore, and skidded
into on-coming traffic. He was struck by a pick-
up truck. He was in a hospital at Livermore when
we got to him. He was being kept alive on a life
support system. He had received a severe injury
to the head. The brain surgeon said that it was
impossible to operate on him. He said that David
was "gone." After several days of recording flat
brain scans, they made Aida authorize the dis-
continuance of the life support equipment. It was
a very traumatic experience for all of us,

especially for Aida. It was a terrible time in our lives and still has an impact on us. It is a dreadful thing to lose a child.

For months, Aida was despondent and then one morning she woke me up. David had come to her in a beautiful dream and talked to her. She said that he told her that he did not want to return but he knew that she was really suffering. He came back to reassure her that he was all right. She asked him what it had been like to die. He said that, at first, he was having a very hard time crossing over. He was pulling on some heavy ropes. Suddenly a blue lady appeared and she helped him. She made everything easy. Aida asked him, "What do you do there?" He replied that he worked in a garage with someone he had met named, Carlos Samayoa. Aida then asked him if he would have a hard time crossing over again. He told her, "Not this time." He pointed to a ladder and said, "Look." She looked at the ladder as he quickly climbed it. The last thing she saw was his heels as he disappeared.

As soon as her dream ended, she awoke. Then she woke me up to tell me of her miraculous experience. After she told me the details of her dream, I asked her about Carlos Samayoa. Aida had a faint recollection of hearing that name in Guatemala, but she did not know any Carlos.

David had loved to work on cars and spent almost all of his spare time working in our garage when he lived with us. It would make sense if he continued working in a garage in his after life. Aida called her Sister Carmen in New Jersey and asked her about the Samayoa family. Carmen knew a girl with that name but I do not think that she knew a Carlos. Aida finally contacted her older Sister Marina in Guatemala. Marina told her that the girl that Carmen knew, had a brother named

Carlos. He was a mechanic in a garage and had recently died. It made the hair stand up on the back of my neck when we heard who Carlos was. A dream was one thing, but how could Aida dream of something that she had no prior knowledge of. Either there was a logical explanation, or David had actually visited with her. Whichever it was, it brought relief and mental peace to Aida. For that we were grateful.

Safetran finally merged the two plants at Colorado Springs and I remained in California. I opened up a Safetran Sales Office and worked as a Marketing Manager.

About a year later, another company, Data Communications Systems, offered me a job as Vice President of Marketing. I left Safetran and went to work for them. I opened a sales office in Mountain View, California. This company eventually went out of business and I stayed in Mountain View. I opened my own Dealership. It was called Traffic Devices, Inc.

I had completed my courses at Foothill College and was concentrating all my energies in getting my own business off the ground. I soon discovered that fourteen hour days and seven day weeks are still not enough time to get everything done. Not when you are doing everything yourself. I had an extremely successful first year. However, I realized that I could easily work myself into an early grave.

I had one job in Los Angeles that I was working on. An electrician that was working nearby suggested that we knock off for a coffee break. I told him to go ahead but I was going to finish what I was doing. He asked me, "Are you afraid of your boss?" I told him that I was my own boss. I owned the company.

He looked at me and said that I was a "self employed slave driver." I thought about it, and he was right. I never let myself take a break. Even when I was sick. I decided that it was time to relax and smell the roses.

EPILOGUE

In 1983, ten years after I had retired from the Navy, I closed up my company and really retired. I became a consultant to the Traffic Manufacturing Industry.

I also do Field Service work for various Traffic Companies. I work on a case basis, strictly part time.

Sometimes it is hard to keep the work part time. Two very good friends of mine, Peter Kohl, a Marketing Manager in the Traffic business and Lyle Burks, a Traffic Engineer for Contra Costa County, have a particular knack for finding me jobs that I just can't refuse.

On one occasion, in 1988, they found me a three month position, in Salem, Oregon, as temporary General Manager of a Traffic Company. Recently, they helped me get a seven month consultant job to help set up a factory in Vista, California.

In addition, Jerry Bloodgood and John Itagaki occasionally keep me busy doing work for their BI Tran (software) Company.

Other friends of mine, Vince Perez, Richard D'allessandro and Gordon Dale of the Signal Control Company, in Salem, manage to keep me supplied with Field Service work.

Frank Ribelin of the General Devices Company, who used to be my boss at Singer, always has work for me. I have made many good friends in the Traffic Industry and I enjoy visiting with them every chance I get.

I also go to ship reunions on occasion. The USS Hornet (CV-8) meets each year with the USS Mustin group. The Mustin was one of the Destroyers that picked up Hornet survivors in 1942. I also attend reunions with the USS Walke group from the Korean War. Captain Marshall Thompson and his charming wife Janet have become good friends of Aida and me as a result of these events. They are fun and it is nice to be able to reminisce with old shipmates.

Aida and I live on our one acre lot in El Dorado Hills in the Sierra foothills. We visit our children and grand children whenever we can. I also keep busy doing stained glass windows as a sideline.

I still remain in contact with some of my childhood friends from Chicago. Howard Emmett, Bernie Saltzman and me, occasionally see each other. Don and Rita Elliott live in Cupertino and have been particularly good friends over the years. Don was the Best man at my wedding to Aida.

I go back to Chicago every once in awhile, but there are fewer and fewer of my family and friends left. My father died in 1960 after a long illness following a stroke. He was 70. My mother died in 1976, from a heart attack. She was 86. My brother Paul died at 64 in 1986, after a long bout with lung and throat cancer. We had both started smoking as young teenagers. I quit smoking, cold turkey in 1964. Paul was never able to quit, even after he developed cancer. We were close in age and had the same genes. I often wondered how I could quit smoking but he couldn't. I guess I was just luckier.

My sister Dorothy's husband, Charley O'Kane, and my brother Bill's wife, Bonnie, both died in the last few years. The family circle is growing smaller all the time.

On the plus side of the ledger, my brother Bill is still going strong at 81. My sisters Dorothy and Marian are still with us and I see them when ever I can. Bill still drives out to California from Ohio about once a year.

Unfortunately, the un-thinkable happened and disaster struck our family again in 1990. Aida's daughter Elizabeth and her husband Michael were both killed in a traffic accident while returning from a trip to Los Angeles and Disneyland.

In our worst nightmares, we had never expected to have such a shattering calamity strike our family a second time. It has been over four years since this latest tragedy and we are still trying to recover from it.

It is now 1994. I am in reasonably good health and still do Consultant and Field Service work. I am in my early seventies, but I feel much younger than that. I expect to live for a great number of years yet and the spirit of adventure still burns brightly within me.

I have thought over many times the statement that, God always was and always will be. I cannot conceive of anything that did not have a beginning, somewhere or sometime. Since I still feel the same way, after all these years, I consider myself as a true, born again, Doubting Thomas.

When I finally do reach the end of my life's journey, I am certainly looking forward to discovering whether there is something or someone, such as God, who is controlling it all. If there is, I am going to ask God, how he could possibly exist, without ever having had a beginning. Maybe I really do like to live (or die) dangerously.

It is just possible that the really adventuresome part of my life will begin at that moment. "Who knows?"

The End

1926, 3 years Old

1929

'Knickers' Nowatzki
1934

'The Teenager'
1936

US Navy Boot Camp, 1941
'Ski' Nowatzki is on the right

PT Base Melville, Rhode Island,
1943

1945 at end of WW II. Rockford, Illinois with relatives. I am
on the Right, my Mother & Dad are on the left. I'm not really
taller than my Dad, I was standing nearer to the camera.

USS Hornet (CV-8)
Aircraft Carrier

USS Walke (DD-723)
Destroyer

USS Onslow (AVP-48)
Sea Plane Tender (Small)

USS Pollux (AKS-4)
Supply Ship

January 1951, aboard the USS Walke in Yokosuka, with the shipyard Foreman who introduced me to 'sukiyaki.'

June 1951, aboard the Walke in Sasebo, Japan in drydock. We were repairing battle damage received during the Korean War.

1959, Warrant Officer

1961 Hunters Point Naval Shipyard. Signing my advancement
papers to Lieutenant, Junior Grade with Captain Curtze.

1964 aboard the Markab at Yokosuka, Japan. We were shifting berths during a snow storm.

1964 Personnel Inspection on the pier at Naval Air
Station, Alameda. I'm always the shortest one.

July 1973, I retired from the Navy as a Lieutenant
Commander at the Naval Communications Command,
Washington, D.C.

1964, three brothers, Paul, Richard and William

1974, back row, Bill & me. Middle row, Dorothy, Paul & Marian. Front row, Mom.

2004, Aida & I in California
Enjoying the 'golden years'

1964, Subic Bay, Philipines, 'Crash' Nowatzki.
"Those were the days, my friend, we thought
they'd never end...."